On the Edge

On the Edge

The contested cultures of English suburbia

Rupa Huq

Lawrence & Wishart 2013

Lawrence and Wishart Limited
99a Wallis Road
London
E9 5LN

ISBN 9781907103728

British Library Cataloguing in Publication Data.
A catalogue record for this book is available from the British Library

Contents

Acknowledgements

I owe debts of gratitude to various people and organisations who have supported this project along the way. The Barrow Cadbury Trust awarded me a generous individual grant that allowed me teaching release to carry out some of the research interviews that informed the book. The ESRC also provided additional funding to bolster the research project into Preventing Violent Extremism funded by the Metropolitan Police. At Kingston University the Rev Stan Brown informed me of the Clapham Sect in our discussions, and my office mate Dr Heidi Seetzen was co-researcher on the PVE research project. Thank you also to Superintendent Paul McGregor.

I was lucky enough to present initial findings at various conferences to which I was invited. Policy Network took me to Berlin and Oslo while I went to Istanbul with the Dialogue Society. Closer to home thanks are due to the IPPR, Smith Institute, CPRE, Young Fabians, Operation Black Vote and Progress. *Tribune* magazine and the *Guardian*'s Comment is Free allowed me to rehearse in earlier column form some of the ideas that ended up here, and I am grateful for that.

Thanks must also go to all of the interviewees: among others these include Jon Cruddas, James Cleverly, Councillor Bert Jones of Redbridge, Councillor Chris Paul from Manchester and various people in Kingston, including students, council officials and mosque stalwart Rashid Laher. Sally Davison has been a diligent editor who has been enthusiastic about this project from the start. I thank her for her sharp insight throughout and for her patience. Thanks also to Ealing Councillor Julian Bell, whose already considerable reputation was enhanced by his deft handling of the riots of August 2011.

To paraphrase the old Chinese proverb: the process of completing this book shows that we live in interesting times. One constant throughout these turbulent events however has been Rafi, to whom this book is dedicated.

Preface

Riots in suburbia

'What happened?', asked a Japanese resident who'd not followed the news at the cordoned off crime scene-cum media circus that was Ealing Green on the Tuesday morning after the Monday night that had brought the worst rioting the UK had experienced for thirty years to the suburbs. I tried to explain the inexplicable. 'But it's so quiet round here and so international', she insisted. 'I thought they were filming something'. But it was really true. Ealing – to London's west, once home of stiff-upper-lip film comedy – had now become a scene of post-riot carnage. And it was shortly to become the site of a murder enquiry.

The fire at the badly burned building on the corner that had housed a convenience store with flats above had been extinguished, but the emergency services were still omnipresent. It was 10am and a sunny day. Many seemed in a zombie-like state of disbelief. Everyone was bearing mobile phones and using them to photograph smashed up shops or to talk into them to describe their surroundings, while the road was being re-tarmacked where it had burned.

Photos taken by my own hand a day later show the world famous Ealing film studios foregrounded by burnt out cars in the process of being lifted away. Behind a smashed shopfront the hairdresser Visage carries on regardless with no glass. False frozen in time by digital imaging are gatherings of gawpers on Ealing Green and by the famous Ealing Horse statue, where volunteers assembled to help clear up. Some young people take pictures of each other smiling amongst the wreckage, as local traders figure out how to 'make good' the damage, replacing smashed windows with boarded-up facades. Nobody ever thought it would happen here.

Ealing's proximity to Sky and the BBC meant that the piling in of both camera crews and live feeds from the Green was predictable. It has also for years been a favourite place for media folk to live in, film in and set fictional sitcoms in. Its nearness to both embassy-land in South Kensington and Heathrow has long made it a draw for diplomats and cabin crew. Yet the circumstances of the attention this time round were unforeseeable – so much so that police in Ealing had been deployed elsewhere to other potential riot locations. Every time Ealing was mentioned in the media it seemed obligatory to prefix it with the word 'leafy'. Its solid Victorian villa housing and its excellent rail and underground connections had given it the moniker 'queen of the suburbs', a classic development marketed as an antidote to the evils of the city. Suburbs equate with safety, middle England and middle age. But, in an unexpected jolt to the suburban dream, Ealing had now become the site for hordes of swarming youths, terrorising police and locals.

Song tracks such as 'London's Burning' and 'I Predict a Riot' were much invoked in the media, but surely the most relevant song was Half Man Half Biscuit's 1986 'Trumpton Riots' (from the album *Back in the DHSS*), in which, incongruously, power is overthrown in a sleepy stop-animation village.

These events clearly demonstrate, albeit in extreme form, a number of the changing features of contemporary suburbia, and what one might call the 'edgyness' that it exhibits at the turn of the twenty-first century. This means that, in the scramble to answer 'why' so many city centres blazed in the summer of 2011, it is also worth looking at what exactly was happening at the same time in the suburbs. Other chapters in this book explore further some of these aspects of suburbia, but for now I want to flag up the way the riots raised a number of suburban related topics.

SHOPPING IN THE SUBURBS

This rebellion looked different from other political demonstrations. The buildings attacked were not symbols of authority. Instead they seemed to have been picked for the gear on their shelves, in an exercise that focused largely on the acquisition of material goods.

Looters in Ealing, Croydon and other suburban areas such as Harrow and Bromley began their rampage after the 24-hour news channels and social networking sites had spread the first images of youth in other parts of the capital ransacking stores and leaving with armfuls of stolen electrical goods and sportswear. The initial motivation – protests at Mark Duggan's killing by a police bullet the week before – seemed to have been long forgotten by Tuesday night. Thrill-seeking and consumerism began to enter the lists of explanations from commentators who had started the week with the police maltreatment of black people.

Some of the looting can be explained by an attempt to buy into the contemporary world of hypercapitalist consumer paradise, where there is the illusion that the next new thing on the market will make you happy. According to store staff in West Ealing, looters targeted high value goods where they could. At Wilkinsons, which was boarded up but soon trading again, staff reported that all perfumes had been taken, as well as DVDs and Ipod accessories. High-value goods stores such as Carphone Warehouse, Phones 4U and Blockbuster video were completely closed or boarded up. As well as these national chainstores, Seba Electronics, run by an elderly Indian couple since the 1970s was targeted, and Goldmine jewellers was reportedly completely cleared out. Maybe this was more of a shopping spree than a riot – or, as the phrase went, 'shopping with violence'. Could this be a peculiarly suburban form of teenage riot?

Shopping is a key issue for once prosperous suburban high streets. Ealing Broadway and neighbouring west Ealing were already in decline before the riots, in the face of recession and the development of the nearby Westfield mega-mall – which was being guarded by Ealing police even while Ealing was blazing. The difficulties facing local shops became one of the key points of discussion at the unprecedented August emergency Ealing council meeting called to discuss the effects of the riot. The area's already struggling independent, family-run small businesses that had been cleared out were not symbols of capitalist multinationalism, and had nothing to do with government cuts or withdrawing youth services. As right-wing blogger notasheep put it: 'Seba Electronics has nothing to do with the Government's cuts (such as they are), Seba electronics has not closed any local council services, Seba electronics has not oppressed the youth'.[1] On WestEalingNeighbours site was the comment: 'I just hope that the looting isn't the final straw that finishes off any of our local businesses. Times are more than tough enough without looting by people who don't care about our neighbourhood or anyone's else's neighbourhood'.[2]

The opportunism of the looters was, curiously, acknowledged in the mitigation allowed to Kingston University student and aspiring actor Pierre Wilkinson 21, who had stolen goods from Seba Electronics. Justice Darling stated: 'I am satisfied your criminality represents opportunistic involvement after the burglary had occurred … It's apparent to me in all respects you are an exceptional young man admired and respected and expected to go far.' Perhaps leniency was accorded to Wilkinson because he appeared in many ways to be an ideal suburban type – the son of an accountant from Pinner in the London Borough of Harrow and enrolled on a drama degree at Kingston University. The judge told him, 'I am told if you go back into custody, you will have lost your place at university and all you have worked for. For what? A stupid and opportunistic moment of madness'.[3] Suburban rioters apparently did not fit the usual stereotypes.

THE POST-RACE SUBURBS?

One of my earliest memories is riot-related. Back in 1981, the last time bits of London were ablaze in a time of recession, I remember being sent home early from my Ealing primary school. Trouble was brewing in Southall, three miles down the road, and the police advice was that it was coming next to leafy Ealing. But the view that such things didn't happen in Ealing remained undisturbed in the 1980s, and the trouble did not reach our suburb.

Thirty years on when I saw that the word from Twitter was that Ealing would be next, I assumed the rumour-mill was in overdrive, just like last time, and scoffed at the idea. Of course we now all know the rest.

In Notting Hill in 1958, or in Brixton, Southall and elsewhere in the 1980s, the disturbances were quickly dubbed 'race riots'. But in 2011 consumerism seemed to be a primary motivation, and the perpetrators appear not to have been drawn from one racial group but from across different ethnic categories. In some ways, therefore, these can be seen as 'post-race' riots, in keeping with notions of a post-racial world following the election of Obama.

The riots were ethnically mixed, and people from across the ethnic minorities were both perpetrators and victims, as they have been in most of great multicultural crises of our times. 'My brothers you are doing your Eid shopping early', said one tweet from a source with a comedy hijabed lady as her avatar. I think it was a joke. Then there was the Malaysian student who was robbed by people masquerading as coming to his aid; the grieving father in Birmingham eloquently pleading for people to get a grip and stop the madness on the streets; and the guy posing gangsta-style with a Tesco value big-sized bag of basmati.[4] All this illustrates that, contrary to the idiotic Powellite 'them' vs 'us' opinions of David Starkey, multiculturalism is a given, and this is as true of the suburbs as it is of the inner city.

We were treated to various memorable images and new riot celebrities. As well as the grieving grey-haired Pakistani Muslim father in Birmingham, there was the woman jumping to safety from a burning building in Croydon, who turned out to be Polish. Pictures from Southall showed large numbers of sikhs guarding their gurdawara on hearing that trouble might be heading their way from Ealing. In Tower Hamlets men coming out of communal prayers at the Whitechapel mosque chased away the would-be marauders, and there were reports of Turkish shopkeepers in Stoke Newington repelling potential pillagers. Those three young men in Birmingham were not so lucky.

In all these images the original motive, justice for Mark Duggan, became more and more of a distant memory. What had started as a protest about police injustice against the black community had become something quite different. But there were many racially inflected elements in responses to the riots. Following the initial outbreak of violence, television pictures switched to portrayals of groups of white Caucasian males in the London suburbs of Eltham and Enfield, who had mounted vigilante protectionist fronts to defend local property. Some of these had far right links. *The Voice* reported that the vigilante patrols in Eltham were the result of 'a community gathering ... hijacked by racist thugs'. Local MP Clive Efford was quoted as stating: 'Unfortunately, members of the EDL came to Eltham to cause trouble and exploit this situation against the backdrop of all the other things that are happening'. David Starkey's inane remark that 'whites have become black' was a further notable example of the way in which race was interwoven into the undercurrents of discussion.

THE NEW INNER CITY?

The mob was now reaching places it had never reached before. As Hari Kunzru observed: 'Early in the evening, watching social media, I was seeing variants of the same joke: "I'm in Chiswick/ Hampstead/Dulwich Waitrose and there's a RIOT! They've run out of POLENTA!".[5] The smug sense of disconnection (this is nothing to do with me, or my comfortable middle-class life – it is an affair of the poor, in places I choose not to go) was soon replaced by panic: 'WHERE IS THE ARMY?'

Perhaps good travel connections help to explain the chosen sites. Ealing and Croydon, as transport termini served by numerous lines, to some extent qualify as London sub-regional hubs that draw in populations from neighbouring areas. Initial postcode analyses of those charged with offences showed that the distances travelled between rioters' homes and the location of their offence was highest in suburban Croydon and Ealing but shortest in inner-London Camden and Peckham.

In 1987 Thatcher declared that something must be done about 'those inner cities'. The thrust of New Labour regeneration too was focused mostly on city centres – pedestrianisation here, a spaceship-like arts centre there. The suburbs were seen as 'out of the way' places, 'where nothing ever happens', 'dormitory towns'. The riots seem to suggest otherwise.

But a surprising result of the reviving reputation of the inner city – which began to be associated with culture, cosmopolitanism and energy – was that it began to make suburbia seem less desirable. This helped to contribute to a disavowal of suburban status from all sides. The current marketing from boroughs like Ealing stresses its 'vibrancy' in its quest to be attractive.

Now the double-edged nature of such edginess was perhaps being seen, as rioting and looting seemed to seal the status of the suburb as the new inner city in 2011. Risk and danger could be clearly be seen to underscore the contemporary suburb.

A year on things appeared to have changed once more. On the eve of the 2012 London Olympic games, torch relay rallies were staged in all the London boroughs, including its far-flung suburban corners. It was a dramatic change of circumstances. Much retweeted was the juxtaposition of two images from the same spot in Ealing Green, chronologically separated by almost exactly a year: a burnt-out car from 2011 and the passing of the torch in 2012. The caption was 'same place, different type of flame'. By 2012 the memory of suburban streets with shops and cars ablaze may have somewhat receded but between these two events a number of themes relevant to contemporary suburbia were raised: national pride, globalisation, multiculturalism, consumerism, protest, and old and new media, all of which contribute to modern life on the edge.

Notes

1. http://notasheepmaybeagoat.blogspot.com/2011/08/its-not-about-cuts-its-not-about-inder.html
2. www.westealingneighbours.org.uk/WEN-blog/2011/08/09/west-ealing-high-street-badly-damaged-in-night-of-looting/
3. 'London riots: judge spares rioting actor whose degree at risk', *Daily Telegraph* 4.11.11.
4. http://brit-asian.com/wp-content/uploads/2011/08/looter-basmati-2.jpg.
5. H. Kunzru, 'These riots reveal some unpalatable home truths', *Guardian*, 12.8.11: www.guardian.co.uk/commentisfree/2011/aug/12/riots-home-truths-culture-fear-greed.

Introduction

Inside the contested culture of suburbia

> 'Those enormous suburban peoples ... are the peculiar product of England and America; of the nations which have pre-eminently added commerce, business, and finance to the work of manufacture and agriculture. It is a life of Security; a life of Sedentary occupation; a life of Respectability'.
>
> C. F. G. Masterman, *The Condition of England*

The aim of this book is to provide a socio-cultural mapping of contemporary English suburbia - with a nod to America - in setting out the groundwork for making sense of the suburbs. Sociology has often dealt with the 'urban' as an analytical category, but, despite the areas at the fringes of the cities being the main motor of the British metropolis, the 'suburban', by contrast, has been relatively under-researched.

The suburbs, once seen as unproblematic, are being made increasingly more complicated as globalisation causes the sometimes complementary and sometimes contradictory processes of solidarity, community and individualisation to rub up against each other. Pile (1998:23) has summarised the raison d'être of the suburb in the following words: 'for many, suburbia offered an escape from the tensions of city life, while still allowing people to be connected enough to gain from its advantages'. And this 'neither here not there' positioning of the suburb has been boon as well as bane. But suburbs and the relationships that sustain them are now themselves being reconfigured, for example relationships between home and work or the city and suburb. They are places of social mobility not so much in class terms but because they offer homes to people who are quite literally on the move: for we know that there is a high level of population churn both between and within suburbs – quite the reverse of the cultural and social stagnation with which suburbs are more readily associated.

This book looks at case studies of suburban phenomena, informed by empirical research on the ground. Suburbs come in many shapes and sizes, and suburban processes may be captured in many ways, both imaginary and real, but this book is concerned with daily lived realities. It seeks to capture suburban imaginaries as well as power structures, and to avoid any sense of dichotomy between structure and agency, through a deployment of both multi-sited fieldwork and textual study.

RESEARCHING THE SUBURBAN MINDSET

Among other sources, this book draws on research from a series of semi-structured interviews that were conducted in a variety of settings, and could be characterised as multi-sited ethnography. In some cases interviews were conducted through focus groups, which at their simplest can be defined as group discussions organised to explore a specific set of issues. Such discussions enable a more textured and qualitative picture of human relations and everyday life to emerge (as opposed to the comparatively blunt instrument of the quantitative survey method). Such ethnographic methods are often employed to enable authors to claim legitimacy for their argument, but the very fact of choosing to interview a particular participant raises a whole set of practical, moral and ethical questions. The logic of inclusion at the very outset biases the findings. Furthermore, in the subsequent analysis one can focus on the average view or deliberately go for the more outlandish comments, in order to upset received wisdom. The same to some extent applies to the choice of suburbs under discussion in this book. Examples I have drawn on include Southall (the well-known west London Punjabi Asian suburb), Dagenham in east London (known for its extreme right BNP vote), and Chorlton (a white middle-class suburb of south Manchester), partly for practical reasons and partly because they represent different class and ethnic mixes. Both Ealing (now a large multicultural borough, once home of the famous 'stiff upper lip' British comedy), where I live, and Kingston (the last corner of south west London before the Surrey countryside begins), where I work, feature heavily.

Interviewees I quote vary widely: council officials, MPs, religious leaders and local council officers as well as attendees of local community groups and those who belonged to no groups. As with the sites of the research, these were chosen for both practical and analytical reasons. The lesson to be learned from this cacophony of polyvocal discourse is that there is no such thing as a typical suburbanite. What follows, then, is a series of dialogues and empirical cases which provide the scaffolding for constructing the category of 'suburbia'. Unsurprisingly, the research raises many questions. Is suburbia a mindset or attitude or a set of coordinates on a map? Is being a suburbanite a reflexive choice of the suburban dweller or is it the decision of transport planners? Is suburbia about belonging (inherited mores), or can it equally be about becoming (moving out and up)? Is the suburb still a place of refuge or does its new diversified self reflect dynamism more than continuity?

The book's interview-based research is complemented by a wealth of material from YouTube and Facebook, which offer a treasure trove of contemporary history. When searching for 'Ilford Lane' for example, there is vivid imagery capturing Eid festivities in this suburban stretch of East London, where one-time Eastender Pakistanis and Bangladeshis have relocated away from inner boroughs such as Tower Hamlets and Newham. The pictures of young Asian men cruising in cars with the Pakistani flag draped around them and loud sound systems blaring out bhangra music are more immediate than any description. The same immediacy applies to footage of celebrations after the T20 cricket tournament victory of Pakistan, which would surely give food for thought to former Conservative minister Norman Tebbitt, inventor of the 'cricket test' for sporting and national allegiances.

A google search of the word 'Kings Nympton', a council estate in Kingston, leads to four Facebook groups devoted to the estate, each containing contributions of a different tone. One page features 'DID YOU EVER GET OUT OF KINGSNYMPTON PARK ESTATE' [sic]; and 'JUST A PICTURESQUE HOUSING ESTATE SET ON THE TOP OF KINGSTON HILL ... OR WAS IT A BLOT ON THE LANDSCAPE'. The framing of the group influences wall postings, for example the quote from Bru 'guvnor' Price: 'If i got life for murder i could get out in 14 years. Instead i got 23years on kingsnympton' (posted 16.3.08). Contrastingly the KingsNympton Appreciation Society encourages more positive posts, for example that of Jeanette Tanner: 'I Love KN – have been here for 17 years and can't see my self ever leaving. A great place for the kids to grow up, a lovely local, fab school, lovely people. Kings Nympton is a proper old fashioned community in a very pretty part of the world what more could you want?' (posted on 6.2.09). The creation of the community of users replicates the kind of communality that Willis (2010) has described in fan-cultures.

Local examples of virtual communities supplementing the real affective ties of neighbourhood abound. The bulletin board of the Chorltonweb site in South Manchester includes posts such as 'What's Nell Lane like to live on?' (andylad9 7.10.10, 5:06 pm). The poster wants to know what the 'catch' is with the area, as property appears to be cheap: 'I'm after a new fresh perspective on what's it like to live on Nell Lane. I'm scared of buying a house in horrible neighbourhood.' Another poster, SkiBum, seeks 'Recommendations for Nanny in Chorlton??' within the same week (11.10.10 6:55 am).

Ealing Today describes itself as an 'Online resource for Ealing, the site for property, restaurants, shops and information on the Ealing Community'. The site's community forum from 2009 to 2010 seemed largely to consist of postings about people lamenting the closure of shops in the area. Some of the same Chorlton themes recur – 'Cleaner needed in west ealing' in the same week as the nanny was sought in Chorlton. In previous times the local newspaper would have provided a slower source of classified ads, suburban gossip and information, with less immediate opportunity to contribute. Today things are more immediate. There are also website versions of print editions of newspapers and local council publications, often linked to Facebook. The ubiquitous small blue F icon in the corner of the screen is illustrative of the symbiotic nature of social networking and commerce. And Twitter has now overtaken Facebook for its efficacy in providing real-time commentary on events: sorting fact from fiction on this micro-blogging site was one of the jobs that the police faced during the August 2011 riots.

In both user-generated local websites and the web versions of local print media, meaning is co-constructed by a website content manager, and the commenters give meaning to the ideal of the active audience.

This rebalancing of power relations towards consumers empowers those who were once mere spectators or onlookers. The form of the electronic posting changes usual media circuits of production, effecting a reorganisation of the production cycle, as Soep (2010) has pointed out. The exit and entry point of a media product become difficult to discern. Comments on a blog live on after the original article and give rise to a 'digital afterlife'. Such data, unlike commentary in newspapers, which are destined to be chip paper, form a permanent online archive. We can therefore now add the fruits of social networking into the source material at the dispersal of the modern chronicler of the suburbs.

Such online data can be compared with that from offline interviewees. The Kings Nympton commentary can be contrasted with the following remarks of a senior council officer from the Royal Borough of Kingston upon Thames (who has never lived on the estate), interviewed in December 2009:

> One of the main things is that it's not easy to be poor, or indeed different in Kingston, because you are seeing other people who really have quite a lot going for them, even if they're professionals who have lost their big finance jobs, they're likely to have a pretty nice house, and a car, and that kind of thing. So I think it must be harder than living perhaps in Tower Hamlets or the inner city where you're all up against it really, but around here … somewhere like Norbiton there are some really nice houses, very close to Kingston Hill which is absolutely top end of the market really. And inbetween that you've got the Cambridge Estate, you've got the Kings Nympton Estate which is actually the beginning of Kingston Hill and backs onto the park, Richmond Park: a lot of people there with a lot of poverty and deprivation. You must feel quite isolated sometimes.

This quotation highlights the complexities within as well as between suburban areas, with their side-by-side affluence and poverty. And it contradicts the line of thinking which 'assumes, with no regard to the diversity of English suburbs, that people live a singular "suburban" life: a privatised, repressed and banal existence behind the net curtains and the front gardens of the suburban home' – as Clapson (2003:152) points out, again using the law metaphor. Suburban council estates and corporation housing modelled on the garden suburb each provide a further different example of the multiply constituted suburban existence.

SOME THEMES

Gender

Suburbia has always been a gendered concept, associated with domesticity. As Walker (1985:107) points out:

> Between 1950 and 1960, the population in the suburbs surrounding America's major cities increased forty-seven percent, and in one study, women asked for their 'principal aspiration' in moving to a suburban area responded overwhelmingly (seventy-eight percent) that they wished to improve the quality of their home lives; as one woman put it, to better fulfil the 'normal family role, being a home-maker'.

In the post-war era the suburb was the refuge for the wife while the man negotiated the daily hustle and bustle of the noisy, dirty city. This state of affairs was not without its critics. In her best-selling *The Feminine Mystique* Betty Friedan identified that it was 'what every other American girl wanted – to get married, have ... children and live in a nice suburb. The suburban housewife ... was the dream image of the young American woman' (1963/2001:60). Yet this had soured: these same housewives 'have a hunger that food cannot fulfil ... women who think it will be solved by more money, a bigger house, a second car, moving to a better suburb, often discover it gets worse.' For Friedan, the culture of the suburbs bred conformity and ensnared people in a life of monotonous unfulfilment, as expressed in the following much-cited quotation:

> The problem lay buried, unspoken, for many years in the minds of American women. It was a strange stirring, a sense of dissatisfaction, a yearning that women suffered in the middle of the twentieth century in the United States. Each suburban wife struggled with her children, chauffeured Cub Scouts and Brownies, lay beside her husband at night – she was afraid to ask even of herself the silent question – Is this all?' (cited *Guardian* 7.2.06).

Friedan's book was groundbreaking in its exposure of this unspoken 'problem': 'the concrete details trap the suburban housewife'; they are 'the chains that bind her … not easily shaken off' (p77). She goes so far as to liken suburbs to 'comfortable concentration camps'. In her introduction to the 2001 edition, Friedan acknowledged that there had been some progress, and argued that women had made strides in the labour market and occupational structure, 'with so many more choices than their mothers had'. But she was also concerned about some aspects of modern life, including the fact that 'only 35 per cent of American families have one meal a day together', and she found 'anxiety and insecurity … growing among American women and men' – a further sign of the changing nature of suburban life as well as in gender relations (p28).

There is clearly a division of labour between men and women in the suburbs, and this has been repeatedly satirised in popular culture. Medhurst talks of 'men who dream of escaping routine and rut, women who unquestioningly accept or at worst, embody them' (1997:241). This comment hints at the possibility of these boundaries being strayed from – which they so often are in fictitious portrayals of suburban life, from well-known US film and book *The Man in the Gray Flannel Suit* to ABC's long running series *Desperate Housewives*, which ended in 2012.

Walker quotes the post-war poetry of Phyllis McGinley, in *A Short Walk From the Station*, in which the breadwinner and housewife perform their respective roles in a pre-dual earner age (1985:107-8):

> many of the descriptions of women depict satirically the pointlessness of women's isolated lives … 'The 5:32,' [is] a poem celebrating the arrival of husbands from the city. At 'This hour best of all the hours I knew,' she describes 'a man coming toward me, smiling, the evening paper/Under his arm' (88). It is clear that no matter how fulfilling McGinley would like to think the hours with hairdryers and slipcovers have been, only the eventual presence of men redeems the isolation of women in suburban setting.

The suburban settlement became an obvious focus of feminist critique; it was the place from which you had to depart if you were to escape its conventions of nuclear single-family-household composition.

Conversely, the anonymity of the city constructs it in the popular imagination as a more tolerant place, where it is easier to be different: suburbia is slower at adapting to social change and quicker to judge. In Allen's study of the gentrification of Manchester's city centre, a location that had become well-known for its gay scene, he notes (2007:672): 'The gay and lesbian people that were interviewed were attracted to the city centre because the emergent "gay village" provided an environment in which they could come out (since this had not been possible in the suburbs where they had grown up). There has been a thread running through suburban fiction about the gay male escaping to the city, for example as documented by Dines (2009) and Oswell (2000), in relation to Kureishi's *Buddha of Suburbia*. There is also popular cultural evidence, however, of suburban morality being replicated within otherwise non-traditional suburban households. In the 2010 film *The Kids Are Alright*, a lesbian couple raise two teenagers, attempting to enforce discipline on a pair who are subject to the usual adolescent storm and stress. In many ways their lifestyle is like that of any other suburban family – aside from their tussles with the sperm donor.

Class

The first expansion of suburbia was largely undertaken to accommodate the middle class, which grew in Victorian and Edwardian times because of the increase in non-manual work. The middle classes sought improved physical surroundings away from their initial habitat, the city, and in districts of exclusivity that marked out their distinction from those in manual work. There was a sense that moving out to suburbia meant moving up the social scale. Pile cites Bromley in south east London as an example of a place where 'people were dreaming of utopian solutions to the horror of Victorian cities' (1998:35). The extension of the public transport network also contributed to greater occupational mobility. It enabled migration both away from people's place of birth and away from their work. For these original dwellers, the function of the suburb was literally as 'dormitory town'. Suburbia became the presumed habitat of the middle class, and the suburban standard of living evolved to include a regularly changed car (or two), a well-manicured lawn and holidays abroad. The flip-side of all this new comfort was that suburbia also became an arena for competition, bound up with petty, small minded one-upmanship and 'keeping up with the Joneses'.

Though people may have felt that they had 'arrived', the suburban way of life has also attracted its fair share of snobbery and disdain. For Lewis Mumford (1991/1961:553), the suburbs of postwar America were:

> A multitude of uniform, indefinable houses, lined up inflexibly at uniform distances, on uniform roads, in a treeless communal waste, inhabited by people of the same class, the same income, the same age group, witnessing the same television performances, eating the same tasteless prefabricated foods, from the same freezers, conforming in every inward and outward respect to a common mould, manufactured in the central metropolis.

An elitist contempt for those pursuing the acquisition of consumer durables is clear. A portrayal of suburbia as a place of competition and cut-throat class infighting can be seen in William Whyte's work *Organization Man*, which includes a chapter called 'Inconspicuous consumption'. White laments the passing of the old virtues of self-reliance and entrepreneurship, which he sees as having been crushed by loyalty to the postwar corporation, which had supplanted any space for individualism by creating a compliant workforce. He describes the suburbs as being packed with 'organization people' (Whyte 1956: 10):

> This is the new suburbia, the packaged villages that have become the dormitory of the new generation of organization men. They are not typical American communities, but because they provide such a cross section of young organization people we can see in bolder relief than elsewhere the kind of world organization man wants and may in time bring about. Here I will go into the tremendous effect transiency has had on the organization people and how their religious life, their politics and the way they take to their neighbors reveal the new kind of rootedness they are looking for. And, finally, the moral of it all as they explain it to their children – the next generation of organization people.

Indeed throughout the book he refers to the 'package suburb'. Whyte was writing during the Eisenhower presidency, when corporations were being marketed as a panacea for previous social ills; their new technology was seen as offering opportunities for the average middle-class Americans to for the first time own goods such as televisions and cars, and partake of lifestyles where fast food was on the menu – against the backdrop of meticulously planned suburban development and the promoted ideal of the nuclear family. Whyte saw consumerism as symbolic of the rootlessness of these new communities and their depthless inhabitants (p314):

> Today, with more people with the money to buy more things, consumers have a bewildering multiplicity of choices to make. In making them, they have less and less tradition to lean on. And the very similarities of suburbia are pitfalls. When everyone lives in an identical house, the most important item on their estate is washed out as a factor, and the marginal purchases become the key ones. How to choose them?

Consumerism has long been a feature of suburban English fiction and its characters have frequently pursued shopping as a leisure activity. For example, for Mrs Pooter a favourite haunt was Whiteleys at Bayswater (no longer a department store and long since a shopping centre). In the early twentieth century series *The Forsyte Saga*, written by Kingstonian John Galsworthy, Harrods is name-checked. Equally, the consumption of material possessions is a crucial part of Wilmott and Young's study of Woodford (1960), a South Essex suburb of London that was once the home of mainly middle-class railway commuters, but was augmented in the postwar period by people moving out from East London, either as upwardly mobile home-owners or into the newly built council housing. Woodford was an aspirational destination, one that was coveted by people moving out from the East End. Wilmott and Young paint a picture of an archetypal landscape of solidly respectable tree-lined pre- and post-war streets, where home-centredness and reserve shine through their interviews with the status-conscious residents. They comment on residents as having a degree of wealth, 'or at least owning the visible badges of wealth – the £8,000 house, the Rover 100, the extra-large refrigerator' (1960:112). One interviewee remarks: 'People say "Mrs So-and so's got one and I'll get it too"' (ibid). There is not here the overtly critical authorial voice of Mumford or Whyte's work, but their choice of quotations includes plenty of disapproval from residents at the 'new money' of incomers. A works manager is quoted as complaining that 'the working class … don't know how to spend their money. They waste money on fridges. Washing machines, TVs and cars. It's the old tale – the person who knows money best knows how to use it, the person new to getting it doesn't'. This is included in a section called 'The tensions of social class' (p118). The authors also suggest that one difference between Bethnal Green – the subject of their more famous earlier study – and Woodford is the absence of tight kinship networks; there is more spatial and social separation. They also note the rise in living standards experienced under the 'you've never had it so good'-promising Harold Macmillan: 'Higher incomes mean that class divisions are not so securely based upon the structure of workplace; the new divisions are based more upon consumption standards' (p132). This is seen as an inherent good rather than a cause for dismay.

Residents also expressed regret for the passing of the 'old' ways:

> All sorts of people have come into Woodford since the war who ought never to have come into it, you know what I mean. There's not such a good class of people here as there used to be (p119).

Others complain of the central line being extended to Woodford, thereby bringing undesirables, or that the area is becoming more 'like Leytonstone'. One interviewee reports that because they have nothing in common with their new Eastender neighbours on either side they have been forced to sell up and move to Worthing – an early example of what later became known as white flight, although colour does not figure in the narrative at this point. Today fear generated by the growing unfamiliarity of once familiar areas is frequently inflected with anxiety about ethnicity. This is the sense one gets from Tim Lott's (1996) book *The Scent of Dried Roses*, which describes his mother's suicide after an adult life spent in Southall, an area promising much in the 1950s when she moved there, before its later decline and settlement by incomers of Asian origin. This kind of anxiety may have also have underpinned the fabled Mrs Duffy's remarks on immigration to Gordon Brown in the 2010 general election campaign.

The suburbia of the middle-class Edwardians and Victorians has been supplemented by successive waves of suburban development. Dagenham became a South Essex suburb of a very different kind from Woodford when huge council estates were developed there by the London County Council, expressly for the motor-trade workers of the Ford factory that was built there in 1931. Later still the Thatcher government's policy to promote the sale of council houses to former tenants probably helped immeasurably to promote the suburban lifestyle, though it also sowed the seed of much conflict over scarce hosing resources, not least in Dagenham.

Mrs Thatcher's belief that there was 'no such thing as society' was much cited as evidence of social atomisation in the 1980s. And perhaps some forms of suburban living could be taken as classic examples of this breakdown of collectivity. Ulrich Beck has argued that we now live in a risk society, where people are disembedded from established structures through processes of 'de-traditionalisation', and markers of social solidarity such as religion or class identification have become less important: 'as a result of shifts in the standard of living, subcultural class identities have dissipated, class distinctions based on status have lost their traditional support, processes for the diversification and individualisation of lifestyles have been set in motion' (1992:91). These changes can be seen in the changing patterns of suburban lifestyle. It is certainly the case that in the last three decades flexible labour markets, accompanied by rising standards of living for the majority (at least until recently), have led to a fragmentation of class-based loyalties. (This is why political parties need to bring together coalitions of different constituencies. Thus New Labour sought to encompass core-message supporters, Guardian-reading public sector workers as well as middle England and suburban converts who had once supported Thatcher and Major.)

Family

Much of the desirability of the suburb comes from its assumed status as a good place in which to raise children and bring up a family. And it is now nearly four decades since Thorns's assertion (1972:111) that: 'The family is crucial both to the decision to move to the suburbs and to the whole suburban way of life'. In those days the old model of happily married male breadwinner with mother/wife performing childcare was presumed to be the norm, and the only valid constitution of family. But this no longer holds in the industrial west. Beck and Beck-Gernsheim (2002:22) have gone as far as to declare: 'We live in an age in which the social order of the nation state, class, ethnicity and the traditional family is in decline. The ethic of individual self-fulfilment and achievement is the most powerful current in modern society'.

In the 1960s Willmott and Young put the issues of family and kinship at the heart of their London studies. But Beck (1999) has argued that the family unit has been reconstituted to mean many things at the turn of the century:

> You can have a hell of a time nowadays just trying to answer very simple questions. What, for example, is a family? What is a household? What is a class? I call these zombie-categories because they are dead but somehow go on living, making us blind to the realities of our lives. Ask yourself: what actually is a family nowadays? What does it mean? Even parenthood, the core of family life, is beginning to disintegrate under conditions of divorce. Families can be constellations of very different relationships. Take, for example, the way grandmothers and grandfathers are being multiplied by divorce and remarriage (without any genetic engineering). They get included and excluded without any say in the matter. The grandchildren meanwhile have to make their own decisions about their families. Who is my main father, my main mother, my grandma and grandpa? And the answers may vary at different stages of life.

The traditional family of course had 'straightness' at its core. Medhurst (1997: 266) argues that: 'Of all the hegemonies of suburbia, it is the hegemony of heterosexuality that cuts deepest' (though Dines (2009) has uncovered a quite different suburban history of gay narratives in popular culture). The breakdown of suburban family hegemony outlined by writers such as Beck is presented by the right – for example in Cameron's 'broken Britain' mantra – as a problem to be approached in problem-solving terms. The family is an area of sociology and public policy where social capital frequently collides with moral judgement.

Changing families in turn change the character of suburbia, sometimes in subtle ways. The breakdown of the male breadwinner model, combined with the high costs of childcare in the UK, mean that if you take a daytime trip to any suburb you will almost certainly encounter pensioners pushing pre-school children around the streets in buggies, while the children's parents, their own offspring, are working. The 2007 reconstitution of the education ministry as the Department for Children, Schools and Families to some extent recognised the interconnectedness of these questions, though it was in part a tactical decision to wrest control of the family issue from the political right. But the Coalition government – perhaps recognising this – have since reversed the decision.

As Beck identifies, the removal of stigma from divorce has also had implications for the suburban set-up. Relationship breakdown (whether partners were married or not) is a factor that has kept the property market moving, even in a time of economic downturn. Parallel to this has been the development of living apart together, which the suburban home can often accommodate better than other housing forms. This can be undertaken because of not being able to afford a total split in jointly owned equity, or 'for the sake of the family'. The subject is increasingly one of sociological enquiry (Ermisch and Seidler 2009; Haskey and Jefferson 2006; Haskey 2005; Levin, I. and Trost, J. 1999; Levin 2004; Roseneil and Budgeon 2004). In some ways it maintains the family unit/coupledom while allowing more opportunity for choice and flexibility. But in others – in interpreting family life in terms of living separately and negating romantic love – this alternative family formation can be seen as symptomatic of the 'decline' of the idealised version of the family.

Gentrification and respectability

There is a strong overlap between an area being respectable and being regarded as family-friendly. As the mayor's Outer London Commission Pre-Publication Report states: 'Many people make a choice to live in outer London because it is less intensively developed and offers a pleasant and attractive place to live, specially for families' (2010:105). A study of Japanese corporate movers in London shows that the drivers of residential area-choice for them are an easy commute to work, safety – described as 'perceived "security" of the local area' – and the proximity to the Japanese school and other Japanese cultural facilities (White and Hurdley 2003: 695). Association with 'areas of high social status' (p691) was another factor. These are all similar to the reasons why Wilmott and Young's suburbanites relocated, with 'people like us' replacing the more clearly defined desire to live near to fellow Japanese. White and Hurdley name Finchley, North Wembley, Ealing, West Acton, Wimbledon and Croydon as favoured destinations. There needed to be an existing network of Japanese structures for an area to 'work'. (West Wickham on the south east London/Kent border had been pioneered by one letting agency targetting Japanese tenants, and they had set up an office there, but 'it was not supported by the companies who saw it as "too English", so the branch moved to Putney where other agencies were already operating' (p694).)

In many ways, however, suburbanisation is the opposite of gentrification. Allen (2007) found in his research into inner city gentrification that, as well as the usual 'yuppie' singletons and couples, this lifestyle was also attractive to counter-culturalists, gays and lesbians and empty-nester older couples who had 'done the family thing' and now wanted to take advantage of the city centre. Younger gentrifiers who go on to move out when they have children frequently come to regard this phase of their lives as a stage as opposed to a totalising life-style – especially if they are seeking good secondary state-sector school provision, which is hard to come by in cities but often more plentiful in adjacent boroughs. It is notable that Trafford bordering Manchester has retained grammar schools, as have Kent and Buckinghamshire on the edges of London. As one of Allen's interviewees (p677) comments: 'You want a big house with a garden as you get older and things like that'.

In some ways, then, it is unsurprising that part of the aim of the gentrifying movement was to 'take back' what had frequently been subdivided. Changing multi-occupancy inner-city period property back into single family ownership was an attempt to suburbanise the city. On the other hand, some parts of suburbia – which, contrary to myth, has often housed the young and thus been a seedbed of popular culture (the Beatles and Stones were essentially suburban boys as were punks and the purveyors of Britpop) – now contain an ageing population. Many older people are staying put, thereby contributing to the shortage of family-sized properties. Linking ethnic diversity with age, a sixty year old member of Kingston's mosque committee told me:

> For the first time I'm now seeing ... as I drive through these leafy

lanes of Surrey, after being here for forty years, for the first time ever I am seeing brown faces. They are the African carers waiting at the bus-stop who go into elderly people's homes.

SOCIO-SPATIAL QUESTIONS

As should by now be clear, the suburbs are places that are defined in the imagination as much as by geography. Understanding this is aided by Lefebvre's threefold theory of 'spatial practice', 'representations of space' and 'representational spaces'. All three are interconnected. Decisions involving socio-spatial relations can be based on choice – for example to leave the slums and the dirt-ridden, insalubrious inner city – or imposed through material constraint – for example being forced to move to less desirable suburbs because of high rents. The effect of the Coalition government's changes to housing benefit to introduce a 'cap' on the limit private landlords can claim is likely to have the effect of forcing people out from the city to outlying, unpopular districts at its fringes. Boris Johnson, Mayor of London, in his characteristically idiosyncratic language predicted that it would amount to 'Kosovo-style ethnic cleansing'. Certainly such measures, combined with rising rents and unaffordable house prices add to the dynamics of change in the suburbs. It is possible that we will see increasing differentiation between and within specific suburbs. Contemporary challenges can in many areas be seen in the physical built environment – decaying infrastructure, vacant retail units, competition from 'out of town' malls, traffic congestion and deserted industrial estates, now replaced by hi-tech business parks that employ fewer people (for some there has also been a radical re-spacing of living and working spaces, as in the increasing numbers of those who 'work from home').

Globalisation and its attendant 'time-space compression' (Harvey quoted in Marsh and Keating 2006:158) has impacted on suburbia and transformed many aspects of it. Can the geographically relegated fringe of the suburb 'cut it' in the brave new world of global village? Globalisation can be seen as a multi-layered and necessarily overlapping set of social and cultural as well as economic processes. Many suburban residents now reflect multiple identities and senses of belonging, with identifications to their country of birth or ancestral home as well as to where they may currently be living. The question is whether the suburbs can attract other connections. The modern suburb relies on the same factors as the modern city – the free flow of capital, goods, services and labour and supporting infrastructures of transport and communications networks.

The much greater flows of a globalised world make constant adaptation necessary. For example cities need to attract multinational companies, but the movement away from town centres has also meant that companies such as Samsung and Daewoo have located away from traditional urban centres in the UK. This produces different patterns of transport and different relationships between dormitory areas and working areas. One factor in attracting investment is 'human capital' – the potential of a location to attract diverse people and talent. This includes culture and the arts, and the presence of universities and skilled workers. Redbrick universities in the old civic city centres have played this role, but many of the post 1992 'new' universities are likely to be found in suburban areas: for example Middlesex and Kingston, to London's north and south. The information exchange aspect of the modern city increasingly applies to its suburbs. Cities can recede in attractiveness and go out of fashion if what they offer can be offered in a more cost-effective way elsewhere. The suburbs of such a city will then also undergo decline, as their fortunes tend to be interlinked. Many cities have tried to counter these trends though cultural initiatives – for example the Northern towns of Newcastle and Liverpool. Other places have found things more difficult as ebb and flow of globalisation gives and takes away. In towns such as Oldham in Greater Manchester, many former mill-workers came from Pakistan and Bangladesh to perform jobs for which there were labour shortages in the 1960s, but twenty years later these were being outsourced back to their countries of origin.

*

Chapter 1 considers historical analyses of the suburbs. Chapter 2 moves on to electoral politics, while Chapter 3 looks at alternative protest in suburbia. Chapter 4, 'Faith in the suburbs', reflects on the Archbishop of Canterbury's 'Faith in the City' report that emerged from an earlier period of rioting. Chapter 5 then turns to consumption and suburbia. Chapter 6 looks at extremism in suburbia, both among Islamic fundamentalists and among right-wing English extremists. Chapter 7 looks at suburbia in hard times: how is the utopian suburban dream faring now that we all are in so many ways living 'on the edge'?

REFERENCES

Allen, C. (2007) 'Of urban entrepreneurs or 24-hour party people? City-centre living in Manchester, England', *Environment and Planning A* 39(3), pp666-683.

Bedggood, D. (2007) 'Stratifying Class', in Matthewman, S et al (eds), *Being Sociological*, Palgrave-Macmillan, pp131-148.

Beck, U. (1999) 'The New Statesman Essay – Goodbye to all that wage slavery', 5.3.99: www.newstatesman.com/199903050020.

Beck, U. (1992) *Risk Society*, Sage.

Beck, U. & Beck-Gernsheim, E. (2002) *Individualization: Institutionalized Individualism and its Social and Political Consequences*, Sage.

Betjeman, J. (2009) *Betjeman's England*, Introduction, by Games, Stephen, John Murray.

Bracchi, P. (2010) 'Twitter and the bomb joke that's blown justice to bits', 16.11.10: www.dailymail.co.uk/news/article-1330049/Paul-Chambers-Twitter-bomb-joke-trial-thats-blown-justice-bits.html#ixzz160th5GOl.

Brook, C., Mooney, G., and Pile, S. (1998) (eds) *Unruly Cities? Order?Disorder*, Routledge

Clarkson, R. (2010) 'Twitter joke conviction: bomb tweet compared to Betjeman's poem "Slough", 27.9.11: http://blogs.findlaw.com/solicitor/2010/09/twitter-joke-conviction-bomb-tweet-compared-to-betjem ans-poem-slough.html.

Conservativehome (2010) 'Cameron promises most family-friendly government in UK history', 22.1.10: http://playpolitical.typepad.com/uk_conservative/2010/01/cameron-promises-most-familyfriendly-government-in-uk-history.html.

Dines, M. (2009) *Homecoming Queens: Gay Suburban Narratives in American and British Culture*, Palgrave Macmillan.

Dorling, D. (2008) 'Cash and the Class System', *New Statesman*, 8.7.08, pp24-7: www.newstatesman.com/society/2008/07/middle-class-british-income.

Dorling, D. (2008) 'Our divided nation', *New Statesman* 14.6.10: www.newstatesman.com/uk-politics/2010/06/election-seats-support-tory.

Ermisch, J. and Seidler, T. (2009) 'Living apart together', in Brynin, M. and Ermisch J., *Changing relationships*, Routledge.

Fiske. J. (1987) *Television Culture*, Methuen/ Routledge.

Friedan, B. (2001) *The Feminine Mystique* [New ed.], introduction by Anna Quindlen, W. W. Norton.

Hargreaves, A. and McKinney, M. (1997) (eds) *Post Colonial Cultures in* France, Routledge.

Haskey J. (2005) 'Living arrangements in contemporary Britain: having a partner who lives elsewhere and living apart together (LAT)', *Population Trends* 122, pp35-45.

Haskey J. and Lewis, J. (2006) 'Living apart together in Britain; context and meaning', *International Journal of Law in Context*, 2, 1, pp37-48.

Lefebvre, H. (1991) *The Production of Space*, Blackwell.

Levin, I. (2004), 'Living apart together: a new family form', *Current Sociology*, 52, 2, pp223-40.

Levin, I. and Trost, J. (1999) 'Living apart together', *Community, Work and Family*, 2, 3, pp270-294.

Lott, T. (1996) *The Scent of Dried Roses*, Penguin.

Marsh, I. and Keating, M. (2006) *Sociology: Making Sense of Society*, Longman.

Masterman C. (1909/2008) *The condition of England*, Faber.

Medhurst, A. (1997) 'Negotiating the gnome zone: versions of suburban British popular culture', in Silverstone, R. (ed), *Visions of Suburbia*, Routledge.

Mumford, L. (1991/1961), *The city in history: its origins, its transformations, and its prospects*, Penguin.

Office of The Mayor of London (2010) *Pre-publication report of the findings of the Outer London Commission*: www.london.gov.uk/who-runs-london/mayor/publications/planning/outer-london-commissions-final-report.

Orwell, G. (1968 edition of 1941 essay) 'The lion and the unicorn', *The Collected Essays, Journalism and Letters of George Orwell, Volume II: My country Right or left?* (edited by Orwell, S. and Angus, I.) Secker and Warburg.

Oswell, D. (1998) 'True Love in Queer Times: Romance, Suburbia and Masculinity', in Pearce, L. and Wisker, G. (eds), *Fatal Attractions and Cultural Subversions: Scripting Romance in Contemporary Literature and Film*, Pluto Press, 1998, pp157-173 .

Oswell, D. (2000) 'Suburban Tales: Television, Masculinity and Textual Geographies', in David Bell and Azzedine Haddour (eds), *City Visions*, Longman.

Pile, S., Brook, C. and Mooney, C. (eds) (1999) *Unruly Cities: Order/Disorder*, Routledge.

Roseneil, S. and Budgeon, S. (2004) 'Cultures of Intimacy and Care Beyond the Family: Personal Life and Social Change in the Early Twenty-First, *Current Sociology*, 52, 2, pp135-159

Soep. L. (2010) 'Web Two Dot Whoah: The Digital Afterlife of Youth-Produced Media', paper presented at *Youth making media, making 'youth'*, ESRC seminar, Loughborough University, 22.9.10.

Simms, A. (2007) *Tescopoly: How one shop came out on top and why it matters*, Constable.

Stamp, G. (2010) 'Englishman's castles': www.faqs.org/periodicals/201004/2003835081.html#ixzz15Scv9Aly.

Thorns, D. (1972) *Suburbia*, Paladin.

Walker, N. (1985) 'Humor and Gender Roles: The "Funny" Feminism of the Post-World War II Suburbs', *American Quarterly*, Vol. 37, No. 1, Special Issue: *American Humor* (Spring, 1985), pp98-113, The Johns Hopkins University Press.

White, P.E. and Hurdley, L. (2003) 'International migration and the housing market: Japanese corporate movers in London', *Urban Studies* 40(4), pp687-706.

Whyte, W. (1956/2002) *The organization man*, Simon & Schuster.

Willis, I. (2010) 'Remixing Global Media: Fan Culture as Participation' at *Youth making media, making 'youth'* ESRC seminar, Loughborough University, 22.9.10.

Willmott, P. and Young, M. (1957) *Family and Kinship in East London*, Pelican.

Willmott, P. and Young, M. (1960) *Family and Class in a London Suburb*, Routledge and Kegan Paul.

1

Re-situating suburbia

> For me, suburbia is a kind of nether place. It's not urban and it's not rural. It's between the two, and the kind of people who live there are the people from middle England. People with middling aspirations. But that conservatism is positively inspirational: it's like being in Stalag 17 – you've got to make an escape plan.
>
> Billy Bragg

Even though it is something so seemingly familiar, there is no universal agreement about what constitutes 'suburbia', notwithstanding the fact that it is repeatedly claimed to be where most of 'us' (i.e. the majority of people in both the UK and US) live. The stereotypical suburban landscape constructs itself in the popular imagination as a place of leafy lanes comprised of identically spotless semi-detached houses in which mundane lives are lived. Always implicitly white nosey neighbours peer out from behind the net curtains to witness comings and goings, and find out what consumer durables the locals are acquiring; besuited males kiss goodbye their wives and kids en route to the daily commute to the office; cars are cleaned at the weekend; and pensioners see out their days here. It is not only a topological construction; it also connotes a set of attitudes, mores and values. It is 'safe' space.

Yet twentieth century migration has given birth to the multi-ethnic twenty-first century suburb, and an expanded range of issues relevant to contemporary society. In the twenty-first century, having experienced massive growth in the previous century, the suburbs have – even if sporadically – been host to extraordinary happenings that have called into question received notions: almost as if a suburban revenge is taking place to silence those who have always seen them as inherently dull. Suburbs have been exposed as being where Islamic extremists live, where stabbings and shootings occur, and where the far right thrive politically. The columnist Rod Liddle has even provocatively suggested (2008) that anyone wanting to be stabbed should take a trip to the suburbs. This is all in contrast to the notion that 'nothing ever happens' in suburbia.

As recently as 2001, Rogers and Power (2001:69) could state: 'Suburbs are residential areas built outside the core of the inner city, at distinctly lower density but linked to it through continuous development. They have a simple, repetitive form with single-family, usually owner occupied, semi-detached or detached houses with gardens'. But such a neat definition is unable to do justice to the complexities of the modern suburb. In fact a typology of suburbs could be sketched: older established public-transport-commuting suburbs; car-culture suburbs; suburbs where the dominant mode of tenure is owner-occupation; planned suburbs with much in common with 'new towns'; suburbs popular with ethnic minority families; corporation suburbia, etc. Even in attempting to spell this out, however, it becomes rapidly apparent that the suburban spectrum eludes easy definition. Many areas exhibit a number of these features, and all are undergoing changes: the Thatcherite 'right to buy' legislation, for example, has destroyed/and or transformed the corporation suburbs. But what does unite all the variants is their relative invisibility from public discourse in media and policy-making circles, certainly until recent years. Beyond the central core and inner fringes of the city, the suburbs are where the often-silent majority reside; and as such they provide a rich diversity of experience that is all too easily ignored by the urban elitists whose commentary renders suburbia absent from sociology textbooks or newspaper comment columns. The old ideas of suburbia as sterile and unchanging are in desperate need of updating. Suburbia has frequently been examined from a town planning or geographical perspective, but there is an urgent need to consider the suburbs as dynamic social and cultural spaces, and to re-centre them so that they are no longer forgotten peripheral spaces.

For many suburbia has negative connotations. One could construct a lengthy list of suburban detractors, going back at least to the early nineteenth century. According to Andrew Motion, Lord Byron was the first person to use the word derogatively (1998:583), when he described suburban dwellers as 'having inferior manners, narrowness of view etc' – in referring to Keats and his circle who, as non-aristocrats, non-classically educated, were regarded as vulgar and suburban. Architect Clough Williams-Ellis, a founder member of the Campaign for the Protection of Rural England, in his 1928 book *England and the Octopus* employed the metaphor of an eight-tentacled sea monster to convey the sprawl of suburbia. (Williams-Ellis's other great career highlight was as creator of Portmeirion in Wales, which gives an indication of his architectural preference.) Donaldson (1969:3) notes that for many people 'the very word "suburbia" carries unpleasant overtones, suggesting nothing so much as some kind of scruffy disease'. Betjeman was another perpetrator of this argument, both in his television documentaries and in his poetry. An early undated poem of his (Betjeman 2009:172) mocks the inhabitants of Hampstead Garden Suburb:

O wot ye why in Orchard Way
The roofs be steep and shelving?
Or wot ye what the dwellers say
In close and garden delving?

(This is an area designed by Sir Edwin Lutyens and others, which is now considered to be an area of great architectural significance.) More usual complaints concern the cramped nature of houses, for although suburban dwellings were originally built at low density, they later were often tightly packed in, by commercial housebuilders and cash-strapped councils. Donaldson (1969:77) outlines 'the suburban paradox ... The escape to the wide open spaces of the countryside leads to a homogeneous life lived in homogeneous homes, every bit as confining as the most crowded city existence'. Privacy was also sacrificed in this process.

Defining suburbia is problematic: it is often done by a process of elimination – we know that the suburbs are not the country and not the city. We know what suburbia is in opposition to rather than what it is (Webster 2000). It is in many ways the territory of in-between. The semi-private spaces of suburbs are derided for their supposed dreariness but aspired to for their merits – which are also their demerits. The two are always painted in opposition to one another, a relationship of opposites:

SUBURBAN	**URBAN**
White	Ethnic mix
Quiet	Noise
Space	Built-up environment
Aspiration/affluence	Multiple deprivation, decay
Choice	Constraint
Uniformity	Difference
Homogeneity	Quirky
Conformist	Bohemian
Boredom	Excitement
Fuddy-duddy	Youth
Privatised space	Community

English suburbia has featured more often in fictitious portrayal than in the literature of the social sciences or as a pressing topic of public policy. And these depictions in fiction often reinforce stereotypes. They have predominantly portrayed the drab, boring existence of the typical suburban-dweller and turned it into situation comedy, as in the 1970s television series *Terry and June* and *The Good Life*. More recent interventions have represented minority populations, but through celebrations of the spectacular, as in Hanif Kureishi's *The Buddha of Suburbia* and Zadie Smith's *White Teeth*, in which the conformism of unremarkable white suburbia is counterposed to a more fashionable embrace of the multicultural and exotic. Meanwhile in the US *Desperate Housewives* has become the emblematic show of suburban lifestyles, depicting bored women conducting extra-curricular activities to relieve the tedium of mass-produced mediocrity, from dwellings that command a vast expanse of space and are surrounded by immaculately manicured lawns. Though fun to watch, this is far from the reality experienced by most of its viewers, the majority of whom inhabit suburban settings but of very different kinds.

The traditional picture of suburbia paints minority ethnic communities as having been 'left behind' in inner-city ghetto districts; it presumes that the latter equate with differentiation whilst the suburbs do not. But this is far from being the case. Indeed the old expression of 'white flight', originally applied in a US context for émigrés leaving neighbourhoods to blacks, is becoming more and more of a nonsense.

Twenty-first century British suburbia has a high degree of social mixing. A suburb such as Southall in West London, positioned near Heathrow airport, has been a long-established Punjabi Sikh neighbourhood. More recently many other minority communities are moving progressively outward to suburbs from inner city bases.

THE RISE AND FALL OF SUBURBAN SPRAWL?

The suburb as understood in this book is very much an Anglo-Saxon formulation, applying to the urban sprawl of the geographically vast US and the more physically compact UK from the 1800s onwards, with a chief period of growth in the twentieth century (Clapson 2003). In Canada and Australia, too, suburbs are a way of life (Harris 2004, Stratton and Ang 1994). According to Lewis Mumford, in *The City in History* (1961:483), the first cities sprung up suburbs on their outskirts, and archaeologists have uncovered and dated the remains of suburbs going as far back as the greater Ur in Mesopotamia thirty centuries BC. But the phenomenon reached new levels in the West with the suburban growth of the nineteenth century (though academic discussion on modernity and the metropolis has tended to concentrate on the central city across both sides of the Atlantic, whether in the domain of planning and architectural design, or in studies of the inner city by sociologists, who have always tended to be interested in people 'at the bottom').

Importantly, in both the US and UK the form and function of suburbia is multiple not singular or unitary, and it plays an important but often under-acknowledged structuring role in the landscape of the city. The phrase *rus in urbe* demonstrates the 'best of both worlds' aspect of the suburbs. A respondent in Willmott and Young's (1960:8) study of the middle-class East London suburb of Woodford describes it as 'the place I've been looking for all my life – a nice country village within easy reach of London'. Suburbia was conceived of as a positive solution to urban ills. Referring to the garden cities of Ebenezer Howard that became the prototype for later planned garden suburbs, Pile et al (1998:25) commented: 'people were dreaming of utopian solutions to the horror of Victorian cities'. In suburbia there are pastoral sounding Dells, Ways, Avenues, Closes and Roads rather than Streets. To begin with, as outlined by Rogers and Power, the main defining feature was a low density layout with a small number of houses per hectare, both in speculatively built properties and suburban council housing. With the advent of the tower block, popular in the 1960s, social housing once more moved away from single houses, but most of these developments were concentrated in inner-city locations. In the UK the first wave of suburbia was built around the railway network to facilitate city commuting. Later suburbs were designed more with the motorist in mind. In the US, too, the construction of the railroad suburb was replaced by the car-led suburb. The suburbs are remarkably widespread as a lifestyle, in spite of the flack they attract; Barker (2009) recently claimed that 84 per cent of people in Britain live them. Much of the original appeal of the suburban lifestyle rested in the twin attractions of privacy and the possibility of healthy living, offering the possibility of a simulated home in the country. The built environment, social and residential mobility, income, age and occupational status are all general reasons that might explain suburban living as a lifestyle choice.

Although the US is seen as more laissez faire than the UK, which has a more historically interventionist welfare state, public policy has played a significant part in the rise of American suburbanisation (and arguably the attendant process of white flight). This began with the redrawn criteria for mortgage lending in Roosevelt's New Deal, which was followed by further housing acts to stimulate house-building through subsidies for construction companies and then the GI Bill, which guaranteed property purchase loans to war veterans. Completing legislative inducements to all parties concerned were Federal highway-building schemes, which ensured that a ready and able workforce could easily access the city (i.e. workplace) from its suburban outpost suburbs (i.e. home). The cumulative effect of such legislation was to put home-ownership within reach of great swathes of the population for the first time ever. Neatly manicured lawns, picture windows and white picket fences are seen as the archetypal symbols of American suburbs, and this idea of the suburb as being of cookie-cutter or identikit construction can partly be explained by the assembly-line produced Levittown model, which standardised – and set the standard for – American suburban housing. Levittown of Long Island New York, which takes its name from the Levitt house-builders, is still America's largest housing development, where 4000 acres of potato fields were replaced by curvilinear streets housing 17,400 family dwellings at a knockdown price. The stream-lined, cost-cutting, mass production process employed has been likened to Taylorisation. On-site construction was carried out by a largely unskilled and non-unionised workforce, using prefabricated parts. However, the suburbs built by the construction industry were more than simply bricks and mortar; they began to connote an entire lifestyle, and this has been now been pervasive for generations. Writing from an architecture and planning perspective, MacBurnie (1995:134) rightly notes: 'In contemporary discourse, the periphery is perceived to have transcended the narrow confines of any specific territory, process or attendant morphology, symbolizing instead a condition or state of mind'. In short, both 'suburbia' and 'suburbs' have become highly loaded terms, synonymous with dullness and backward-looking conformity.

Despite the predominant image of private wealth and wealth display in suburbia, the expansion of social housing also extended into the suburbs. Co-existing with the inter-war suburban semi, with its sunbeam gate, neo-baronial turreted gables, mock Tudor exterior and – depending on taste and wealth – double-garage and stone cladding is 'corporation suburbia', the shorthand applied in the UK for the peripheral estates of council housing built on the edge of cities by local authorities. In her book which refutes the stereotypes of social housing, Lynsey Hanley (2007:7) writes: 'Play word association with the term "council estate". Estates mean alcoholism, drug addiction, relentless petty stupidity, a kind of stir craziness induced by chronic poverty and the human mind caged by the rigid bars of class and learned incuriosity'. Yet before tower-block concrete became fashionable in the 1960s as a quick solution to the housing of populations in bombed-out inner cities, the ambitious suburban estates of council houses of the inter-war years were modelled on the garden cities built for artisans as envisaged by the philanthropist Ebenezer Howard, who pioneered Letchworth in Hertfordshire in the 1900s. Other examples built along similar principles include Bournville, built by the Cadbury family in Birmingham, Lord Leverhulme's Port Sunlight and Dame Henrietta Barnett's Hampstead Garden Suburb. Ackroyd (2000:732) refers to 'the erection of "cottage estates" on the fringes of London', noting that 'the Cockney need not necessarily be a product of the slums'. This building template was subsequently followed in numerous cities across the country, for example Wythenshawe and Burnage in South Manchester. In the 1980s the Thatcher government's policy of 'right to buy' allowed council tenants to purchase their homes at a knockdown below-market rate, and the fall-out from this policy was a general devaluing of the entire notion of social housing and estates. These now became a refuge of last resort for those at the bottom (the literal margins) of society. But the social composition of the some of the large estates was also transformed, with many houses now becoming privately owned, often by buy-to-let landlords.

The constituency of Jon Cruddas, the Labour MP for Dagenham and Rainham (Olechnowicz, 1997; Wilmott 1963), includes a great deal of this type of housing:

> *How does suburbia fit?*
>
> Erm, you know I don't really understand what the term suburban means. It's quite an interesting concept ... I think the socio-economic profile of Dagenham is slightly at odds with its geographic position.
>
> *It's not a Romford ...*
>
> No, or a Southgate or ... but that to me just demonstrates the trouble with the term 'suburban'. It implies a homogenised community, a white community, a relatively prosperous community – the Terry and June thing – whereas if you scrape beneath the veneer it's a much more complex thing in terms of spatial-economic development ... when you've got net migration into London of 200,000 a year, the simple demographic dynamics are absolutely extraordinary ... including on housing and internal migration within the city. In Dagenham what you've basically got is a lot of people still migrating from inner East London out into the borough of Barking and Dagenham, just as people did forty, fifty years ago. The difference is this that time they're black. It's a very similar physical journey, it's just different groupings, and that reflects the changing class composition – the interesting thing to me is that if you talk about class nowadays you usually don't have the word black in front of it. You know, there is the 'white working class' – which constructs the sociology of the more or less degenerate white mob, but the working class is actually a much more fluid, heterogeneous group. That's witnessed by the repeating patterns of white working-class migration from inner-east London to Barking and Dagenham. You've always

> had certain wards that have had an Asian element, like Abbey ward in Barking, and a greater Asian element in some of the privately-owned wards in Dagenham – Chadwell Heath, for example. But now the most recent driver of demographic change are the black Africans, west Africans, from Nigeria, Sierra Leone, Ghana, who are moving in. These changes are connected with patterns of kinship linked to family, villages and churches, young families moving out of central London.

James Cleverly, the London assembly member for the very different borough Bexley and Bromley, also describes a mixed picture of different land uses and housing styles in his constituency, which encompasses the 'model' Thamesmead estate as well as Bexley, which is more stereotypically suburban:

> The parliamentary constituency of Bexleyheath and Crayford, which is basically this middle band of Bexley, has the largest proportion of semi-detached houses of any parliamentary constituency in the country, so if you were going to look at something which was iconically suburban, that is it. So it's exactly as you'd expect it to be, slightly older than the citywide average, slightly whiter than the citywide average, slightly more affluent than the citywide average. An awful lot of Jaguars and Rovers in the front drive, nice gardens, a working population typically commuting up into London, train to London Bridge. If I made you shut your eyes and I took you there you'd go 'yes, this is what I meant' … The northern bit of the London borough of Bromley, north east bit, again is very much similar, very comfortable, suburban, semi-detached houses, nice cars, gravel driveways, getting gently more affluent as we head south.

When I asked Jon Cruddas if he foresaw a change that could reposition Dagenham, if it could make a transition to become a Bexley, he was realistic about the prospects. (After all, it is an area overshadowed by the vast Becontree estate, about which Wilmott (1963:3) commented: 'The estate seems unending; and it is, in fact, immense'. It was 2,700 acres of what he called 'tedious architecture', houses with 'a bare, sad look about them … a wasteland air' (Wilmott 1963:4). Today the Rainham end of the constituency is the more archetypally suburban part of the seat.) When I asked whether Dagenham would ever become a desirable suburb he answered:

> Well, it's a working class community. It's changing actually but ... I think it's a great place. I have a good time. It's very honest in terms of its frustrations. People will tell you what they think. That's partly what lies beneath the BNP thing. They're very frustrated ... their inability to navigate through the complexities of the modern world, especially when it's changed so quickly. The dynamics at work in terms of the sheer velocity of change.

In other words people are aware of the rapid changes in their own part of suburbia, though they may not know how to deal with them.

James Cleverly argued an interesting proposition:

> I would suggest that, unlike many cities around the world, certainly many European cities, Londoners are suburban at heart generally. If you're a Parisian, as you become more affluent you move closer to the centre, and the idea of having a family of 5 in a flat right slap bang in the heart of Paris is an aspiration, something to aspire to ... That makes complete sense. That's where the restaurants are, the galleries are, that's where all the transport converges. Who wouldn't want to live in a smart urban flat? You'd be crazy not to. Whereas in London you could give them the keys either to a flat in Eaton Terrace or to a 5-bedroom semi in Bromley and a lot of them would take your big house with a gravel drive – you know, near Parkland in Chislehurst ... No Parisian would ever do that. For the French it would be a complete no-brainer. If I handed someone two and half million quid to spend on a property ... they would be straight slap-bang into the heart of Paris. But I would say a significant proportion of Londoners, probably the majority, would go for the big house in Chislehurst you know. And why is that? ... big cultural differences, which is why affluence congregates in Paris, Berlin, a lot of these big urban cities, and in London to a large extent it kind of scatters.

THE AMERICAN DREAM

The suburbs are also part and parcel of the American dream, and the US is the world's most suburbanized nation. Examples are manifold: as well as the Long Island Levittown there is the Levittown in Bucks County, Pennsylvania. Other cities contain other examples: Bloomington/Minnesota, Westport/Connecticut, Park Forest/Chicago and countless others. Donaldson (1964:64) cites Henry Ford as a factor in their growth: 'The internal combustion engine and mass-produced automobiles shortened the distance from city to suburb, and new roadways sliced through the greenbelt between railroad stations throwing up radial eyesores in their wake'. The most sustained growth of suburban homes took place under Eisenhower around New York, Boston, Los Angeles and Detroit, as a building boom took place to fuel demand from families that were reuniting after the war or making up for lost time. It is a natural sentiment to want to seek space away from overcrowding, and GI loans made this a real possibility. Donaldson (1969:68) explains how the suburban imperative became lodged in the national psyche:

There remains today a feeling that great cities are places to visit, not to live, and many mid westerners believe that New York, for example, is not only dirty, crowded and hectic (and it is all these things) but also, somehow evil. So Americans pack up and move to the suburbs, living by the village myth, preferring to travel several hours a day to avoid the great city.

Outside space is a key part of the suburban domain, allowing for the staging of garden parties, and for suburban inhabitants to occupy themselves in maintaining its greenery. In the words of Donaldson (1969:71): 'Americans might like to persuade themselves that in caring for their front lawn, they were satisfying some kind of primeval urge to return to the good agrarian age'. As early on as in 1899 Thorstein Veblen in his well-known work on proto-consumerism and wealth display also draws a parallel between the well-kempt lawn and cow pasture. In this sense the acquisition of land with the suburban home is what John Major might have called a 'back to basics' desire.

'Those who could afford to choose where they lived abandoned the city centres … to philanthropists … the working classes and urban poor', claims Iain Chambers (1986:22). Rogers and Power (2002:29) also paint a picture of suburban population diffusion: 'the outward flow of people who have choice and jobs, who leave behind depleted services, boarded up shops, half empty classrooms, derelict homes and spaces'. This fits with the notion that inner-city dwelling is a constraint rather than a choice. It should be noted, however, that for many philanthropists the inner city has been selected as their base; the historian David Kynaston (2009:424) argues that in recent times 'the moral superiority of the inner city over the suburb or new town was a given'. Indeed there has been a sense that moving to the suburb was a conscious removal of oneself from the 'real life' of the decaying inner-city for the blandness beyond it – as the 'white flight' concept implies. This term is American in origin and US sociologist William Frey (1979:426) summarised it thus: 'After the war, the increased availability of suburban housing permitted an outward movement of central city whites as well as an expansion of blacks into previously white neighbourhoods.' Figures of city depopulation substantiate the sense of exodus from the metropolis on the part of the populace, but social reformers have often chosen to situate their work (and even selves) in the inner city – from Booth's famous Victorian poverty-mapping of the capital to the postwar siting of the Institute of Community Studies (now renamed the Young Foundation) in Bethnal Green, the subject of the seminal *Family and Kinship in East London*. The decision of the Edwardian C.F.G. Masterman to take up rooms in a tenement block in the inner south London district of Camberwell in London, in order to get a taste of the working-class experience, went further still.

However, the direction of travel has mainly been away from the inner city. MacBurnie (1995:136) has explained: 'In the American context, where the urban has seldom existed as a cultural project, the suburban has become the hegemonic ambition, representative of the nation's collective identity. The urban, defined oppositionally, has necessarily come to signify the marginal.' This is also a widespread view in the UK. The last Labour housing minister, Caroline Flint (2011:203) (while simultaneously pouring scorn on critical social commentators on the grounds that they are disconnected from reality – 'penning articles from the comfort of owner-occupied leafy suburbs and country cottages') outlined a list of the priorities of voters that to all intents and purposes constituted a suburban checklist. She argued: 'The desire to be close to family, invest, improve, move to the nice neighbourhoods, leave behind something for the next generation, or just have a few square metres of your own – conservatory and all – is instinctive, and the drive to own [property] is unshakeable'. The broad thrust of UK public policy thinking has long conceptualised the inner city as a problem to be approached in problem-solving terms – from

Mrs Thatcher's 1987 declaration that after eight years in power the government should do something about 'those inner cities', to New Labour's Urban Task Force and 'Excellence-in-cities' programme.

To date no government has unveiled a comparable 'excellence-in-suburbs' policy agenda, though there have been sporadic initiatives. In September 2009 a report was published, claiming that outer London boroughs were being starved of money in favour of inner-city regeneration: 'Eighty per cent of people in the UK live in suburbs; we are the vast majority of the population. We need to stop suburbs declining. Some may say they are already in decline. This is our response to that challenge (London Councils 2009).' Boris Johnson as London Mayor initiated the Outer London Commission, which found a range of suburban problems, including congestion, blighted high streets, lack of educational provision, affordable housing and crime, but his administration has done little to address such problems.

MODERNITY V TRADITION

The suburbs are steeped in mythology as unchanging and conservative. They are associated more with 'tradition' than 'futurism'. Ackroyd (2000:733) sees 'cultural nostalgia ... evident in the architectural style of the new suburbs'. This is most famously evident in the suburban mock-Tudor semi-detached house or in the flourish of a neo-baronial turret. And much new-build suburban architecture continues to be constructed in traditionalist styling. Historically, however, while suburban housebuilding could now be seen as 'playing it safe', styles such as Mock Tudor also included innovatory elements. This was particularly true of the Arts and Crafts designers, and in early 2010, for example, the work of Ernest Trobridge (1884-1942) was celebrated at the Museum of Brent in a major exhibition, 'Ernest Trobridge: Visionary of the Suburbs'. This was a huge leap forward from the ribbing of such styles as being suitable only for the nouveau riche, as in the phrase 'Stockbroker Tudor', as cartoonist Osbert Lancaster termed middle-class 1930s housing. There were contradictions in the nature of the 1930s semi and the suburban housebuilding of the Edwardian era: though they were a new development, their design can be seen at the least as echoing the past.

But though the consequences of modernity are most apparent in the urban landscape, the forces that shape the city also apply to the suburbs at the city's edges: the suburbs grew of the city, and questions of economy, planning and history equally apply to them, as do power relations and inequalities. As MacBurnie (1995:135) rightly points out: 'The rise of the suburban metropolis exposes some of the inherent conflicts and contradictions in the unfinished project of modernity.' However, the champions of modernity have often been enemies of suburbia, which is seen as stultifying in its echoes of the past.

Alongside all the housing reassuringly built from traditional materials and with an emphasis on continuity, there was also more dramatically modernist building in the suburbs, signalling a more fundamental break with the past – particularly in public projects. Among the most striking of these were the London Underground stations of the interwar years. These made appeals to the potential customer through technology, stressing 'fast electric trains' and the prospect of escaping the slums for new suburban pastures. 'You will find real comfort and happiness in Edgware', or 'Why not live in Hounslow?' were the typical appeals, presented through suitably modern art advertising, with posters that were indebted to the avant garde movement. Charles Holden's Piccadilly Line creations such as Southgate and Bounds Green to the north or Park Royal and Boston Manor in the west all followed a modernist European template, particularly in their clean lines. Chiswick Park, on the district line, also resembles this style, with its brick 'box' type structure, glass panelled square windows and imposingly tall semi-circular ticket hall of reinforced concrete that announces the station name to the world. Green (2009) has claimed of Arnos Grove that when it arrived, its futuristic neon was 'like a bombshell in the countryside', with Southgate being more radical still, resembling a spaceship.

Contemporary suburban building certainly adopts modern technological forms. Workmanship and the traditional crafts and trades have become increasingly dislodged by new methods in building across the board: the recently completed L1 shopping mall in the centre of Liverpool is almost all concrete and steel with only a few bricks used. Suburban precincts are also becoming less timid in appearance, though Bicester in Oxfordshire was modelled on twee design principles. In contrast, the sheer scale of Manchester's Trafford centre has emboldened it.

Those who critique suburbia have included both those who have celebrated futurism and traditionalists who have attacked its newness and destruction of the rural past: the past and present frequently unite in their hatred of the periphery. As early as 1935 Anthony Bertram, in his book, *The House: A Machine for Living In*, declared: 'The man who builds a bogus Tudoresque villa or castellates his suburban home is committing a crime against truth and tradition. He is denying the history of progress, denying his own age and insulting the very thing he pretends to imitate by misusing it' (cited in Sharp and Rendel 2008). In 1956 Betjeman (2009:153) referred to his own aristocratic heritage, and his inability as a child to shoot like the best of them, in his poem about Hertfordshire, while at the same time condemning the houses that had sprung up there:

One can't be sure where London ends,
New towns have filled the fields of root,
Where father and his business friends,
Drove in the Landaulette to shoot

Tall concrete standards line the lane,
Brick boxes glitter in the sun:
Far more would these have caused him pain,
Than my mishandling of a gun.

Betjeman himself is something of a paradoxical figure; his thoughts on the disappearing world of the England of yore were communicated by the then technological sophistry of television; the arch critic of modernity used advances in film to rail against progress in social settlement.

The desire for the reassurance of the past in the building of the present, designed to last into the future, has perhaps recently been most evident in the building of Poundbury, Prince Charles' heritage styled town in Dorset, newly built from scratch in the 1990s.

THE IMPORTANCE OF PLACE

While some areas have gone unremarked on by academics, other locations seem to have acted as magnets for sociological study. East London has been a favourite since Charles Booth's landmark studies, although the area has subsequently tended to be viewed in a 'parish pump' idealising manner. Willmott and Young (1964:65), for example, refer to 'the kind of informal general "matiness" which characterises the old East End communities'. This conjures up the idea of jolly cockneys who triumph through adversity. The idea of authenticity is implicit in the East London setting for Downes' (1966) work on delinquency, and that of Cohen (1972) on skinheads. The latter is known for its much quoted perspective that skinhead activity is a response to a disappearing way of life: the young victims of urban renewal, and the slum clearance that has cut through their traditional communities, come to see the manifestation of aggressively working-class sartorial style as a compensatory solution. Clarke (1976:8) argues that 'the East End from a sociological point of view has been seen as the archetypal working-class community'. But for the traditional East End inhabitant, a move to suburbia is a definite step-up.

As we have seen, Willmott and Young flag a series of differences between Bethnal Green and Woodford – one of the key ones being the split between public and private. In their words: 'In Bethnal Green people are vigorously at home in the streets, their public face much the same as their private. In Woodford people seem to be quieter and even more reserved in public ... endorsing Mumford's description of suburbs as the apotheosis of "a collective attempt to lead a private life"'. Both locations are, as the authors stress, part of East London, but the former is inner-city and the latter suburban. However there is considerable interplay between such districts in suburban drift, illustrating that the suburbs have long been sites of diaspora. The follow-up study of the East End undertaken by Dench et al (2006) tells a tale of disenchantment, anger and resentment on the part of the whites who remained behind, with much friction between the established residents and the new arrivals, against a backdrop of an increasingly transient population.

Does place matter any more? Postmodern social theory suggests increasing de-territorialisation, although Nayak (2003), who conducted fieldwork amongst youth in the North East, passionately argues against this line of reasoning. In an era of globalisation, the neologism 'glocalisation' has been coined to capture the ostensibly contradictory processes between the global and local. All mainstream parties in Britain currently subscribe to some kind of 'localism' but there is a good deal of opportunism in this. Thus the Coalition government has been strategically astute in passing on many of its cuts to local councils through cutting their revenue support grant – a classic buck-passing exercise. Its 'Localism Bill', with the underpinning premise that 'Localism holds the key to economic, social and political success', claims to empower communities, but its main effect has been a defraying of expenses. Elected mayors have also been seen as a way of establishing local identity and autonomy. Others argue that the national is the main level of identity that people identify with. Labour shadow minister Ivan Lewis MP (2001:241-2) has written (in relation to the royal wedding in 2011: 'In the market-towns, villages, council estates and suburbs there is a desire to express pride in Englishness, partially born out of patriotism, partly as a cry of defiance from people who feel alienated from the mainstream political establishment'. The word 'cities' is curiously absent from his sentence – the suburb is generally felt to be part of quintessential Englishness, while the city itself retains dangerous connotations of cosmopolitanism. It is interesting that the EDL have chosen suburban areas for the holding of their provocative anti-Muslim marches, for example marching past Harrow mosque in 2009, and planning a protest against halal meat in school meals at Harrow Civic Centre in 2010 (though the latter had to be abandoned).

CONCLUSION: SITUATING SUBURBIA IN THE TWENTY-FIRST CENTURY

The twin currents of continuity and change have informed the unfolding of twentieth-century suburban history. The 'ethnicisation' of suburbia has contributed to its political reshaping: many parts of Britain's electoral map that were in my memory (dating from the 1980s onwards) obstinately blue, have been red from 1997 onwards. Bill Schwarz (1997), charting of the ending of Tory rule in 1997, sees the moment of victory as a fundamental 'break-up of the Conservative nation'. He writes: 'The old Tory vision of the Union had, in the 1990s, come to mean little more than the politics of a contracting England … Electorally, the conservative nation resembled nothing so much as the geographic cluster of subscribers to *Country Life*' (Schwarz 1997:27). Though the Tories returned to power through coalition in 2010, their hold on many areas will remain fragile inasmuch as they fail to shake off their old-fashioned version of Englishness. Equally, the 'ethnicisation' of suburbia brings with it challenges for the Labour Party. Following the rise in the BNP vote in Barking and Dagenham in outer east London, the respected pressure group Operation Black Vote called the borough 'the racist capital of the UK'.

Although its net effect was to lessen the supply of affordable housing, and there was very little social building in its wake, the right to buy has succeeded in opening up tracts of suburban estates to a more socially diverse range of people, with a quicker turnover of residents than was customary for the secure tenancy holders of the past (for example through sub-letting and buy to let). As Hanley (2007:59) rightly notes, the criteria for the original tenants of these estates were strict: 'these attractive health-improving homes were only open to those whose earnings were higher than the average worker'. When I interviewed Dagenham MP Jon Cruddas in 2007, his view of the dynamic and mixed nature of modern Dagenham was in sharp contrast to Wilmott's (1963:13) sketch of the area as 'a "one-class" community' at the time when it was originally built, identifying 'common criticisms, and indeed reasons for moving out of the area [were that] "Dagenham was too uniform, too depressing, or too limiting"' (1962:112). Contrastingly, a lack of uniformity seems to be the new contemporary norm:

> I think what is extraordinary about Dagenham is the way it's dealing with extraordinary forces rather than the way it isn't ... If you had these patterns of demographic change in the middle of Surrey ... you would have a political earthquake. They wouldn't deal with it. Actually what is extraordinary in Dagenham is the ability of the community to deal with all the changes ... There's not violence, there's no riots. It's safe, stable, quiet, honest, so I think the BNP will go, and what will be left, in hindsight, will be the extraordinary ability of the community to accept and adapt to these changes – if it was a rich middle-class community in the middle of Surrey, I tell you it wouldn't be such an orderly series of changes. The golf club would be on fire ... I don't know demographically any community that's changed as quickly as this historically ... this is unprecedented ... I've been the MP since 2001 and the demographic change in that time is absolutely extraordinary.

When I interviewed James Cleverly I told him that I was a bit worried that this book would focus on atypical suburbs. He told me that there is no such thing as a typical suburb:

> Every suburb is an atypical suburb. If you look at Croydon, Croydon is a very urban suburb, it's the third largest financial services centre ... They've striving for an independent city status and they have tall glass and steel ... It looks and feels more like the City/Canary Wharf than it does like Bromley, though it's literally just over the border – and yet that's a suburb. My neck of the woods doesn't have a huge amount of ethnic diversity but if you go to places in west London there's a huge amount ... Bexley until one generation ago was heavy industry, but Bromley's never been heavy industry ... Move around to the Richmond and Twickenham kind of area – incredibly white middle-class, very typical outer London – you know all the images you'd get, millionaires' row. You go up to Havering ... Havering's nothing like Richmond ...

It has been claimed that in modern times all the characteristics that were once cherished about suburbia – stability, safety, respectability and whiteness – are under threat, replaced by the risk and danger which now lurk around suburban corners. No longer can we comfort ourselves with the notion that an Englishman's home is his castle, or count on a suburban retreat into a privatised world untouched by external forces. It is certainly true that traditional urban-suburban dichotomies are indeed undergoing twenty-first century upsets, but alarm at new developments is a very old phenomenon. Thus, for example, the essayist and sometime Liberal MP C.F.G. Masterman (1909/1960:169) decried the time-space compression that he saw as being ushered in by technological advance: 'In all our mechanical ingenuities we have constructed masters for us, rather than servants; being compelled ... to adjust our lives to the new conditions which these, and not we ourselves, henceforth dictate and impose.' Telephones and express trains were among the examples he named as 'expedients which are adapted to acceleration, rather than to happiness'. In a chapter on suburbs (1909/1960:57), he described how the middle class's hard-working male population was 'a life of Security; a life of sedentary occupation; a life of Respectability ... [with] a male population engaged in all its working hours in small, crowded offices under artificial light'. For Masterman suburbs were part of the evils of modernity, but Richard Littlejohn (2007) has more recently sought to defend a suburbia that he sees as under siege: 'Not content with screwing the south of England to subsidise his native Scots, Gordon

Brown is now screwing the suburbs to pay for the burgeoning client state in the inner cities … Of course, the suburbs tend to vote Tory, which is why [he] hates them'.

But, as we by now have established, any idea of suburbia as singular or static is deeply misguided. Urban relations are dynamic, never static: they are shifting landscapes both culturally and socially. As Doreen Massey (1993:65) has commented: 'If it is now recognized that people have multiple identities then the same point can be made in relation to places. Moreover, such multiple identities can be a source of richness, or a source of conflict, or both.' As the following chapters will show, suburbia in the twenty-first century is as much about urban jungle as it is about the village green. Politicians and policy-makers ignore this at their peril.

REFERENCES

Ackroyd, P. (2000) *London: The Biography*, Chatto & Windus.

Barker, P. (2009) *The Freedoms of Suburbia* Frances Lincoln.

Bertram, A. (1935) *The House: A Machine for Living in*, A. and C. Black.

Betjeman, J. (2009) *Betjeman's England*, Introduction by Games, Stephen, John Murray.

Betjeman, J. (2009). *Betjeman's England*, Introduction by Games, Stephen, John Murray.

Bragg, Billy (2006), in 'Suburban special: what is a suburb?' http://www.timeout.com/london/big-smoke/features/2331/6.html.

Brodkin, K. (1998) *How Jews Became White Folks and What That Says About Race in America*, Rutgers University Press.

Campbell, S. (1999) 'Getting High: The Adventures of Oasis'. review in *Popular Music*, Vol. 18, No. 1, pp158-160.

Campbell S. (2004) '"What's the story?": rock biography, musical "routes" and the second-generation Irish in England', in *Irish Studies Review*, 12(1), pp63-75(13).

Carey, S. and Ahmed, N. (2006) 'Bridging the Gap: The London Olympics 2012 and South Asian-owned Businesses in Brick Lane and Green Street': www.youngfoundation.org.uk/publications/reports/bridging_the_gap.

Caesar, E. (2005) 'Hard-Fi: The Staines Massive', *Independent* 22.7.05.

Chambers, I. (1986) *Popular Culture: The metropolitan experience*, Methuen.

Childs, P. (2000) 'Suburban Values and Ethni-Cities in Indo-Anglian Writing' in Webster (2000).

Clapson, M. (2003) *Suburban Century: Social Change and Urban Growth in England and the USA*, Berg.

Cohen, P. (1972) *Subcultural conflict and working class community*, CCCS Selected Working Papers

Dench, G., Gavron, K. and Young, M. (1996) *The New East End: Kinship, Race and* Conflict, Profile books.

Donaldson, S, (1969) *The Suburban Myth*, Columbia University Press.

Downes, D. (1966) *The Delinquent Solution A Study in Subcultural Theory*, Routledge and Kegan Paul.

Economist (2007) 'Et in suburbia ego? With age, cities go centrifugal – but maybe not for ever', 3.5.07: www.economist.com/node/9070632?story_id=9070632.

Engel, M. (1997) 'Hallelujah Chorus Sings Leader's Praises', *Guardian*, 4.11.97.

Flint, C. (2011) 'A State in Society for All: Better Homes in Stronger Neighbourhoods' in Philpott, R. (2011) (ed) *The Purple Book*, Biteback.

Frey, W. (1977) 'Central City White Flight: Racial and Nonracial Causes' in *American Sociological Review*, 44, pp425-448.

Green, O. (2009) 'Suburbia: Transformed by the Tube', Talk delivered at London Transport Museum on 18.11.09.

Hanley, L. (2006) *Estates: An Intimate History*, Granta.

Head, D. (2000) 'Poisoned Minds: Suburbanites in Postwar British Fiction' in Webster (2000), pp71.

Harris, R. (2004) *Creeping conformity: how Canada became suburban, 1900-1960* University of Toronto Press.

Heath, S. (1999). 'Young adults and household formation in the 1990s', *British Journal of Sociology of Education*, Volume 20 Number 4.

Heath, S. and Kenyon, E (2001) 'Single young professionals and shared household living', *Journal of Youth Studies*, 4 (1), pp83-100.

Heath, S. (2004) 'Shared households, quasi-communes and neo-tribes', *Current Sociology* (special issue: 'Beyond the Conventional Family: Care, Intimacy and Community in the 21st Century'), 52, 2, pp161-179.

Kynaston, D. (2009) *Family Britain, 1951-1957*, Bloomsbury.

Lawson, M. (2007) 'TV matters: Is there more to EastEnders?': http://blogs.guardian.co.uk/tv/2007/05/tv_matters_is_there_more_to_ea.html.

Lewis, I. (2011) 'One nation Labour: tackling the politics of culture and identity' in Philpott, R. (2011) (ed).

Liddle, R. (2008) 'How to get stabbed: you, too, can be knifed in a public', *Spectator*, 4.7.08: www.blnz.com/news/2008/07/08/stabbed_you_too_knifed_public_4219.html.

Littlejohn, R. (2007) 'Sending Out an SOS ... Save Our Suburbs', *Daily Mail*, 7.9.07.

London Councils (2006) *Successful suburbs: the case for investment in London's suburban communities*, www.londoncouncils.gov.uk.

Nayak, A. (2003) *Race, place and globalization: Youth cultures in a changing world*. Berg.

Olechnowicz, A. (1997) *Working-class Housing in England Between the Wars: The Becontree Estate* Oxford University Press.

Orwell, G. (1937) *Coming up for Air*, Penguin, 1937.

Manzoor, S. (2004) 'Don't knock crap towns. We need them', 29.9.04: www.guardian.co.uk/britain/article/0,2763,1315132,00.ht.

MacBurnie, I. (1995) 'The Periphery and the American Dream', in *Journal of Architectural Education* Vol. 48, No. 3 (Feb. 1995), pp134-143.

Massey, D. (1993) 'Power, Geometry and a Progressive Sense of Place' in Bird, J. (ed) *Mapping the Futures: Local Cultures, Global Change*

Medhurst, A. (1997), 'Negotiating the Gnome Zone: Versions of Suburbia in British Popular Culture' in R. Silverstone (ed), *Visions of Suburbia*, Routledge 1997.

Melly, G. (1970) *Revolt into Style: the pop arts in the 50s and 60s*, OUP.

OBV at www.obv.org.uk/index.php?option=com_content&task=view&id=344&Itemid=127.

Motion, A. (1998). *Keats*,: University of Chicago Press.

Peach, C. (1996) 'Black Caribbeans: class, gender and geography', in Peach (1996) *Ethnicity in the 1991 Census, vol 2: the ethnic minority populations of Great Britain*, HMSO, pp25-43.

Peach, C. (2005) 'Does Britain have ghettos?' in *Transactions of the Institute of British Geographers* 21(1), pp216-35.

Philpott, R. (2011), *The Purple Book*, Biteback publishing.

Pile, S. (2000) *Unruly Cities?* Open University Press.

Robinson, V. (1996) 'Indians: onward and upward' in Ceri Peach (ed.), *Ethnicity in the 1991 census, vol. 2, The ethnic minority populations in Great Britain*, HMSO.

Rogers, R. and Power, A. (2001) *Cities for a Small Country*, Faber and Faber.

Sandhu, S. (2004) *London Calling: How Black and Asian Writers Imagined a City*.

Sandhu, S. (2000) 'Paradise Syndrome': www.lrb.co.uk/v22/n10/sand01_.html.

Savage, J. (1996) *Time Travel: pop, media and sexuality 1976-96*, Chatto and Windus.

Schwarz, B. (1997) 'The Break-up of the Conservative Nation', *Soundings*.

Sharp, D. and Rendel, S. (2008) *Connell Ward and Lucas: Modernist Architecture in England*, Frances Lincoln.

Stratton, J. and Ang, I. (1994) 'Sylvania Waters and the Spectacular Exploding Family', *Screen* 35(1), pp1-21.

Veblen, T. (1899/2004) *The theory of the leisure class*, Constable.

Webster, R. (2000) (ed) *Expanding Suburbia: Reviewing Suburban Narratives*, Berghahn.

Williams-Ellis, Clough (1928) *England and the Octopus*, reissued in 1996, Council for the Protection of Rural England.

Willmott, P. (1963) *The Evolution of a Community: A study of Dagenham after forty years*, Routledge & Kegan Paul.

Willmott, P. and Young, M. (1960) *Family and Class in a London Suburb*, Routledge and Kegan Paul.

2

Suburbia at the polls: the periphery as political centre of gravity

Josh: 'Average people' is a pejorative phrase ...
CJ: This may come as a shock to you, but 80% of the people in this country would use the word 'average' to describe themselves. They do not find the term deprecating. Indeed, being considered an 'average American' is something they find to be positive and comforting.

Lies, Damn Lies and Statistics, The West Wing, 10.5.00

The May 2010 UK general election saw Labour crash to defeat, with its worst share of the vote since 1929. A prolonged bout of left soul searching broke out within the party, cemented by a lengthy leadership election process. A clutch of publications by Labour party thinkers (Byrne 2010, Diamond and Radice 2010, Painter and Moussavi 2010, Hamid and Scholes-Fogg 2011, Philpott 2011, Thomas 2011) called for rethinking the party's aims and values, and learning the lessons of 2010, and a wide variety of proposals have been put forward for future success. Notwithstanding the lack of consensus in these responses, one thing is clear: the type of territory to which any political party needs to appeals if it is to win power next time around is essentially suburban.

Many of the comments made have a ring of familiarity. In 1989 an article in Old Labour magazine *Tribune* stated:

> Victory requires at least some seats from the south and it will be built on sand unless the substantial support of groups in plates like Surrey is won, reinforcing the mood for change and reform throughout the whole of the country. I reject the old Labourist contention that

> many of these areas can be written off, because this time around the fragile presence which Labour has over large swathes of the southern region will disappear altogether (Rowlands 1989).

As early as 1959, in the aftermath of an earlier defeat, Merlyn Rees wrote a Fabian pamphlet urging Labour to acknowledge suburban aspiration in its politics, to counter Macmillan's narrative of 'you've never had it so good' (Clapson 2003). However in 2010 there was a distinct unease about living standards amongst many suburban voters, part of 'the politics of anxiety' according to Labour MP Gareth Thomas (2011), who won once-Tory bastion Harrow West in 1997 and has held it ever since. In fact all politicians need to understand that since the late twentieth century suburbs have subtly shifted in meaning; they are no longer the outposts of nondescript nothingness they were once taken to be. It is legitimate therefore to ask whether there is a distinctly suburban electorate, with distinct concerns and needs, as distinct from those of the inner-city electorate or rural voter.

The core Ealing Acton parliamentary constituency (a constituency with elements of both inner city and suburb) is an ideal test-case to answer this question. Lord Clive Soley of Hammersmith has stated that there is a pronounced difference between what he called 'the inner city' and 'outer London' parts of his former constituency (then called Ealing, Acton and Shepherd Bush). At an event to mark fifty years of Ruskin Hall, home of Ealing Borough's Labour Party, Soley encapsulated the difference in the following story:

> I was elected MP for Hammersmith in 1979 and then in 1997 this part of the world [Ealing/Acton] was added. Just after the election I had a phone call from a lady in Ealing Broadway who said to me, 'Look I didn't vote for you, I don't agree with your politics, but you are my MP now, so I wanted to ask you to help me with a very important political issue. The issue is that of … squirrels. They're really annoying me. I want to know how I can shoot them'. I told her, 'you should come to Hammersmith, we shoot people there'.

Soley also recalled that when he was canvassing along the redrawn boundaries spanning the two boroughs, officers from the Ealing/Acton side of the constituency invited him and all the other candidates to a dinner: 'I'd never been to a dinner in Hammersmith, well if you'd have been invited to a dinner you'd be wise to take a food-taster with you'. The implication was that political life is cut-throat in the inner city while conduct is more gentlemanly in suburbia.

The Ealing Acton constituency, nestling alongside inner-city Shepherds Bush, is the innermost of three in the London borough of Ealing. And Ealing itself forms a backdrop to this chapter – it was my childhood hometown, and my base while writing this book. Ealing North includes the 1930s ribbon development of Greenford, and the more 'new-town'-type areas of Northolt; while Ealing Southall encompasses one of the UK's best-known areas of UK Punjabi settlement. Within this trio most types of UK suburbia are represented: the genteel late nineteenth-century detached villas of affluence in Ealing Broadway; the model estate of Brentham, built as cooperative housing, on which Hampstead Garden Suburb was modelled; the local authority-built tower blocks of the South Acton estate; the 1930s ribbon development in the north of the borough; and Southall's Edwardian and Victorian terraces, which have been favoured by Indian immigrants since the 1960s. Ealing Acton, however, within the one constituency, captures the difference between inner-city and suburb in its boundaries. In May 2011, at the Ealing Mayor-making ceremony, I talked to Angie Bray MP (who had been elected a year earlier), about how she characterised the constituency, and the ways in which it was touched by gentrification:

> Ealing is much more of a traditional suburb as you'd understand it. Acton tends to lean more towards being an inner-London area. London does tend to move outwards as central London becomes more expensive – as Hammersmith becomes more expensive you get Acton becoming more expensive.

These comments reinforce the classic inner-city/suburban divide, and they also show how the patterns shift. As we have seen, many outer London boroughs stress their urban qualities in their publicity materials, but Bray argued against the disavowal of suburbia: 'The people who move from central London don't want to replicate central London. That's not why they moved here'. There are a number of tensions here.

Suburbia has characteristics in common with the inner city, but also with the mythical territory of 'middle England'. (This is one reason that it is difficult to categorise.) It shares many features with the 'middle' that has been the electoral holy grail of recent decades – Mondeo Man, Worcester Woman and the 'squeezed middle' are just three post-Thatcher variants. In other words elections cannot be won without appealing to suburban voters – though defining what the 'middle' is can be as difficult as defining the suburbs.

The Economist (2010) has talked of people …

> around the middle of the national income distribution. They have jobs of middling status … Their nondescript semi-detached houses are neither in the inner cities (from which they, or their parents, often migrated) nor in the kind of suburbs conventionally described as 'leafy' (to which they aspire to move).

These people are viewed – and would probably view themselves – as average voters, but it is a mistake to overlook the specificities of different kinds of suburbia.

Suburban sentiment has been a key, if under-acknowledged, driver of electoral strategy in the post-war years, for both the Labour and Conservative parties. The tussle to be the most suburban post-war prime minister of them all must surely be between the self-styled Finchley housewife Mrs Thatcher (a premier curiously devoid of a first name in everyday parlance), and her successor, son of a garden gnome-maker John Major, who, while simultaneously presenting himself as a Brixton boy, famously praised English suburbia, and in fact hailed from what Gilbert (2003:144) calls 'the decidedly vincible suburb of Worcester Park'.

The switching of the suburbs to New Labour was decisive in 1997. Geoffrey Wheatcroft (2005:231) offered the following descriptive account of election night as the extent of Labour's victory sunk in:

> Meanwhile in the offices of the *Daily Mail*, the visage of the editor grew not merely pensive but blacker as events unfolded. Then in the small hours Finchley fell from Tory to Labour, Finchley, the heart of suburbia and the seat which Margaret Thatcher had represented for more than thirty years. As that 'Labour gain' was announced, Paul Dacre shouted at the newsroom television, 'What the fuck's

going on? These are fucking *Mail* readers!' So they were, but the *Mail*'s beloved Middle England had deserted the Tories at last.

Barker (2009) has claimed that 84 per cent of people in Britain live in some form of suburbia. But, as we have seen, with the spread of ethnic minority populations outward from traditional inner-city ghettos, and the proliferation of gated developments beyond the central core, we have been seeing both an urbanisation of the suburbs and suburbanisation of the inner city. The 'ethnicisation' of suburbia has contributed to its political reshaping. Seats like Birmingham Edgbaston, Harrow West and Ealing North aided New Labour's victory in 1997 and have remained with the party ever since. This is something the Conservative Party needs to understand if it is to ever form a majority government again.

In 2010 the electoral landscape changed once again. It is commonplace to speak of Labour as weak in the south and strong in the north, but it is perhaps more helpful to think of Labour as having a suburban (vs urban) electoral deficit rather than a southern (vs northern) one – with London being the exception to both these rules, since many of its suburbs have remained with the party. It remains to be seen how these suburban voters – who now constitute a substantial section of the 'squeezed middle – will react to what is at the time of writing their downward mobility.

The rest of this chapter will look at past precedent to argue that English suburbia has been a key battleground of electoral politics. It will contend that, contrary to the received wisdom of suburban seats always returning Conservative politicians, the volatility of the vote in the suburbs has contributed to the complex mosaic picture of the twenty-first century political map.

SUBURBAN VOTING PATTERNS

The constituency of Ealing Southall was the scene of great rejoicing in 2007 when, in an early test of Gordon Brown's popularity, a by-election was handsomely won by Virendra Sharma for Labour. The borough was subsequently selected by Brown for the unveiling of his plans to raise the threshold for stamp duty in 2008. The *Telegraph* headlined the event 'Ealing, Queen of the Suburbs, welcomes Gordon Brown, King of doom'. It praised the area's 'parks, shops, well-regarded schools and streets of late Victorian and Edwardian villas', and alluded to the 'leafy' town's Victorian nickname, but also pointed out that the new threshold of £175,000 was virtually meaningless in Ealing, given the average price of houses (Wallop 2008). By 2010 circumstances had changed, though Sharma held on to his seat. Following its defeat the Labour Party embarked on a long drawn out leadership election campaign, in which the Ealing constituency duly participated.

I played a small part in leadership candidate David Miliband's low-key suburban home-based campaign, when I hosted a meeting in my front room in the Northfields district of Ealing, when, as well as David Miliband it was occupied by Laura Kuenssberg, the BBC's chief political correspondent, and a camera crew. The idea was to have a low-key discussion with ordinary party members. In later weeks this campaign tactic of meeting members in their homes was widely ridiculed, derision was heaped upon a document available on the web with instructions on 'How to host a David Miliband house-party (Freeman 2010, Kirkup 2010), and such events were likened to the archetypal suburban Mike Leigh drama *Abigail's Party* (BBC Newsnight (2010). But perhaps normality as a personal attribute is becoming a new currency in politics – certainly there was much emphasis on being 'ordinary' by all the other Labour leadership contenders. My 'at home' in Ealing was arranged at short notice to tie in with other campaign visits nearby on the same day, including to a factory in Southall, which also offered a good framing for the reaffirmation of normality, in the works canteen. Miliband also adopted the principles of community organising in his campaign ethos and literature – something that has since been taken up more widely in the party. The 'David Miliband Movement For Change' had people seconded to it who were members of the London Citizens campaign group – perhaps an example of traditional politicians learning from grassroots activists. Certainly Miliband's willingness to engage in a small-scale domesticated setting with members over a cup of tea is a significant change from the noisy and disorganised meetings of trade union 'brothers' that used to constitute paying your dues. He even adhered to the house rule of removing footwear. Our meeting was held in the type of domestic environment in which many women, of ethnic minorities in particular, feel comfortable – rather more so than in a pub, where party meetings have often tended to take place. Issues raised clustered largely around anti-social behaviour type issues – noisy neighbours were mentioned by one young couple; while an elderly gent worried about the council's closure of public toilets (enacted presumably to combat their use as drug dealing spaces.)

In their historical account of the Conservative Party, written in the depths of their period of opposition, when it was uncertain whether the party could win again following three election defeats, Seldon and Snowdon (2004:228) wrote:

> In the late 1990s, the Conservatives could not rival New Labour's appeal, which seemed to chime better with the socially progressive attitudes and cosmopolitan lifestyles in the last decade of the twentieth century. Not one single inner-city constituency (outside London) elected a Conservative MP in 1997 and 2001.... The Conservatives had become the party of rural and suburban South-East England, and little else.

The situation had dramatically altered from that of only a decade earlier, when the Conservatives had looked to be invincible, not only in their heartlands of suburbia but also in gentrified inner city seats, including Battersea, Putney and Walthamstow. It was getting to grips with an expanding conception of suburbia that would eventually help the Conservative recovery.

In the twentieth century, suburbia had been seen as naturally Conservative voting territory. Posters from the long run of Conservative rule from 1951 to 1964 show a direct appeal made by the party to suburban families, as in the two children and young couple seated round the dining table with the slogan 'Life's Better with the Conservatives, don't let Labour ruin it'. Kenneth Clarke has described Margaret Thatcher as Finchley woman, the classic epitome of the suburban wife (quoted in BBC 2008). Indeed analyses of Thatcherism often attribute her working-class support as deriving from her personal qualities as a grammar-school educated girl with a shopkeeper father (though in fact the deferential non-class aligned Conservative vote long predated Thatcher). Whatever the case, Thatcher's policies of 'popular capitalism' were directly linked to an electoral dividend in home and share ownership when council houses and public utilities were sold off to 'ordinary people'. In this way

Thatcher managed to recruit support from 'those inner cities' – partly by helping to make their residents more suburban.

New Labour knew that they also had to appeal to the suburbs. The late Philip Gould (1998) wrote of his frustration during the Thatcher-major period that Labour had not understood the aspiration of suburbia in crafting their appeals to the electorate, something that he was aware of from his childhood in Kent:

> my party was to betray ... ordinary people with suburban dreams who worked hard to improve their homes and their lives; to get gradually better cars, washing machines and televisions; to go on holiday in Spain rather than Bournemouth. These people wanted sensible, moderate policies which conformed to their daily lives and understanding. Labour had failed to understand that the old working class was becoming a new middle class: aspiring, consuming, choosing what was best for themselves and their families. They had outgrown crude collectivism and left it behind in the supermarket car park.

This project to make Labour acceptable to suburb-dwellers – more often collapsed into the catch-all category of 'middle England' – was at the heart of the New Labour project. Gould had learned from polling techniques used on the 1992 Clinton campaign, where the strategy adopted was the incessant running of focus groups with swing voters in the suburbs. He and others were able to refocus Labour strategy in the 1990s around the recognition of the suburbs as the key battleground of elections, and the need to broad out from wooing Labour's traditional heartlands. Vindicated by Labour's best election result ever in 1997 he wrote:

> The unfinished revolution is rooted not in Labour's traditional industrial heartlands but in the sprawling suburbs of an emerging middle class. Labour lost elections because it turned its back on this new constituency, ignoring the postwar rise of a newly aspirational electorate (1998).

SUBURBAN VOTING PATTERNS: THE ETHNIC VOTE

A subset of the suburban electorate, of increasing value to political parties as time has passed, has been the 'ethnic vote', which has generally been presumed to be Labour-adhering. This has been of crucial importance in a number of seats. Thus in the 2007 Ealing Southall by-election of July 2007, all the three major parties fielded Asian candidates to in order help attract this group.

Founded in 1997, the British Asian Conservative Link declares on its website:

> We believe the Asian culture, as a way of life, goes hand in hand with the doctrine of conservatism and the economical contribution made by the Asian community is remarkable. However, politically, the Asian community is largely underrepresented. The BACL recognises the need for greater political participation and it aims to support prospective parliament candidates (PPC) to parliamentary post as well as other political roles.

One of a group I interviewed in Bury was at the time a Conservative PPC, and I asked him whether he thought that Asian voters were really natural Conservatives:

M: Looking after your family, looking after your community, paying your taxes, contributing to your society ... they're all sort of Asian traits really aren't they? I think Labour has taken the Asian vote for granted, but things are changing for a number of reasons. I think women within our communities are far more empowered to making their own decisions, and that includes who they're voting for. I think families don't vote as a bloc as a bloc-vote as it used to in the past. Young people are learning about the democratic system so I think now more than ever before you're finding households that are voting for different parties rather than all voting for one.

U: Before it used to be the inheritance vote, so whatever your father votes or your parents voted you'd vote for at the same election, but I think you can see that slowly eroding. In our family household we voted completely different parties. Our parents still voted Labour because they see themselves as staunch supporters, but the rest of us all did our own thing. I think partly that's a reaction against centralised politics anyway, because we're seeing that there is no distinction any more between Labour and Conservative because they are all so centralised. I think that has played a role, but I think people are also more polarising their

> opinions because they want to say 'I'm in this camp or I'm in that camp'. They don't want to be in the middle. In Conservative foreign policy and Labour foreign policy – or New Labour foreign policy should I say? There's nothing there to differentiate them.

Once more we see change taking place in the suburbs, this time generational. And here the Iraq war has played a major role.

When in May 2011 I interviewed Liam Byrne, he described how his local Labour Party had followed community organising principles in his constituency of Birmingham Hodge Hill in order to keep the seat in the face of anti-Iraq war opposition. (Something the Bradford West CLP might wish they had learned from!) In a large number of other seats (for example Cambridge, Manchester Withington, Bethnal Green and Bow and Hornsey and Wood Green), an alliance between Muslims and anti-war intellectuals had led to a shift towards Lib Dems, whose Ethnic Minority Liberal Democrats (EMLD) group is headed by Haringey councillor Fiyaz Mughal. Byrne, however, argued that the Birmingham Asian vote consisted of a large number of different communities. For example, Pakistanis went for 'the bigger houses, extensions, planning'. But he also thought that women's participation was crucial:

> About four to five years ago we felt Pakistani women were being excluded so we thought about service delivery on a range of issues, and that evolved into targeted training. We found that if the men were asked along they were a bit uncomfortable about that, so we put on women-only events. I'm the only man.

He also believed that local activity was crucial:

> In some of our wards we have 40 per cent contact, in some 50 per cent. We are trying to build the social capacity of people running different organisations, negotiating with the council. The ambition is to take over the management of the new school.

I put it to Conservative James Cleverly that the ethnic vote is normally presumed to be pro-Labour, and that Labour have continually been accused of taking this vote for granted:

> That's because they mistook ethnicity as the drivers for voting … When the ethnic population of London was heavily weighted towards inner London and less affluent, they tended to be in public sector jobs – you know the Windrush generation, more public sector jobs – [and so they] happened to vote Labour. It just so happened that in inner London, less affluent, public sector employees voted Labour. It just so happened that that's where ethnicity tended to be clustered and I think the lazy assumption was therefore that brown and black people vote Labour because of their ethnicity.
>
> Whereas actually what you tend to find is that as those brown and black people started to become increasingly employed in the private sector or increasingly become self-employed – which is a driver to Conservative voting – and as they decentralised geographically, as the things that they felt passionate about mirrored the things that the settled white middle-class affluent population felt, they shifted their voting patterns. When I talk to some of the Asian business people around Chislehurst, they say exactly the same things as a lot of the white business people. Their ethnicity is not a factor in their voting decisions.
>
> The traditional white van man, it's man in a white van, it's not a white man … When the man in the white van has got brown skin and he's keeping his business afloat he will vote in the best interests for himself, and that's what's slightly catching the Labour Party out.

Though it is true that ethnic embourgeoisement is a factor, in other interviews with Asians I have found that Enoch Powell's intervention in 1968 helped solidify attitudes against the Conservative Party. I asked Cleverly specifically about the Asian vote:

> Again I think it's one of those areas where the whole block vote mentality is really damaging – the assumption that all non-white voters have the same issues and drivers, whereas a Ugandan Asian that came over in the 1960s will have very, very different views to a Bangladeshi Asian that came across ten, fifteen years ago, who in turn will have very, very different views to a Muslim Somali family who came across say three or four years ago, who will have very, very different views to a black West Indian family who came across in the 1950s, who themselves will have very, very, very different views to a black African family that came across in the 1980s. To say 'you're all

BME' –it's a phrase that I absolutely hate. To me it's insulting ... I think the left in politics keeps looking for these blocks ... so you have a union block, a public sector employees block, the ethnic block, the women – and they talk about these things like somehow by virtue of your gender your views on everything will be the same.

How do people react to Cleverly on the doorstep, I wondered – as someone of mixed race parentage, visibly not the archetypal 'white' Tory candidate. Cleverly downplayed any discrimination, positive or otherwise, in his advancement, pointing out that his profile fitted that of the traditional Conservative in every other respect bar pigmentation:

I'll be somewhere and people will say, 'James, with you doing so well it shows that Central Office [Conservative HQ] is changing'. But if it weren't for the colour of my skin I would be so out of central casting. I mean I would be every Conservative casting you could ever imagine ... from a small business family, went to a private school, joined the army, started a business, live in suburbia with my wife, two kids, dog and an estate car. Look at myself. I cringe at how embarrassingly Tory I would be. And yet people hold me up and say 'great change'. Half of my association, if you turned round to them and said 'what's it like having a black representative?', it's not an issue, it's so not an issue, because for them I tick the boxes they want me to tick. Ethnicity, I wouldn't say it's really important.

If you knock on the door in Biggin Hill, it's as geographically far away from central London as it's possible to get. It's built round what used to be army air-stations, it's outer, outer London. I go and knock on a door, I just don't ... or maybe I'm desensitised to it. I don't know, I don't get, I don't notice that.

I raised the subject of John (subsequently Lord) Taylor, the black barrister who lost what was until then a safe Tory seat as Conservative candidate in Cheltenham in 1992 to the Liberal Democrats. Was this not evidence of racism by Conservatives?

The point I would make is the real Tories are the ones that continued voting for him. I love the fact that it is seen as the Tories are racist because they didn't vote for John Taylor, they voted Lib Dem. But

> didn't it make the Lib Dems racist? My take would be the people that didn't vote for him were racist ... Also that was the election when Chris Patten lost his seat. People forget that we lost a lot of seats in 1992. Everyone thinks we lost all our seats in 1997. We lost a lot of seats in 1992. We let go of a very big majority. And then there's tactical voting, the fact that Taylor was basically imposed on the local association ... If there was some local council leader that they [local Conservative Party members] really wanted and an external candidate is forced upon you, there's always friction. It doesn't matter if you're male, female, black, white. That can create issues.

THE SUBURBS AND LOCAL POLITICS

To paraphrase Michael Portillo circa 1997, the 2008 local elections were a truly awful night for Labour, particularly when the jewel in the crown of local government, the London mayoralty, fell to Boris Johnson, and London assembly's first BNP member was elected. One compelling argument repeatedly propounded regarding the Tory triumph in the capital was that it was the suburbs that won it. Tony Travers (2008) of the LSE declared that 'suburban England and Wales deserted the prime minister'. According to Simon Jenkins in *The Times*, 'The suburbs, long moribund as political cockpits, came alive to deliver victory for Johnson'. Johann Hari (2008) wrote:

> I have just forced myself to read the detailed election stats from last Thursday. It seems the media cliché is true: it's the angry, whiter outer suburbs that elected Boris, out of rage with the congestion charge and council tax. Boris will forever be the mayor of Zones Four to Six, the chief executive of Watford and Bromley and Amersham.

Yet although the suburbs had seemingly taken a rightward turn, the election results confirm the underlying volatility of the twenty-first century suburb – socially, demographically, economically and of electorally. James Cleverly rejected the claim that Boris had simply 'used' the suburbs as a convenient stepping stone on his route to power:

> The ... lazy assumption is that Boris won it in the suburbs, which is only half true. The counts were all done in different places. I was

certainly one of the first, and I knew that I'd win big. When the figures came, it was 'bloody hell that's a huge margin'. I mean my majority was 75,000 … [but] the point when I knew Boris had won was not when I got my result, but when I heard the result in Lewisham and Greenwich, which was a strong Labour constituency. And whilst [Labour's] Len Duvall won, the margin was much, much tighter than before. So it wasn't just that the Conservatives in outer London came out in big numbers, the Conservatives in inner London came out in big numbers as well. It wasn't noticed because they didn't win the seats, but they kept the margins tight … Boris did win because the outer London boroughs came out in force, but that wouldn't have been enough if Livingstone had created enough vote differential in the inner London boroughs … Boris did ok in the inner London boroughs. He wasn't crucified in inner London in the way that Livingstone was crucified in outer London … He spends a lot more time in outer London than Livingstone ever did, but he hasn't sacrificed inner London in order to make that happen and he still gets a really positive reception when he goes to places in inner London … it's not about 'using outer London', it's about galvanising London and giving people a reason to vote, Livingstone never did. That's not *using*, it's politicians saying 'vote for me and I will pay attention to your needs'.

… there is no doughnut, there is no homogenous outer London with the same issue … I remember the *Evening Standard* asked me about Conservative factions in the new [Conservative GLA] group, as it was now a much bigger group, and I said there aren't any. She said 'come on, there must be factions', so I said 'I'll rephrase that, there are 11 different Conservative factions on the GLA [i.e. all 11 members]'.

At the GLA level, the suburbs were far from having all rejected Labour: for example the party held the outer north London seat of Enfield and Haringey, contrary to expectations, and gained Brent and Harrow. However, the election of a London-wide BNP London assembly member through targeting the votes of disaffection in outer borough votes such as Havering, Sutton (St Helier estate) and Barking and Dagenham was a low point of the night.

The highly differentiated nature of twenty-first century suburbia was reflected in the 2010 local election results. Newham and Barking and Dagenham became all-Labour councils, and Labour also took Harrow, Hounslow and Ealing from Conservative control. (As a consequence I was appointed Deputy Mayoress of the London Borough of Ealing.) In an early *Simpsons* episode, the Mayor of Springfield's seal has the motto 'Corruptus in Extremis'. This is not quite the descriptor I would choose for the activities of the Labour leadership in Ealing during the municipal year 2010-2011, but, like all local authorities, the council was put under extreme pressure to deliver services in the face of drastically reduced budgets and increased demand, including the need to expand the number of school places available. Labour had campaigned on a manifesto promising both to freeze the council tax and councillors' expenses. Tapping into a populist vein of anti-banker sentiment, there had also been a promise to cut the bonuses of senior officers, but other decisions were more difficult.

In a year of observing full-council meetings from a prominent position in the council chamber many things struck me. The meetings always began with a prayer delivered by the borough chaplain. The format was modelled on the House of Commons 'debating' style, with highly partisan 'yah boo' boorish behaviour on both sides and insults regularly traded. Subjects dealt with included the closure of a special needs centre, against which a large-scale community mobilisation took place; dangerous road crossings; stop-and-shop bays for motorists in retail parades to keep them viable; and, most notably the cuts to the borough's library services.

During the consultation period on library closures petitions against them were delivered by local mums, who spoke passionately on the need to keep smaller branches going. Houses in the streets near me started displaying 'Save Northfields Library' window posters. Through Facebook and my local (Tory) councillor's blog I saw the campaign gather momentum, with plans to chant from the public gallery and unfurl banners on the day. For the Labour administration the decision was a difficult one. In the chamber they faced taunts from the Tories of asset-stripping – even though the only reason the closures had been considered was because of their party's dogmatic decisions in central government. In the end Ealing decided to close none of the libraries on the list, but its mobile provision was cut, and in a dangerously 'big society' way it was announced that volunteers were to staff some of the branches some of the time. Savings were also to be achieved by trimming the management structure.

Central government decision makers rarely have experience of the bread and butter of local politics. In the last Conservative government there was John Major and Malcolm Rifkind, but of the current party leaders or holders of great offices of state few have ever served in local government. Among the current coalition cabinet there is Eric Pickles, who was a councillor in 1980s Bradford when it was a Thatcherite experiment, and Vince Cable, who was a Labour councillor in Glasgow in the 1970s. In fact it seems that the selfless calling to represent one's local community can be bypassed now that national politics has become professionalised as a career – and as politicians are getting ever-younger.

The first major test following the 2010 general election were the GLA and Mayoral elections of May 2012. Ealing Labour launched their campaign at 9.30am on a Saturday in October 2011, in the draughty Labour hall in Acton where this chapter began. Fifty or so members turned out for Ealing North MP Steve Pound's opening address. He told us that Boris was not up to the job. 'It's all very well to quote Plato, Socrates and Catullus,' he opined 'and all those other Argentinean footballers ...'. Part of his knockabout rhetoric ribbed Johnson's privileged background as being incongruous with the experience of the average Londoner. Yet class war as a tactic has not always been helpful to Labour – famously, it flopped in the 2008 Crewe by-election. Pound also pointed out that despite making much of his claim to be a mayor for the suburbs, none of Johnson's actions have really lived up to this rhetoric – record fare hikes had done nothing for those in outer London. The much heralded outer London commission that was touted at the time of 2008 Mayoral election turned out to be a gimmick that had largely sunk without trace. (Pound himself had seen the seat he won from the Conservatives in 1997 climb to a 15,000 majority by 2010. But he has always shrugged off any personal factor in the solidifying of his majority to buck the current trend and attributes his wins to changing demography and an increasing ethnic minority electorate.)

Sometimes these occasions can be a bit of an excuse for anyone who likes the sound of their own voice to mouth off, but here suggestions seemed in the main constructive. Housing and transport emerged as the big issues. It was pointed out that the area effectively had a five-day-a-week tube on the district line, due to all the weekend closures; while younger people wanted a way out of the situation in which it seemed that they would never be able to afford home ownership. Unnoticed by most, Johnson had removed the proviso that any new-build developer must include 50 per cent of the dwellings as affordably priced. These were the kinds of issues that really mattered to local people, but celebrity spats seemed more likely to dominate press coverage. We also heard from Ken Livingstone himself, who concentrated on the issues that faced London – in stark contrast to a *Guardian* weekend magazine interview that had appeared the same day that had focused on his offspring fathered to different mothers. The day was rounded off with Livingstone and entourage conducting some high visibility campaigning on Acton High Street, while the rest of us were made to do some leafleting/canvassing on the dense and unloved South Acton estate – which is separated by the north London railway line from posh Chiswick – another reminder of the stark contrasts in our borough. Such is the stuff of the suburban political campaign.

SUBURBAN INSECURITY

The suburbs, once fixed points in an ever-changing world, are now more than anywhere else the place where people are feeling the pinch: the rising cost of filling up at the pumps, their fixed rate mortgages ending, perceptions of escalating crime and the supposed influx of immigrants. Heathrow's siting in West London long made it a hub for Punjabis, now they have been joined by large numbers Poles. In East London the Pakistanis of Newham are being joined by Lithuanians, and while Morrissey sang of Dagenham Dave back in 95, Nigerians have settled there more recently, reflected in the African shops on the Heathway.

C.F.G. Masterman wrote (1909/2008:222):

> of all the illusions of the opening twentieth century perhaps the most remarkable is that of security. Already gigantic and novel forces of mechanical invention, upheavals of people, social discontents, are exhibiting a society in the beginnings of change. It would seem likely that a very rapid disintegration … has taken place in a period of external tranquillity, in beliefs and ideas.

By 2012 insecurity is almost a given. Many suburban voters are feeling disenfranchised, and their inclination for aspiration has become tempered with multiple insecurities. Thomas (2011:20), for example, warns of 'those across the commuter belt ... whose incomes are being squeezed, who worry about whether their children will find it harder to get on, who want lower taxes and better public services but who are open to stronger co-operative and mutual ideas'. This phenomenon of insecurity cross-cuts with issues such as immigration, the spectre of unemployment, fear of crime and struggling with finances in the face of planning for the future (pensions, tuition fees, childcare, etc).The Conservative solutions include the 'big society' of volunteerism. A number of Labour strategists have argued that this linking of anxieties about financial insecurity with issues of immigration should be recognised: thus Ivan Lewis (2011:231) argued that: 'The party's instincts to be internationalist, liberal and champions of multicultural societies jar with the growing sense of insecurity of citizens buffeted by rapid economic and social change.'

At the start of his premiership Tony Blair was able to embody a sense of optimism and aspiration, and this helped to keep his broad tent together. But the mood in 2010 was very different. Gillian Duffy's comments in the run-up to the 2010 general election identified the flashpoint issue of immigration and its repercussions on employment; while housing is an inter-related issue that the Labour government should have done more on. For the insecure in the suburbs, Labour became known as the party of benefit scroungers, immigrants and the unions. Clearly, it had failed to win support for the 'globalism is good' argument.

But rather than writing off suburban voters as narrow-minded petit-bourgeois culturally suffocated hinterland dwellers who bizarrely prioritise having a neat front lawn and keeping themselves to themselves behind their net curtains, it should be the goal of any party who seriously seeks power to understand suburban aspiration. For the fact is that the suburban experience is the majority experience – though, as we have seen, it is also extremely diverse. The suburban electorate is not an amorphous blob; politicians of all hues would do well to not lose sight of this fact. In the next chapter we turn to the utopian visions of alternative protest in suburbia, the messages of which, contrastingly, stress the concept of the 'greater good', and the notion that 'another world is possible'.

REFERENCES

Abrams, M., Rose and Hinden, R. (1960) *Must Labour Lose?* Penguin Special.

Applebaum, A. (2001) *The Strange Death of Tory England*: http://www.slate.com/id/109898.

BBC (2008) *Making of the Iron Lady*, BBC4 documentary, 12.6.08.

BBC Newsnight (2010): 20.8.10: http://news.bbc.co.uk/1/hi/programmes/newsnight/8936842.stm.

Byrne, L. (2010) *Why Did Labour Lose – and How Do We Win Again?* Progress pamphlet.

Clapson, M. (2003) *Suburban century: social change and urban growth in England and the USA*, Berg.

Clarke, K. (2010), in *The Making of the Iron Lady*, BBC documentary 5.1.10: www.bbc.co.uk/programmes/b00c13bf.

Cosgrave, P. (1992) *The strange death of socialist Britain: post war British politics*, Constable

Dangerfield, G. and Stansky, P. (1988[1935]) *The Strange Death of Liberal England* University of Stanford Press.

Economist (2010) 'Class and politics: The misinterpreted middle', 25.3.10: www.economist.com/node/15777629.

Flynn, D., Ford, R. and Somerville, R. (2010) 'Immigration and the election' in *Renewal: a journal of Social Democracy*, Vol 18 No 3/4, pp102-114.

Freeman, J. (2010) 'How to host a party, David Miliband style', *Total Politics*, 18.8.10: at www.totalpolitics.com/blog/26943/how-to-host-a-party-david-miliband-style.thtml.

Gabbatt, A. (2010) 'David Miliband's guide to hosting a house party', *Guardian*, 21.8.10: www.guardian.co.uk/politics/2010/aug/21/david-miliband-guide-hosting-house-party.

Gilbert, D. (2003) 'Sex, power and miracles: a suburban triptych', in J. Kerr & A. Gibson (eds), *London from Punk to Blair*, Reaktion.

Gilmour, G. and Garnett, M. (1997) *Whatever Happened to the Tories?: The Conservative Party Since 1945: History of the Conservative Party Since 1945* Fourth Estate.

Gould, P. (1998) 'A roar from the suburbs', *Prospect*, 20.12.98: www.prospectmagazine.co.uk/1998/12/aroarfromthesuburbs/

Gould, P. (2007) 'Tony Blair's thoroughly modern journey: The case for ten years of new Labour', *Times*, 26.6.07: www.timesonline.co.uk/tol/comment/columnists/guest_contributors/article1985553.ece.

Hamid, H. and Scholes-Fogg, T. (2011) *What Next For Labour? Ideas for a New Generation*, Queensferry.

Hari, J. (2008) 'Livingstonite Republic of Central London', 6.5.08: http://blogs.independent.co.uk/openhouse/2008/05/livingstonite-r.html.

Harvey, D. (2009) *The Enigma of Capital and The Crisis of Capitalism*, Profile Books.

Hassan, G. (2010) 'After "new Britain": The Strange Death of "the Labour Nation"' 27.9.10: www.gerryhassan.com/?p=1374.

Huq, R. (1998) 'Currying Favour?: New Labour's Relationship with the British Asian Community', in Perryman, M. and Coddington, A. (eds), *The Moderniser's Dilemma* Lawrence and Wishart, pp59-74.

Jenkins, S. (2008) *Times*, 3.5.08.

Kirkup, J. (2010) 'How to host a David Miliband house party', *Daily Telegraph* 21.8.10: www.telegraph.co.uk/news/politics/labour/7957537/How-to-host-a-David-Miliband-house-party.html.

Masterman C. (1909/2008) *The condition of England*, Faber.

McLaren L.M. (2010) *Cause for Concern?: The Impact of Immigration on Political Trust*, Policy Network: www.policy-network.net/publications/3889/Cause-for-concern?-The-impact-of-immigration-on-political-trust.

Palmer, C., Ziersch, A., Arthurson, K. and Baum, F. (2005) '"Danger lurks around every corner": Fear of Crime and its Impact on Opportunities for Social Interaction in Stigmatised Australian Suburbs', *Urban Policy and Research*, Volume 23, Number 4, December 2005, pp393-411.

Painter, A. and Moussavi, A. (2010) *The politics of perpetual renewal: the changing attitudes and demographics of Britain*, Demos/Open Left.

Philpott, R. (ed) (2011) *The Purple Book*, Biteback.

Rowlands, M. (1989) 'Coming to terms with the suburbs', *Tribune* 2.7.89.

Seldon, A. and Snowdon, P. (2004) *The Conservative Party*, The History Press.

Shirlow, S. and Pain, R. (2003) 'The geographies and politics of fear' in *Capital & Class*, Summer 2003 vol. 27 no. 2, pp15-26.

Taylor, I. (1995) 'Private homes and public others', *British Journal of Criminology* 35 (2), pp263-285.

Thomas, G. (2009) 'Beating Boris will require new ideas and learning from errors', *Tribune*, 27.2.09.

Thomas, G. (2011) *The Politics of Anxiety: How commuterland holds the key to Labour's revival*, Cooperative Party and YouGov.

Travers, T. (2008) 'It is clear – the suburbs have deserted Brown', *Guardian*,

3.5.08: www.guardian.co.uk/politics/2008/may/03/london08.localgovernment.

Wallop, H. (2008) 'Ealing, Queen of the Suburbs welcomes Gordon Brown, King of doom', *Daily Telegraph*, 2.9.08.

Walks, A. (2004) 'Place of Residence, Party Preferences, and Political Attitudes in Canadian Cities and Suburbs', *Journal of Urban Affairs* Volume 26, Number 3, pp 269-295.

Wheatcroft, G. (2005) *The Strange Death of Tory England*, Allen Lane.

3

Alt. Suburbia: citizenship on the periphery

> SchNEWS warns all readers not to attend any illegal gatherings or take part in any criminal activities. Always stay within the law. In fact please just sit in, watch tv and go on endless shopping sprees filling your house with endless consumer crap … you will then feel content. Honest.
>
> *SchNEWS* Disclaimer

> *Council official*: Just who do think you are, Mrs Leadbetter?
> *Margo*: I am the silent majority.
>
> *The Good Life*, BBC1, May 1975

If suburbia is a contested concept, 'community' is another term which eludes easy definition. In this chapter we use it to refer to political and pressure group direct action outside the electoral cycle.

For some, the notions of suburbia and community are incompatible. Kynaston (2009:86) quotes Labour's 1945 manifesto architect Lord Young as claiming, in 1951: 'One suburb is much like another in an atomised society. Rarely does community flourish'. Other writers also have clearly defined notions of the suburban dweller. For Masterman (1909/1960:57), '"the suburbans" … form a homogeneous civilisation – detached, self-centred, unostentatious – covering the hills along the northern and southern boundaries of the City and spreading their conquests over the green fields beyond.' For others on the other hand, consumerist ostentation has been one of the accusations levelled at suburb-dwellers; while for yet others preserving greenery (rather than its destruction as described by Masterman) has been a hallmark of recent suburban protest. This chapter looks at examples of different suburban protests that in varying degrees demonstrate a vein of what might be called 'alt.suburbia': the Eco

Village, Kew Bridge Road, Brentford TW8; the squatted home of Mr and Mrs Expenses, the at-the-time serving MPs Ann and Alan Keen at Brook Road South Brentford TW8; and the anti-road protest at Claremont Road, Wanstead London E11. At all three of these sites, green-tinged protest was enacted through squatting. This chapter also looks at Town Hall protest at Ealing.

Suburban protest can range from marches and petitions to non violent direct action. There is also a burgeoning interest in urban new social movements inspired by sociologists such as Castells, linked to the idea of Temporary Autonomous Zones (TAZ), as theorised by the US based a anarchist Hakim Bey (1991). These raise questions of alternative politics and lifestyles as well as extra-parliamentary political action as a means for voices from the margins to be heard – be these suburban in an imagined or real sense. Such political activism often brings perpetrators into direct conflict with authority – in spite of the new-found enthusiasm for citizenship started under New Labour and continued by the coalition government.

New Labour's take on citizenship was most usually in its notion of the third way, while the Cameronite Tories favour the Big Society: neither of these positions has much room for the politics of antagonism. In 2005, Gordon Brown declared in the context of a speech on the role of the voluntary sector: 'Politicians once thought the man in Whitehall knew best. Now we understand that the … mother from the playgroup … might know better' (Wheeler 2005). This comment juxtaposes the men in suits with the constituency often known in the US as 'soccer moms' or the school-gate mothers. Mobilisations by such groups are very often around localised issues – as with the protests about library closures in Ealing. Unlike the formalised structures of, say, the trade unions, groups may form on an ad-hoc basis, in support of or in opposition to flashpoint events (no to a supermarket chain, yes to expanding a local primary school). On becoming prime minister in 1997, Tony Blair, in a celebrated speech at the Aylesbury Estate in South London, proclaimed: 'The next decade will be defined by a simple idea: "we are all in this together". It will be about how to recreate the bonds of civic society and community in a way compatible with the far more individualistic nature of modern, economic, social and cultural life' (Wheeler 2005). Such ideas are malleable enough to be welcomed by people of all political stripes and none – as was the later flagship policy of the Tories, the Big Society.

Indeed the very phrase 'we're all in this together' was later appropriated by Chancellor George Osborne (although the tax cuts he subsequently awarded for the super-rich in the £150,000 plus income bracket suggest otherwise).

Community can be all things to everyone. In her study of the interplay between social control, community relationships and interaction with officialdom and institutions, written in the aftermath of violent disorders of 1991, Beatrix Campbell argues (1993:266):

> Community is dead, long live community politics. Just as the very notions of neighbourhood, collectivity, class, consensus and solidarity were alleged to be waning as the organising principles of British progressive politics, community was reincarnated by liberals and radicals and conservatives alike after the Sixties as a political constituency. Community politics appeared like a golden egg, immaculately conceived, small and perfectly formed, bringing classes together, reforming the quality of life within the neighbourhood. For progressives the promise was a politics made in heaven – a carnival of convivial campaigns that would re-engage the people in the political process.

Campbell sees community as a convenient way of negating class consciousness. Certainly the 'end of class' language, once beloved of Blair and Brown, has now been appropriated in the narrative of the big society. In the past decade or so the adjectives 'cohesive', 'vibrant' and 'diverse' have been mentioned as positive attributes in the same breath as 'community' – for example in local authority literature branding different neighbourhoods. In the mean time, 'social exclusion' has become the accepted terminology for all that is bad, and has replaced 'poverty' in the modern political vocabulary.

But yesterday's estates built as model developments in the safe haven of suburbia are today's areas of urban decay. Describing breaking and entering as 'the conquest of space, other people's space', Campbell (1993:244) argues that for some groups shared values are partly forged around lawlessness and delinquent subculture: at the time of which she is writing, joyriding and ram-raiding were entering the urban vernacular. The concerns of the majority electorate around such issues gave rise the memorable Blair soundbite 'tough on crime, tough on the causes of crime' in the 1990s, and the pre-election epithet 'Broken Britain' from David Cameron. But none of the mainstream parties is in the habit of acknowledging the social causes of such breakdown. The idea is always that individuals can sort out their own problems without conflict. The overarching philosophy of the 'big society' is described on the Cabinet Office website as being about 'helping people to come together to improve their own lives. It's about putting more power in people's hands – a massive transfer of power from Whitehall to local communities'. Its implementation is buttressed by the Office for Civil Society within the Cabinet Office, whose brief is to support voluntary and community organisations (this was one quango that was spared in the spending review). The implication is that all that is needed is a bit of good will – there are no clashes of interests or inequalities of power and resources. Equally, political battles are seen as being restricted to electoral politics. Thus New Labour championed citizenship education when in government, but the Crick report of 1998 that kick-started this movement was mainly focused on participation in electoral politics, with its sub-text being the arrest of the decline in plummeting UK electoral turnouts. A further impetus for flurries of commentary on community and citizenship have been the 'disturbances' (official terminology) or 'riots' (common parlance) that break out from time to time in Britain. Thus, those in 2001 in the three former northern English mill towns of Bradford, Burnley and Oldham (Huq 2003) hastened the rush to citizenship teaching, which became a national curriculum requirement from September 2002.

This chapter adopts a wider definition of citizenship, community and politics, and now turns to examine grassroots protest in suburbia, and examples of 'alternative citizenship', where participants are engaged in non-traditional forms of political organisation.

SUBURBAN ANGST: PROTESTS IN SUBURBIA

As well as being a veteran of many a national protest, I have also been a stalwart of demonstrations in the suburbs, including the angry mob march variety and the attending of squatted premises. In October 2010, when I arrived at the neo-gothic splendour of Ealing Town Hall for the first full council meeting of the new season, a protest on the steps outside allowed me to witness the other side of the process. The issue at stake was the closing of the Albert Dane daycare centre for the disabled in Southall at the western edge of the borough. Inside the town hall those involved had taken up places in the public gallery, and campaigners were adorned in t-shirts with SAD emblazoned on their chests – 'Save Albert Dane'. While political demonstrations are associated more naturally with the political left, the Conservatives had championed this case, in keeping with their role as the local political opposition, supported by the Liberal Democrats, thereby demonstrating a localised example of the national coalition government. The ruling Labour group nonetheless ploughed on with the decision, to jeers from those present from the campaign; Labour was easily able to force through the closure because of their comfortable majority. This was a straightforward reversal of the position two years earlier, when I had been on the outside of the same building as part of a gathering protesting against the withdrawal of the grant awarded by the council to the domestic violence pressure group Southall Black Sisters, in the face of cuts by the then Conservative majority on Ealing Council (Hundal 2008). On that occasion the initial funding cut was reversed by a later High Court decision (Royston 2008). Such protests have become a more regular occurrence since the onset of the financial crisis – as with the public libraries campaign later in 2010. All such protests were of course cast into the shade by the disturbances of summer 2011.

Perspective is everything. Different features of the suburban landscape are visible from different vantage points. It was while on the top deck of a 65 bus going back and forth over Kew Bridge that a squatted site known as Eco-village came to my attention in autumn 2009, thanks to the bird's eye view my elevated position gave me. The site was surrounded by hoarding put up by St Georges, a newbuild housing company, and the protestors were camped on the land inside. I had been past the hoarding umpteen times on my way to work in Kingston before I noticed the ramshackle settlement, with its 'tent-city' appearance. But by mid 2010 the camp had vanished from view and bulldozers began moving in. By late 2011 the first show home of the new high-end flats was up and running. The developers had been able to bypass the former regulations requiring an affordable housing element because of new rules that allowed them instead to offset their luxury apartments in one part of a borough with the construction of other housing, aimed at more downmarket tenants, elsewhere in another – thereby keeping the riff-raff at arms length. During the history of the site I had seen the hoarding change from an advert for a newly released housing development in West Drayton, depicting affluent people eating al-fresco in sunny climes, to a navy-blue coloured background adorned by the logos of St Georges and Brentford Football Club, and then to printed and blown up drawings submitted by pupils of the local primary school, before all of these were finally replaced in autumn 2011 with adverts for the finished product.

The squatters were opposing what Bridge and Watson (2002:452) have described as 'developer-led speculative suburbanization – as a result of more rapid transport, the baby-boom, and changing practices of mortgage lending'. Among their criticisms was that St George had wanted to build a multi-storey development with 130 parking spaces. As Freddie, one of the eco-villagers later said to me, 'Just imagine the traffic that would have been added to Kew Bridge'. The advent of the automobile is often seen as a key driver of suburban development, but it is also being increasingly opposed by green and alternative protests – often involving people who are themselves from the suburbs. Such protests often promote a different and better way of living than the usual rat race, most usually in American context but also in the UK, for example in the opposing of ribbon development (McCreery 2002).

One October Sunday afternoon in 2009 I ventured inside the gates through a gap in the hoarding – on which the adverts had been modified with slogans from the eco-villagers. The day had been billed to the outside world as a 'family fun day'. On a day of mixed weather, and following the subsiding of the drizzles, I had decided to go along for a closer look, accompanied by my five year old son. As we walked over Kew Bridge we'd seen the colourful tents and what looked like two gatherings of people. A 'No drugs/alcohol' warning was a noticeable feature of the entry. The first person we met as we made the transition to the other side was a young man, probably in his twenties, who told us that the main activity for the day was building a cob house. This would form winter shelter for the campers until their possible eviction the following year. He began to explain how this was a structure of clay mixed with mud, and then took us round to show us. At the far corner of the site, three young men and a middle-aged woman stood near what looked to be a large mud circle undergoing construction; this would eventually form the foundations of a house.

In a study of squatting in inner London boroughs Kearns (1979:596) wrote that squatters 'forge a sense of community and perceived territoriality becomes an integral factor in group solidarity, as evidenced by exhortations to defend "our street" or "our block"'. Certainly the protesters at Eco-village defined themselves as being literally under siege from the authorities and developers. They promoted their way of living as being community-focused, for people not profit, and ran it along utopian principles of participatory democracy in decision-making. Their power networks were painstakingly non-hierarchical; collective action had assumed more importance than individual action in their non-formalised social organisation.

The developers boast on their website that: 'St George has built an impressive reputation, and won awards for regenerating disused parts of the capital and transforming them into vibrant communities in attractive landscaped grounds, offering on-site facilities such as fitness suites, business centres, concierge service, shops, cafés and restaurants.' But the eco-villagers had their own vision of a vibrant community – though none of the on-site facilities St George envisaged were there on the open day, save for the cups of tea that were offered to helpers, which had been heated on an open fire at another part of the site. Hand-washing facilities for those working with mud were basic: a square blue plastic washing up bowl for rinsing hands. 'It's not for eating food with but good enough to get your hands clean', the woman present tells my son.

Freddie was enthusiastically thwacking away at the mud. Balls were being constructed that then got patted into the wall. He told me that he was 19 and was supposed to have gone to university that year but had chosen not to. I asked him why he had made that decision. 'I wouldn't have been learning anything about sustainable living,' he answered. 'The thing about squatting is that it's usually seen as quite intrusive, going in with crowbars and that. This wasn't like that at all.' Another eco-villager Richard chipped in: 'It's not mutually exclusive. You can study and live here. India [a fellow eco-villager] goes to college and is saving a fortune in accommodation.' The population of the Eco-village conformed to Kearns's (1979:591) findings that 95 per cent are usually aged between 20 and 35 years old. One can only guess that, written when it was, his statement that 75 per cent of his sample were native to the UK can be read as meaning that they were overwhelmingly white. This overwhelming whiteness is something I have seen in various alternative protests since the 1990s.

Of those present on the open day not all lived there. Some were commuting; one dreadlocked camper lived on the Queen Caroline council estate at Hammersmith. He told me that the council there wanted to move tenants on, so that they could develop private housing in its place: 'They're not offering money to go but mortgages elsewhere. It's a systematic effort to push out the working class.' The middle-aged woman turned out to be from Hackney, though she had grown up nearby: 'I think there's more money round this part of London so the attitude of people is very different. I live in East London, Hackney, and where I live it's very different. When there's wealth around people react differently'. I pointed out that there had been local public support over the squatter protests earlier in the year at the home of then Hounslow MPs Ann and Alan Keen. Someone else commented that Brentford itself was not an affluent place – 'just look at those tower blocks there'. Indeed in the distance the Brentford Towers loomed large. Though their name sounds like something from a fairly tale, maybe a castle inhabited by Rapunzel, the reality is a 1968-built stretch of four tall, slightly tired-looking high-rise council blocks, which only that week had been condemned on BBC local tv as lacking suitable escape routes should a fire occur. This mixed view of whether or not the area was affluent was symptomatic both of the variety of housing in the area and the changes that were taking place. Brentford had been touted for a number of years as the next big thing in terms of desirable places to live, but had not yet quite made it.

'Do you still want me to go to university mum?' Freddie asked, turning to the middle-aged woman. I was taken slightly aback. I hadn't thought that our party of two might not constitute the only mother and son team there. 'Not right now this instant maybe, but I think you still should go', she answered. 'That's your lad then?' I asked. 'Yes I'm just coming to visit him.' She couldn't imagine Freddie living in a hall of residence, sharing a student kitchen, the implication being that the 'who stole my cheese' pettiness of student living would be a shock after his present experiences – before coming to the Eco-village he had already squatted in the Ocean Estate in Stepney Green. Like the Brentford squatters discussed below, the Eco-villagers saw their role as building an alternative future, constructed against officialdom, who were cast as the villains of the piece. To them education had been rendered as land had been under capitalism – just another commodity to be bought and sold.

The people at the Eco-village were incredibly industrious in generating the cob mixture, moulding cob-balls and patting them into the wall. Kearns (1979:592) named renovation as a function of the squatters, including 'voluntary labor, mutual aid, shared tools and expertise, unorthodox and second-hand materials, innovation and determination'. In his words, they were 'uninhibited and imaginative in shaping their physical environment'. On the open day we had plenty of sightings from onlookers and even some largely good-humoured mild abuse from people crossing Kew Bridge. I heard 'get a job' being shouted from two women passing. As quick as a flash the retorts came back. 'I *have* got a job', said one villager.

Another non-villager took photos with a large lensed camera for his 'uni project on social documentary'. One of the villagers was also making a film, but on my asking whether they were well networked they replied that although they had a Facebook page they were 'not very good at it'. At the nearby Brook South Road South squat (see below) house there had been constant e-campaigning with the aid of a dongle, but apparently the internet was not regularly in use here.

The composition of those present was fluid. A group of girls aged between 9 and 11 came by later, pupils at the nearby Strand on the Green primary school in the W4 postcode of posh Chiswick, and at Gumley House convent. The five of them – two black and three white – got stuck into making the cob wall, as did my five year old. As the sky became dark one of them was being phoned by a dad. We all downed tools together, although my son wanted to continue. The Eco-villagers were planning a week-long programme of half-term events. 'It'll be bigger than this; Halloween party, face-painting and stuff. Spread the word', said Richard. The dream was short-lived, however. By mid 2011 construction was well underway, the marketing suite was complete and the show-home had gone up.

A PROTEST SQUAT IN BRENTFORD

In July 2008 further unusual goings-on had occurred in New Road, Brentford, just down the road from eco-village. Indeed there had been an overlap in the personnel involved. Events centred around a rather modest corner house which for a brief period of time in the summer of

2009 was positively fending off camera crews and press photographers. This was the unoccupied home of MPs Ann and Alan Keen, who had been exposed in the *Telegraph* for their expenses claims (though this additionally owned house was not actually part of their claim). Initial attempts to make contact with the squatters drew a blank, probably because my attempts to knock at 9am after completing school drop-off were bad timing. Finally I got to see the squatters, on their penultimate day in the property. On that occasion, in addition to the provocative banners festooning the property inviting passers-by to 'fight corruption', there was a placard advertising their court appointment later that day, urging well-wishers to turn up and support them. I got the details and at lunchtime made it through the heavy police presence and camera crews for a ringside seat at the case of Alan Keen and Ann Keen v persons unknown, in which the two MPs won their case for an interim possession order against the squatters who had, as they put it in court, 'occupied/ recycled/ liberated' the couple's house.

Colourfully attired squatters filled the pews of the courtroom at the Brentford County court, treating onlookers to a Yellow Submarine style chant of 'We all live where the Keens have never seen'. The MP couple were absent. Kearns (1979:593) wrote of the squatters he studied that they had 'a strong sense of accomplishment and pride in home possession, preferring the retention of dweller control over their squat to acceptance of rehousing in council tenant estates'. The squatters of Keen-gate also had a sense of pride. They were not prepared to go down without a fight and, abandoning their house in the middle of a decorating project, were now representing themselves in court, squaring up to the Keens' barrister Robert Latham. The case had no named respondents at the start, but one by one the squatters stood up from various positions in the congregation, providing their names and thereby becoming enabled to present their case, but also liable for any damages sought further down the line. There were 11 defendants by the end. The only cast members missing were Mr and Mrs Expenses, but they hadn't needed to be there in person and their barrister easily won the interim possession order.

NOTES FROM THE MARGINS: SUBURBAN PROTEST IN THE 1990S

For me both events were a flashback to 1994, when for the purposes of my PhD I began frequenting meetings of the Advance Party, a ravers' campaign set up against the then proposed Criminal Justice and Public Order Bill, which threatened curbs on newly made illegal gatherings (Huq 1998). I combined my study with writing about the subject for radical red/green magazine *Red Pepper*, a status that helped me gain access to the group. Interestingly, the campaign had multiple centres, sometimes in suburban locations. For example, in order to draw attention to the new offence of aggravated trespass there was a nonviolent occupation of then Home Secretary Michael Howard's Kent constituency-home back garden, while there was also a legendary 1992 party at Acton Lane, West London. At around the same time, Claremont Road in suburban east London, condemned to demolition to make way for the M11 link road, also became a major focus of protest. Although the Department of Transport had attempted to empty the street pending its bulldozing, some residents were digging in their heels, and were joined by a younger energetic squatting crowd. Here again continuity with the past was stressed: Dolly Watson, a resident who had been born in a house in the street, became a figurehead of the campaign for her stubborn refusal to succumb to the compulsory purchase order served on her, until her eventual forcible removal, followed by her death shortly afterwards.

The culture of immediacy inherent in the idea of not simply trying to influence events (e.g. writing to an MP) but wanting instead to lead them was integral to these campaigns of nonviolent direct action, which thrived on the creation of visual stunts and the attraction of media attention. As McRobbie (1994:23) remarked: 'Far from being overwhelmed by media saturation, there is evidence to suggest that these social groups and minorities [neo folk devils] are putting it to work for them'.

As the original residents of Claremont Road were moved out to accommodate the Department of Transport's plans, squatters moved in to occupy a number of houses, which then took on different functions – cafe/bar space, live performance-space, dance-floor etc. The 'occupation' had the effect of turning a mundane space into a site of resistance sealed off from the outside, so that being there felt like participating in a perpetual rave, without the usual barriers of entry price and start and finish times, and also like being on a film set, because the street was cordoned off from everyday use. Much of the campaign was shaped by middle-class protagonists of suburban origins. Meanwhile DIY community centres, squatters' cafés and creative workshops up and down the country reworked the government's programmes of 'care in the community' and urban regeneration – for example Justice?, based in a squatted Brighton court-house, who produced *SchNEWS*; the Rainbow Centre, a squatted church in Highgate; and Brixton's Cooltan Arts, a former dole office where John Major (allegedly) used to draw unemployment benefit in his youth; and the Luton Exodus collective, which organised raves, and ran a squat housing thirty people and a community farm. Much of the rhetoric around these campaigners' yearning for an olde England was not dissimilar to William Morris's imagined medieval-styled world of happy people and greenness.

If the legislation's purpose had been to appease the electorate of the Tory shires, then the politicisation of substantial sections of middle-aged, middle-class, respectable England through the anti-Criminal Justice Bill and anti-road campaigns, particularly inasmuch as they opened their eyes to police brutality, was surely an unintended consequence. Aware of losing ground among their natural supporters because of television news pictures of grandmotherly individuals being roughly treated by the police in the anti veal transportation protests at around the same time, *Police Review* (Spring 1995) called for 'a change in tactics to prevent the service losing public faith'. John Stewart of road-protesting group Alarm UK told me in 1995: 'Protesting is becoming almost respectable for the middle class. The middle classes are experiencing the same uncertainties the working class always had. No job is safe anymore. People are much more critical and more prepared to take on the establishment'. McCreey (2002) sees links between the 1990s protests in suburban London of Claremont Road and the situationists of the 1960s Paris left bank; while one popular contemporaneous website enthused: 'As the recession deepens throughout the decade, the co-operative free festy/rave/squatter/new age techno traveller tribal crossover counterculture scenes are the real green shoots in the Communal Economy which will grow unstoppably.' The commercialisation of the alternative in the form of supermarket organic produce and high street herbal medicine can be dated to the 1990s, a decade in which green consumerism's empowering potential had already been noted by academics (Nava, 1991:168).

In the eyes of its perpetrators their actions were rooted in natural justice (Reasons and Rich, 1978), with a moral higher value than the simple criminal sanctions of legal law. This is seen in a leaflet from the East London M11 Link Road protesters urging: 'Resist the road-builders, they are strong but we are right.' When I visited the condemned Claremont Road in 1994 it felt almost like a Glastonbury-style festival, with a number of attendees literally dancing in the streets. The bay-fronted two-storey brick-built villas which had been subject to compulsory purchase order had taken on new uses behind the steel sheeting. I returned on another occasion in the daytime and both times took numerous photos as everything looked like a spectacle. There were clear links to the eco-green protest movements. One photo shows a disused car full of overgrown plants, and the slogan 'rust in peace' can be seen. McCreery (2002:229-230) has included a picture almost identical in her essay on the subject, remarking that: 'Claremont Road had never been a particularly impressive street … just a single strip of about thirty late-nineteenth-century bylaw terraced houses squeezed in beside the railway … transformed into an extraordinary festival of resistance'.

Many of the protests drew on ideas of historical rights and traditions. Thus in the road protests at Twyford Down and Solsbury Hill, legitimacy was derived from the fact that both were ancient festival sites. The right to rave was presented as part of British cultural heritage, as in one participant's references to 'our inalienable right to hold parties and dance as our ancestors have done for hundreds of years'. Lord Justice Hoffman's affirmation of 'an ancient and honourable tradition of peaceful public protest' adorned a pro-active campaign postcard pre-addressed to the Department of Environment. And the 1996 utterance of a High Court judge in a post-Act case – 'What Mahatma Gandhi did was certainly against the law … but most people approved of what he did' – elicited similar applause from the NVDA lobby. The genealogy of CJB protest was traced to Woodstock (Manchester Freedom Network leaflet), and to the suffragettes, diggers, levellers, poor laws, poll tax and the peasant's revolt (Nottingham Campaign Against the Criminal Justice Bill leaflet of 1994; Harding 1998:80). The 1990s saw a strong growth in green movements, and particularly those that sought to 'conserve'. And many of these involved participants from suburbia.

COHESION AND EXCLUSION

It seems, then, one can make a strong case for alternative politics being alive and well in suburbia, especially in the green and conservation movements. However, it is also the case, from the examples discussed, that many of those involved in such protests were not from the suburban localities in which their actions took place (Brentford and Wanstead) but were instead 'passing through' – though in fact many were also originally from other suburbs.

Earlier commentators who have written about associative life in suburbia have often seen such areas as ripe for the sort of people who are 'joiners', but the types of groups they were thinking of tended to be choral societies and women's institute branches rather than non violent direct action protest. However there is much activity at local level that is more alternative than the women's institute while not involving bold acts of direct action. For example at local government level there are many campaigns on issues such as schools, pedestrian crossings, the opening up of new supermarkets and planning applications, traffic measures, fares and a whole range of other bread and butter issues. These campaigns often involve overwhelmingly middle-class participants. Dahl (1961:297) has noted that community politics will inevitably only be able to command a segment of popular opinion:

> Because of differences in objective situations few decisions of government affect citizens generally and uniformly. Most decisions have strong and immediate consequences for only a relatively small part of the population and at best only small or delayed consequences for the rest. By and large only those citizens who expect the decision to have important and immediate consequences for themselves or for those with whom they feel strongly identified, try to influence the outcome.

The most vociferous are frequently from the middle class.

Writing on the 'right to the city' movement, Mayer (2009:363) observes 'the barrenness which Fordist zoning and suburbanization had brought about' in the 1960s. Perhaps we can now trace a 'right to the suburb' movement – illustrated by all the protests described in this chapter – as the suburban dream itself has become increasingly unobtainable given the upward spiralling of housing costs. Among the arguments made by those demonstrating in all these instances is the need to improve the quality of life in the suburbs, and for more opportunities to participate in the community. All would see themselves as transformative in their aims, and frequently adopt a rights discourse to articulate their views.

There are obvious inter-connections between the suburban resistance movements described here, as well as differences between them. The protests at Ealing Town Hall cuts are probably most in the 'traditional protest' mould. As squat protests, the Eco-village, occupation of the Keens' home and Claremont Road anti-M11 protests all had deep socio-spatial implications: they literally could not be divorced from their context, making their respective locations far from interchangeable. In some sense they were also against privatization. Squatting indicates a refusal to conform to social norms, a refusal to budge from the space in question. Squatters are also often driven by wants rather than needs: stemming from the desire to live the alternative lifestyle rather than a necessity. Marcuse (2009) importantly draws the distinction between the claims of the discontented and the deprived. Our suburban protestors are more likely to be drawn from the former than the latter. 'Community cohesion' and 'social exclusion' have become popular terms in recent years, but there is a sense that some involved in alternative suburban situated protest are electing to be socially excluded, or are even excluding themselves from conformist society.

Commenting on the Criminal Justice Bill campaigns, Doreen Massey (1998:127) scorned attempts by the Conservative government 'to control what was evidently – to them – a disturbingly high degree of mobility and lack of desire to "settle down" on the part of significant numbers of young people'. 'These young people apparently did not *want* to own their own "nice home" in some salubrious avenue (or, at least, not yet); they appeared to reject the strings of the already established.' Press (1995:798) too makes this point: 'they don't want (or can't afford) to live in straight society under a landlord's roof'. The philosophy behind squatting equally rested on a sense of 'natural justice' in drawing attention to the situation of the number of empty UK properties outstripping its homeless population.

Perhaps another unifying factor between the protests described in this chapter is the class base of the participants. In this sense what was once 'alternative' has become normalised for a substantial minority of the middle classes; there has been an 'imitation ... of the lifestyles of artistic subcultures (bohemians, avant-gardes) in contemporary metropolises amongst the young and highly educated' (Featherstone 1991:97). And this trend has embraced the suburbs as well as the inner city. Kearns (1979:597) remarked that 'Westminster, Camden and Islington are regarded as "trendy" boroughs noted for a liberal ambience generally attractive to squatters.' But, as we have seen, squatting is no longer confined to these areas. Indeed squats in Wanstead, Kew and Brentford were partly explained by opportunism, as communities sought out space away from inner London. It would be tempting for some to read these suburban protests as demonstrating the crisis of legitimacy in capitalism, but the cases described almost transcend traditional left/right divides. Mayer (2009:364) refers to 'a panoply of middle class-based movements embracing a variety of concerns', and locates them across the spectrum, 'from NIMBY to environmental, from defensive, even reactionary to progressive'. The potential elasticity of the terms employed is great: the term 'new politics' (Lent and Jordan, 1999) was applied to the anti-criminal justice bill protests and the contemporaneous road and animal campaigns, as a way of describing issue-based, extra-parliamentary activity; but since then new politics has also been repeatedly called for by practically everyone, including David Cameron, Ed Miliband, Nick Clegg, Gordon Brown and Tony Blair.

Perhaps the examples in this chapter demonstrate most clearly that suburbia is multi-faceted, and its politics are multi-perspectival, and that they incorporate ballot box struggles as well as alternative mobilisations. It is also affected by the twentieth-century fragmentation of traditional understandings of class, and the emergence of other fault-lines, giving way to a politics of difference. In other chapters we will see how the suburbs have also been affected by other forms of 'new politics', including the newly politically assertive brand of Islam, whose young followers can be seen as a by-product of 'the war on terror'. The rhetoric of 'community cohesion' may sometimes today come up against other new policy agendas, for example support for faith schools, where religious groups are educated apart from the mainstream. These are in keeping with support for 'choice' and a conservative emphasis on faith, but they separate off communities in precisely the way the Cantle report warned of, in its findings after the

2001 riots in the northern towns. While uniformity is impossible to impose in a heterogeneous population, ways of living with difference are crucial. Britain's demographic picture is incontestably more mixed than ever before, and the suburbs are no exception to this, many of them now qualifying for the adjective of 'super-diverse'.

It is in some ways the supposed facelessness of suburbia that makes alternative protest in suburbia so noteworthy. The silent majority are finally afforded a voice. McCreery (2002:241) has commented of Claremont Road: 'had the area not been rendered anonymous and banal, then the activists would not have been able to impose themselves upon it so emphatically'. Yet suburbia is not in fact characterless. In many ways it has specific characteristics – spatial distance from the city centre, self-containedness. The suburban arena potentially allows new voices to enter political debate, both in official and alternative politics. Perhaps in an ever-more unpredictable world this is one certainty that can be foreseen and welcomed.

REFERENCES

Barthes, R. (1975) *The Pleasure of the Text*, Jonathan Cape.

Bey, H. (1991) *T.A.Z.: The Temporary Autonomous Zone, Ontological Anarchy, Poetic Terrorism*, Autonomedia.

Bridge, G. and Watson, S. (2002) *Blackwell Reader on the City*, Blackwell.

Campbell, B. (1993) *Goliath*, Methuen.

Coote, A. (2010) 'Ten Big Questions about the Big Society', New Economics Foundation: www.neweconomics.org/publications/ten-big-questions-about-the-big-society.

Dahl, R. (1961) *Who Governs?: democracy and power in an American city*, Yale University Press.

Featherstone, M. (1991) *Consumer Culture and Postmodernism*, Sage.

Hall, P. (2007) *London Voices, London Lives: Tales from a Working Capital*, Policy Press.

Harding, T. (1998) 'Viva camcordistas! Video activism and the Protest Movement', in McKay, G. (ed) *DiY Culture: Party & Protest in Nineties Britain*, Verso.

Hart, H. (1963) *Law, Liberty and Morality*, OUP.

Hebdige, D. (1979) *Subculture: the Meaning of Style*, Routledge.

Howe, D. (2011) 'My father curfewed me and I jumped through the window', at SocialistWorkerOnline 20.8.11: www.webcitation.org/6110nDPVN.

Hundal, S. (2009) 'Funding u-turn will help women groups', 30.1.09: www.pickledpolitics.com/archives/2832.

Huq, R. (1999) 'The Right to Rave: Opposition the Criminal Justice and Public Order Act 1994', in Jordan, T. and Lent, A. (eds), *Storming the Millennium: the new politics of change*, Lawrence and Wishart, pp15-33.

Huq, R. (2003) 'Urban Unrest in Northern England 2001: rhetoric and reality behind the "race riots"', in Lentin, A. (ed), *Learning From Violence: the youth dimension* Council of Europe, pp42-52.

Jordan, T. and Lent, A. (1999) *Storming the Millennium: the new politics of change* Lawrence and Wishart.

Kean, H. (2003) 'The transformation of political and cultural space' in Joe Kerr and Andrew Gibbon (eds), *London: from Punk to Blair*, Reaktion, pp148-156.

Kearns, K. (1979) 'Intraurban squatting in London', *Annals of the Association of American Geographers*, Vol 69, Issue 4, pp589-598.

Kynaston, D. (2009) *Family Britain, 1951-1957: Tales of a New Jerusalem*, Bloomsbury.

Lévi-Strauss, C. (1955) *Tristes Tropiques*, Plon.

Marcuse, P. (2009) 'From critical urban theory to the right to the city', *City: analysis of urban trends, culture, theory, policy, action*, Volume 13, Issue 2-3.

Massey, D. (1998) 'The Spatial Construction of Youth Cultures' in Skelton and Valentine (eds) (1997) *Cool Places: Geographies of Youth Cultures*, Routledge, pp121-124.

Mayer, M. (2009) 'The "Right to the City" in the context of shifting mottos of urban social movements' in *City: analysis of urban trends, culture, theory, policy, action*, Volume 13, Numbers 2-3, June 2009 , pp362-374(13).

McCreery, S. (2002) 'The Claremont Road Situation', in Borden, I., Kerr, J. and Rendell, J. and Pivaro, A. (eds) (2002) *The Unknown City*, Routledge.

McKay, G. (1996) *Senseless Acts of Beauty: Cultures of Resistance since the Sixties*, Verso.

McKay, G. (1998) (ed) *DiY Culture: Party & Protest in Nineties Britain*, Verso.

McRobbie, A. (1994) 'Folk Devils Fight Back', in *New Left Review* 203, Jan/Feb, pp107-116.

Nava, M. (1991) 'Consumerism reconsidered: Buying and power, in *Cultural Studies* Vol 5 (2), pp157-173.

Press, J. (1995) 'The Killing of Crusty', in Savage, J. and Kureishi, H. (1995) *The Faber Book of Pop* Faber and Faber.

Reasons, C. and Rich, R. (1978) *The Sociology of law: A conflict perspective*, Blackwell.

Royston, J. (2008) 'Sisters celebrate as council caves', 18.7.08:
www.ealingtimes.co.uk/news/2403179.sisters_celebrate_as_council_caves/.

SWP (2011) 'Jail the Tories, not young people', 16.8.11: http://www.webcitation.org/6110sO9Rv.

Wheeler, B. (2005) 'The politics of volunteering', 2.6.05:
http://news.bbc.co.uk/1/hi/uk_politics/4576541.stm.

Wind-Cowie, M. (2010) 'Civic Streets: The Big Society in Action', Demos: www.demos.co.uk/publications/civicstreets.

4

Faith in the suburbs: identity, interaction, belonging and belief

> I marched through Golders Green, passing by the rows of Jewish stores. The little world my people have built here. The kosher butchers' shops frowned at me, asking why I hadn't tried their chopped, now only £2.25 a quarter. The recruitment agency smiled widely, inviting me to apply for a job with a Sabbath-observant company, half-day Fridays only. Moishe's salon raised an eyebrow at my hairstyle and wondered if I wouldn't like something, maybe, a bit more like everyone else
>
> Naomi Alderman, *Disobedience* (2006:121)

This next chapter turns to the practice of religion in the suburbs. While the famous 1985 Archbishop of Canterbury's Commission on Urban Priority Areas report that so irked the Thatcherite Conservative Party was entitled 'faith in the city', this chapter looks at faith in suburbia.

Despite the fact that religion was a key consideration of all three theorists now known as the sociological 'founding fathers' – Marx, Weber and Durkheim – there was for a long time a tailing-off in its consideration by modern sociology and funding by research councils: they tended to focus more on vogueish consumerist or identity topics. The 'cultural turn' by the social sciences in the 1980s is usually understood as a shift in emphasis away from questions of structure in sociology and towards the study of culture, especially popular culture. But culture in this case is not usually understood as an approach that needs to pay much attention to faith or religious cultures. However, in the last ten to fifteen years this has begun to change. The £8.3k 'Religion and Society' Research Programme, launched jointly by the ESRC and AHRC 5 in 2007, to run over five years, is a sign of this shift away (back) from a post-enlightenment lack of social-science interest in questions of faith, to be replaced by a recognition of the need to take religion seriously. Certainly the academic study of religion need not be confined only to concerns of theological position. The 'Religion and Society' programme seeks to look at various other identity markers, and notes the need to consider religion 'on a local and global scale ... in historical and comparative contexts as well as through the perspectives of gender, age, sexuality, class, economic status, dis/ability and ethnicity'. It also attempts to be outward-facing, in keeping with the multiple wider community dimensions of religion: 'to engage publics, religious groups, policy makers, charities, creative and cultural sectors and others in dialogue about the role of religion in society'. This is broadly the approach that will be adopted in this chapter.

But if the importance of religion as a social force is growing in academic respectability, the link between faith and suburbia remains one of contestation: many critics of the suburbs have seen them as places where consumerist materialism has triumphed over belief in divine power. Popular cultural readings have frequently depicted this mismatch. In Leslie Thomas's steamy novel *Tropic of Ruislip* (1974), a tale of suburban wife-swapping as practised by the species 'Flat-Roof Man', local vicar Reverend Boon attempts to drum up business/new congregation on the new estate of the book's setting, only for nonchalant resident Polly Blossom-Smith to retort: 'I don't know. They go back to the places they came from originally for such things as Christenings and weddings. I suppose they think things are more *established* there' (Thomas 1974: 133). The word 'established' is a play on words, as remarked on by the vicar, but this goes unnoticed by Polly. The novel is typical of a 1970s view of materially and individually focused suburban lives, wherein a godless people dwells, who have no time for anything other than G-plan furniture, and certainly not for putting down roots in their new community. But the 1930s suburbs were also viewed as godless places. In George Orwell's 1939 novel *Coming Up For Air*, the central character, reluctant suburbanite George Bowling, embarks on a short sojourn to the countryside of his childhood to escape his current suburban tedium, only to find that it too has become suburbanised, with cranes moving in before his eyes to continue this process. Part of Orwell's metaphor for the decay of this former beauty spot of the Thames Valley are the untended graves of Bowling's parents and the old church he attended as a child, where the same vicar is in attendance but no longer recognises George. This too seems to be telling us that the modern suburbanite has no time for religion. And the sentiment has also been echoed by sociologist Steve Bruce (2002:13):

> When the total, all-encompassing community of like-situated people working and playing together gives way to the dormitory town or suburb, there is little left in common to celebrate ... the plausibility of any single, overarching moral and religious system declined, to be displaced by competing conceptions ... privatised, individual experience [with] little connection to the performance of social roles or the operation of social systems.

The same argument is made in Bruce (2000:17). Yet US theorist Putnam (2000) sees religion as a key component of social capital, and religion is certainly playing a role in community life in some parts of modern suburbia. Religion has in fact literally made its impact on the face of suburbia in the many buildings used for congregational worship – which in many cases have been recycled for newer migrant communities, while in others they have taken the form of grand constructions built from scratch. The picture of religion is today is in fact very mixed – just as are the suburbs themselves.

In the traditional suburbs it was generally in earlier eras that the church as a physical presence and spiritual force assumed a more central role in the life of the suburb. A celebrated example exists in the 'the Clapham Sect', an English ecclesiastical movement with a strong zeal for social reform that sought to influence suburban morality by modelling a particular kind of suburban life away from the evils of the city. William Wilberforce was a leading light of the movement, and among Clapham Sect causes was the abolition of slavery. A parallel emphasis was placed on the centrality of family life. The two can be seen to combine in stories of important meetings in the Anti-Slavery campaign being adjourned whilst everyone went to play with the children on the Common. The template was of suburban life as an imitation of rural idyll, where homes and gardens plus women and children were kept separate from the grime, danger and vice that lurked in the contemporaneous city. This suggests that there were deep and complex moral-religious motivations at work in this creation of suburban life. Whilst campaigning for women and children to be protected from the abuses of the industrial revolution, members moved their own families to what was then an embryonic suburb-cum-village of Clapham (though it is now considered to be inner city); but the men's work continued to be focussed in the city. Such 'women and children first' imperatives resurfaced in 1930s suburbia, with its concern for respectability fused with the vision of a rural idyll. Flat-roofed churches later followed as a new feature of the suburban landscape as more modernist development began. Tim Lott, in his memoir *The Scent of Dried Roses* (1998:25), describes how he returned to Southall where he had grown up as a child following his mother's suicide: 'I drive past the anonymous shops. There is an ugly 1950s church, Our Lady of the Visitation just before Cardinal Wiseman School.' His criticism of the building reflects his hatred of suburbia itself, which he and his brother are embarrassed to live in and dream of escaping. The book's new edition in 2009 included the subheading 'One family and the end of English Suburbia – an elegy'.

Ruxley Church in Ewell, Surrey, a joint Anglican-Methodist church formed from the former church of St Francis of Assisi and Ruxley Lane Methodist church, provides another example of changing times. It is housed in the former Methodist building, a simple frame structure incorporating wood construction that was erected cheaply and quickly as a dual purpose building-cum-community-centre in the 1950s. The obituary of Ernest Hunt, aged 103, in the June 2011 edition of the church magazine *Ruxley Star*, detailed the achievements of one of the church's founders. As well as the claim that people active in faith communities have higher life expectancies, the obituary records the origins of the church in a 1948 Sunday School for children in the local primary school, after which its success justified a new building (originally a multi-use community hall). Then in 1960 a 'Society' (Methodist terminology for a local church or congregation) was formed as adults started to attend. Two hundred yards down the road the Anglican church built to serve the new estate has now been demolished: this ostensibly more substantial brick building was found to have huge structural cracks due to subsidence, and these made it unsafe (it is built on London clay). The suburban house of god, built to a rigid structure according to a traditional pattern, had failed, whilst its more flexible, semi-temporary neighbour survived – though advanced plans are afoot to build a new united church in what is to be one more a substantial and rigid building.

The developing character of suburban faith spaces and spirituality is evident across the built environment and material infrastructure of present day suburbia. Structures such as the Russian Orthodox Church by the A4 in Chiswick, the Regent's Park Mosque or the Neasden Temple in London NW10 have each been welcome additions to the suburban London skyline, in each case greeted with initial curiosity but now integrated into their surroundings, an accepted as 'part of the scenery'. Kadish (2011) has claimed that many synagogues in twentieth-century Britain were built in bold architectural styles (for example Byzantine Style/Orientalism in Sunderland; Scandinavian Modernism in Greenbank Drive, Liverpool) precisely to be highly visible. Suburban faith spaces may indeed be purpose-built, but they often also demonstrate great ingenuity in recycling buildings formerly used for other purposes, religions or denominations. The imposing grey-stone structure of Our Lady Mother of the Church in Ealing Broadway is now one of the UK's oldest established Polish Roman Catholic churches, although from 1867 to 1972 it was a Wesleyan Methodist church. The mosque in West Ealing, as was the case with many others in the UK, began with worshippers congregating in a late Victorian terraced house before moving to its current premises. In Naomi Alderman's *Disobedience*, quoted at the beginning of this chapter, the synagogue is a pair of 'semi-detached houses, glued together and scooped out' (2006: 56). And the adaptation of housing for congregational prayer space also questions the easy assumption of suburbia as a space of the private rather than public realm. Kingston may to the naked eye have only one mosque, but informal arrangements often take place: Muslims can pray elsewhere; and in New Malden our interviews uncovered evidence of a community centre being used for Friday worship. In these many different ways places of worship and religion can in their own way play a role in suburban place-making.

For, though the 'flat roof man' of the new suburb of Plummers Park was resolutely WASPish, the practice of faith in suburbia today is a story of diaspora, immigration and social networks as much as it is of spirituality. In considering suburbs and ethnicity, much sociological literature talks of population displacement, and looks at 'push' and 'pull' factors associated with outlying districts of the cities. At one time moving to the suburbs and away from the city was regarded as a positive choice, but more recently there has been an over-turning of these traditional geometries of power, as the inner city is becoming unaffordable for many, particularly in big cities such as London. This reversal is undermining the concept of 'flight' from inner urban areas. Some years ago the American sociologist William Dobriner (1963:64) outlined the classic position with regards to this suburban drift:

> suburban migration presupposes the negative images of the city (flight) and positive values which encourage a new life in the suburbs (search) … The city has long been the center of alien ethnic groups, crime and violence. Cities are becoming increasingly concentrated with the nonwhite races … Flight to the suburbs may be a polite assertion of the principle of white supremacy.

Indeed the term was often expanded to 'white flight' – away from the minorities who had clustered in the inner-city. However today many minorities have themselves moved to the suburbs – sometimes from choice and upward social mobility, but also sometimes through constraint. And this has once more changed the face of suburban religion.

A suburban setting that sustains religion rather than abandoning it can be seen in Alderman's *Disobedience* – in this case its tight-knit Orthodox Jewish community. The novel draws a pen portrait of Hendon in north west London as a suburb rooted in religious custom and practice. Its moral seems to be that close communities result in closed minds. Ronit, the narrator of the opening quotation, performs a 'return of the native' type role, returning from her new life as a city-slicker sophisticate from New York City to the ultra-orthodox Jewish community of her childhood. At one point, stifled by the claustrophobic atmosphere, she remarks of her suburban surrounds (Alderman 2006: 115):

> It's this place, that's the problem. It's being back here with all those little couples sitting in their identical houses producing identical children. It was seeing them in synagogue, all those women in smart Shabbat suits and their perfectly matched hats and each woman appropriately paired to a man, preferably with a child tugging at each arm. They just fit together, the whole set – like Orthodox Jew Barbie: comes complete with Orthodox Jew Ken, two small children, the house, the car and a selection of kosher foodstuffs … it all seems just so neat.

The book depicts the Orthodox Jews of Hendon as having preserved cultural traditions and practices and created an air of exclusivity – and the area is also continually personified, as in this description of a Saturday night (110): 'The place was utterly deserted; Hendon rested contented and perhaps a little over-full from the Sabbath. Hendon might walk out later to buy bagels or for a cinema outing, but for now was satisfied to remain at home.' Hendon is also often judgemental and disapproving of alternative lifestyles. (Of course *Disobedience* describes only one side of the communities of Hendon. It is home to a campus of Middlesex University, which brings in numerous young people of different ethnic backgrounds that reflect the cosmopolitan nature of the UK's capital, as well as to the orthodox Sara Rifka Hartog Memorial Day school.) Here we can see a minority group with its own take on suburban mores, in which religion plays a role not so dissimilar from that of Anglicanism in other areas. The suburb may be home to a minority community, but it remains the height of respectability.

Britain's move to become a multicultural society is underscored by its multi-faith character, though the nature of the relationship between faith and community varies widely. The UK's capacity to accommodate cultures is a cornerstone of the diversification it has undergone since the middle of the twentieth century; and since religion has been an important aspect of most major migrant groups, the country has shifted from having one dominant denomination to its current patchwork of all faiths and none. This means that as people move to the suburb, the faith mix in the suburbs also changes. There is thus clearly a need to locate a consideration of faith groups within the context of a wider system of (sub)urban, national as well as transnational networks of social organisation.

Perhaps the religion that this applies most clearly to is Islam, which has become central to discussions of identity within Britain. Even before the 'war on terror' began, Britain's Muslims were subject to 'unprecedented scrutiny and examination' (Open Society Institute 2002:71). In this sense British Muslims face unprecedented civic and spiritual challenges. This chapter therefore now turns to Muslims in Kingston, and findings resulting from research in the borough conducted under the aegis of the government's Preventing Violent Extremism programme from 2008 to 2010 (though the focus in this chapter is on attitudes to Islam rather than extremism, which is a separate subject from faith and will be dealt with in chapter 8, where Islamic fundamentalism will be considered alongside extreme-right anti-immigration policy). Interestingly, the Kingston project was eventually broadened out to also look at Tamils and South Koreans in the borough, and the interview evidence seemed to suggest that the faith identity of these two groups had also hardened in diaspora: it was through Korean pastors that contact was made with this community, which proved to be the most 'closed' of the three. My main focus here, however, is on the Kingston Muslim data; and further interview material with staff from an inter-faith project from Bury, a leafy suburb to the north of Manchester.

KINGSTON CASE-STUDY

Kingston – or to give it its full legal-administrative title the Royal Borough of Kingston upon Thames (RBK) – is often thought of as an archetypal suburban borough. The classic tv series *The Good Life* was set in Surbiton, part of the borough. In their responses to the Place Survey for London Councils (2009), designed to investigate how residents' views have changed over time in relation to their quality of life and local public services across all the 33 London boroughs, 83 per cent of people in Kingston stated that in their local area people of different backgrounds got along well together; 85.3 per cent recorded general satisfaction with the area; and 74.7 per cent believed there was fair treatment in local services (though Kingston came lowest of all boroughs in the percentage wishing to be more involved in local-decision-making.) The mere mention of Kingston evokes classic suburban images: it is not usually associated with hotbeds of Islamic – or indeed any type of extremism. And most existing published research into Islamism and youth disengagement has been conducted in more obviously 'ethnic' areas – such as the 'pathfinder' borough of Hounslow (Cantle 2007). So the central premise of the 'Preventing Violent Extremism' study, which focused on respondents of Tamil, South Korean and Muslim backgrounds, itself served to unsettle a key presumption about suburbia in classical academic sources – that it is ethnically homogenous. At the time in which the research took place, both the Muslim and Tamil communities were featuring prominently in the public eye, as various failed 'terror plots' came to trial implicating Muslims, and a prominent Tamil rights demonstration took place in Parliament Square.

Our interviewees had moved into the area for a number of different reasons. One perception was that Bangladeshis in Kingston and its environs were those who had 'made it', as opposed to their more down-at-heel counterparts in the multiple-deprivation blight districts such as Tower Hamlets. One British-born Bangladeshi man, who as a child in the 1980s had moved there from the East End with his family, described how the restaurant trade had been a motivating factor:

> When I was growing up it was four or five families and we were all sort of related. There were other people from our village that were there. Other than that there weren't very many families when I was very young. While I was growing up more and more Bengali families came, because Surrey is a goldmine for Bangladeshi restaurants and they all do really well because it's a wealthy county and they all like Indian food ... so a lot of families started emerging. I'd say from mid-90s onwards there was this kind of rush, they'd say, 'it's too far from east London, and we work in Surrey, we have a business in Surrey, we might as well move there'. So people actually moved out from East London and set up businesses in Byfleet, Weybridge, Tadworth, Epsom, places like that. Bengalis in Epsom are actually growing at a higher and more accelerated level than Bengalis in Kingston, but the number of Muslims in Kingston has significantly increased since I was young.

Another interviewee, a Bangladeshi aged 21 who was an undergraduate at Imperial College, praised Kingston for being ethnically mixed but recognised that there was a degree of conscious or subconscious segregation at play in choice of residential district. When I asked whether the stereotype of Kingston as a white leafy suburban borough was now outmoded, he replied:

> ... well I think it is, but the values – the white leafy values – are still around, as you seem to have all the white people living in a certain area, and all the Asians and Africans also seem to live in specific areas. You have all the Koreans living in New Malden, all the Sri Lankans in Coombe and everywhere, and all the Africans seem to be

living in Cambridge estate. I don't know if it's a financial thing or cultural thing. Then you have all the English people tending to be living Kingston Hill or nearer town, in the Charter Quay development ... So obviously there are the different sectors, but people cope with it. There's no, you know, difference or resistance or anything.

I was born in 1989. During the early 1990s there were a lot of white people but since 2000 a lot of people have emigrated to Kingston, a lot of people like Africans, Pakistanis and Bengalis. The mosque has had a part to play in it, because it's the one that they can find, and there's this madrassa school and everything. A lot of parents are keen for their children to go, and it helps with the schools as well, because nowadays the competition for schools is so large.

Kingston Mosque or masjid is a mainstream Sunni Mosque. Even though it is not necessarily representative of all Kingston Muslims, many of our interviewees in official positions referred us to the mosque. The committee member we spoke to was at pains to stress its inclusive nature:

I stood down as chair of the mosque, and the vice chair is a black man, and do you know the number of Punjabis who've said 'why have you got a black chairman?' And yet he's far more scholarly than I am. He knows the Qu'ran far better than I do, prays 5 times a day and all that – except a Somali doesn't have a big beard, his hair doesn't grow. It never grows, it's just a growth. On Eid we have a black, brown and white Imam, did you know that?

Some interviewees perceived it to be a 'Pakistani' mosque, while others felt more comfortable to pray at home or attend events at Regents Park, the central London mosque. The Mosque has a good relationship with the local authority and police, and is seen by officialdom as encouraging diversity and thus as an important tool in the engagement process – but it is only the tip of the iceberg in terms of the borough's Islamic population.

Also present in Kingston are Ahmadiyya Muslims, who follow different prayer rituals and have suffered the long-term experience of not being accepted as an Islamic faith by more mainstream Muslims, to the point where they are persecuted in some countries. The Ahmadiyya Mosque is in the neighbouring south London borough of Merton.

Such cultural differences raise the difficulties of the concept of a single demarcated Muslim community in Kingston, or indeed anywhere. This mosque committee member saw the rural/urban divide as the most important:

> The majority who came here from the 60s, 70s, came here from rural areas of Pakistan and Bangladesh. If they had come from a big city, say Bombay, it would have been different ... if they come from rural lands, how do they cope with completely different structures?

The picture that emerged in our study was of a changing and diverse population, but with the majority of Muslims now being British-born, with English as their first language, as is the case in the rest of the UK. (This necessitates the asking of new questions, such as how to manage the multicultural settlement, rather than immigration per se.) To use the old cliché, immigration itself is becoming a less 'black and white issue'. On the other hand, the old questions of race can sometimes come back in new ways – and particularly through the new discourses on Islam, which will later be explored in more detail.

Within the 'Muslim' sample we spoke to were Shi'as, Sunnis, Ismailis and Ahmadiyyans, between whom there are many similarities but also some differences. Ahmadiyyans are more common in South London than other areas because of the location of their main masjid in Morden, and throughout our study there was evidence of Muslim factional aggression directed towards them from other Muslims in Kingston, including the distribution of anti-Ahmadiyya leaflets in Kingston town centre – although it has been difficult to ascertain the exact origin of these and the mosque committee has denied any involvement. And it should be remembered that Tamil people can also be Muslim in faith background. Policy-makers need to take account of such differences. Future research could also include looking at Muslims from eastern Europe and Muslim converts – these are minorities within minorities.

BURY AND ILFORD: FURTHER EXAMPLES OF RELIGIOUS DIASPORA

It has sometimes been claimed that a history of Manchester Jewry can be traced on the ground as you walk up Cheetham Hill (Lipman 1966;

Kadish 2011). Manchester's Jewish population dates from the 1780s, and its history can be seen even in the location of the Manchester Jewish Museum, which has been on Cheetham Hill Road since 1984, in a former Synagogue of the Sephardi denomination dating from 1874: the synagogue fell into disuse as a result of northward Jewish suburbanisation, as the population moved away and further North, to Prestwich and Whitefield. Indeed these suburbs at the end of the four-mile stretch are described by Waller and Criddle (1987:122) as among 'the most exclusive and desirable of the residential areas in northern Greater Manchester'. As they describe, 'many members of the Manchester Jewish community … did … well, and moved north and up out of the original Cheetham Hill ghetto'. The popularity of these suburban neighbourhoods amongst the Jewish community, and their distinctive mark on the area's character and institutions, can be seen in the educational provision in the borough of Bury, which includes the Manchester Jewish Grammar School in Prestwich and the Bury and Whitefield Jewish Primary School. The suburban character of the surrounding areas as commuter towns servicing Manchester was sealed in 1992, when the Manchester Metrolink light rail system was opened serving Whitefield, Prestwich and Heaton Park, with Bury as the northern terminus. (There was a joke at the time that the Conservative government had put in a tram system passing through the city centre linking the only two Tory-voting parts of Greater Manchester.) Yet the Bury borough is also increasingly becoming a destination for Asian Pakistani settlement. At the time of writing there are multiple synagogues and mosques in Bury. In late 2009 I was lucky enough to interview three staff on the interfaith Adab project in the borough: Usma, Eram and Musadir (all of second-generation Pakistani ethnicity).

> **Usma:** We're trying to break down barriers by actually engaging the white community, by engaging with the Jewish community. Bury is quite unique in its fabric in that outside London it's got the largest Jewish population as well as the largest Muslim population in the north west. There isn't much interaction going on there at all. We're trying to break down those barriers and provide a Muslim Women's Forum for women to engage with Jewish women and explore similarities. There is an unparalleled amount of similarities between them.

Eram: There's quite a lot of orthodox in the Prestwich area.

Usma: Prestwich, Salford, Whitefield. Some of those orthodox Jews are then resonated in the wider Jewish community. And that's when you first realise the similarities that they do have to us, as opposed to what you see in the jingoistic nature of the press, or local peddlers of hate or vicious prejudices.

When I asked what reaction they had got to their approach Usma replied:

In the process that we've set up, we haven't sought to desert the existing infrastructures – we know Bury is quite renowned for its interfaith set-up. We've got the shalom salam forum, we've got the Muslim Christian forum. We're seeking to strengthen those by working in conjunction with them and with liaising with them. In the Muslim Women's Forum, through getting speakers to come in and slowly raising ideas about the need for exchange, the need for a dialogue, women recognise that, and they want that, but they want to do it in a safe space and forum, so it's a case of facilitating that. So the women who do come in, we don't say straight off 'this is what we plan to do'. We don't want to scare them off. It's a case of offering them a carrot at the end of the stick and saying to them that something can come from this. And generally they're quite intrigued by it. It's not all good – we do have some people who say 'you shouldn't really be liaising with Jewish people', and that we're infidels for doing that. But you're going to get that in every society. The thing is to try and concentrate on the ones that are open-minded and work with them and help them to become more reasoned and tolerant women.

I asked whether the two groups lived in the same wards:

Usma: The Jewish families tend to be in more affluent suburbs, whereas Muslim women are generally located in lower socio-economic backgrounds, in more deprived wards, more centrally based and near the central business district. The Jewish ladies tend to be more towards Prestwich, Whitefield, the more leafy suburby areas – and Fairfield, Ramsbottom and Greenmount as well. You don't really see many Asian people there, or Muslim people. I think there's two reasons for that. One, I think the sense of family and community is very great in the Muslim community, and if you move further and further away people think that elongating your distance means you're severing your ties with the family, or straining those ties, and if you're close to them you've got a closer link to your family … something along those lines anyway. And there's other people who think 'we know this area off by heart, we know everybody in this area, it's a nice area so we may as well just stay there'.

Musadir: I think both communities basically like to stick together … I think generally in the north there is a culture of families moving into suburban middle-class white areas when they do well in business or their children have become well-educated, and got good jobs – these families are tending to move out. I think one of the other key issues is that with white leafy suburban areas come good schools, and these young Muslim professionals are quite conscious that they want to send their kids to good schools. I think that's an important factor.

A parallel can be drawn between Bury and Ilford in the London Borough of Redbridge, outer East London. In its Gants Hill neighbourhood, served by London Underground's central line, a longstanding Jewish community is being supplemented, some would argue replaced, by Muslim families of Pakistani and Bangladeshi descent. In June 2010 I interviewed three Labour councillors from Redbridge in Ilford. Their description of the area also illustrated changing demographics:

KT: It was originally a Jewish area. After the war most of the Jews moved out of the East End and came via Ilford. Ilford at one stage had I think the largest concentration of Jews in Europe, and the synagogues had something like three to four thousand members just in this area. The Jews then moved on, some a bit further into Essex but mostly into North London and Hertfordshire. And now there's really quite a small Jewish population. I think we never really had a large Afro-Caribbean community growing here, but certainly Jews – and the Sikhs came in probably from the 1960s onwards, and subsequent to that we've had other groups.

> … the area is polyglot or multicultural, certainly if you look at the ethnic mix it is really quite mixed, predominantly Asians … and in fact we had a Chinese man as the last mayor, there's a small Chinese community as well. It's always been quite peaceful.
>
> **BJ**: It's an area of mixed affluence.

According to Peter Hall (2008:204):

> Ilford … was originally settled by Jewish and other white inhabitants whose families moved from the East End in the 1920s and 1930s when the area was being built. In the 1980s and 1990s they have been supplanted and in part succeeded by waves of arrivals from the Indian subcontinent, now in the second and third generation, whose families also started in East End slums – indeed in many cases the same slums – but who have moved in search of a better quality of life.

One of the Redbridge councillors I spoke to observed: 'an interesting thing that comes to mind is wherever there's been a large Jewish population it's followed by a Muslim population, not just here [but] everywhere. Just the way it seems to go.' A good standard of local schooling was frequently mentioned by interviewees in all three locations as reasons for moving there.

KINGSTON AND BURY: THE HEADSCARF

Recent years have witnessed much debate around the headscarf, as when government minister Jack Straw called it a barrier to communication. It is worth highlighting how this debate is perceived from the other side, and noting how this item is worn in different ways and for different reasons:

> I wear it and I don't wear it, I am not too bothered with the headscarf. Sometimes I wear it, sometimes I don't. It depends how I feel, if I feel I want to wear a beautiful headscarf with my make-up I wear it, if I don't want to I just leave my hair open and I'll go, enjoy …

However, what most participants had in common was an increased experience of discrimination when wearing a headscarf:

You get comments and name-calling, especially when you've got your hijab on. I live in Surbiton, where it's predominantly English people, and I think I am the only one with the headscarf sticking out there.

Focus Group participant, December 2009

Another time was on the bus. I was just doing my A-levels. There was a time when I wore the Jilbab for two and a half years, and this lady looked at me and said, in a very patronising way 'Are you not hot, wearing that?' And I said 'No I'm not, but even if I was it's something for me to be bothered about and for you to just ignore, you just mind your own business.' And to be honest the Jilbab, it's like this light material. But you get this assumption that I'm being forced to suffocate myself in the way I dress. And I said 'No, I'm not sweating. There's nothing wrong with me.' And she said 'oh god, I don't know how you put up with it.' Luckily it was my stop, so I got off.

Focus Group participant, November 2009

In particular many participants resented its interpretation as a sign of oppression. Among Bury participants the following exchange took place:

How long have you worn it?

U: I've worn in since I was in Germany, so 2006. That's three years now. I think that's when I was engaging with Muslims directly, Muslim women …
I was staying with a German girl who had converted to Islam anyway, and another who was a German Turk, and she was covering.

In France as well?

U: Yes, it was a major issue in France. I didn't want to go there. My sister's there at the moment, in Lyon. She said that initially it was quite hard. You're at university, with all the work and everything … she found it quite hard. And things have changed quite a lot in France, quite rapidly. I mean the only people you see in France wearing headscarves now are old women, and when people do see you with a headscarf on they assume you're from north Africa and can't speak a word of French. They expect you to speak pigeon French or something. They underestimate your intelligence, and you get quite a lot of looks – but that spurs you on to a certain degree.

E: I've worn it five years. Five to six. At uni.

M: I've not started [laughter] …

U: I've not really noticed. You usually get some nutters at the supermarket who presume that you can't speak English, and who say things really slowly, so you speak to them and – ok fine.

In a Lancastrian accent …

U: But you know in Germany people are quite vociferous in their distaste for it. You'll get people stopping in the street and just staring at you, and you'll get people saying out loud 'why is she wearing that on? They're taking over the country'. It was a lot more vociferous over there, so when I came back to Manchester everything seemed relatively easy. You can walk round in Manchester and nothing gets said to you at all. They don't give you a second glance.

Not even in those Jewish areas we talked about?

U: Yeah, it's just no problem. I don't really feel it. I think if you went to an area such as Yorkshire or somewhere really down south, you know Surrey or Suffolk, where there's a completely different social or ethnic fabric, then you might encounter a completely different reaction. But you know I personally feel that there's so many rights and so many liberties here that we don't realise, and it's not until you go on the continent that you realise how restricted those European Muslims are.

KINGSTON AND BURY: POLITICS, GENERATION AND POLITICISATION

There has for some time been a sense in popular culture and media representations that religious identities were to some extent underplayed by first-generation immigrants, or that religion was practised more privately, but that it is now becoming a greater source of identification for the second generation. This was a topic we wanted to probe in interview:

> *Are you more religious than your parents were?*
>
> **E**: In my view, yes, because my parents are more cultural. My mum wouldn't wear the headscarf. My mum and dad are more cultural than we are … so 'yes you *should* read your prayers … if you want.' 'Yes you should read the Koran … if you want' … if you do it you're a good person, if you think about doing it you're still good, but it's not such a bad thing to not do it. It's good that word you used 'reawakening' [see below], because that's what it feels is happening.
>
> **U**: I'd say I'm more practising than my parents. My mum's really now started praying, but before she couldn't abide it … when I first started wearing the headscarf on it was quite an anathema to her. She felt … maybe she felt intimidated by the fact that I had it on. She actually said to me 'do you think that you're being a better Muslim by doing this? If you're such a good Muslim then you shouldn't watch tv and you shouldn't listen to music.'

We also heard from some participants that their experience of discrimination or racism had increased since 9/11 (for example, 'dirty looks' in the immediate aftermath of the events were reported by one hijab-wearing woman) – though younger interviewees had no real memory of these events that had occurred a decade earlier. Many participants also reported a qualitative change in the type of racism they were experiencing. Thus, whereas beforehand their experience of racism tended to be focused on their ethnicity, it was now quite clearly focused on religion, and its perceived association with terrorism.

> Before it was racism now it's become anti-Muslim. As you were saying, before it was about where you were from, you were from Pakistan … and about … the colour of your skin. And now it's

> about being a Muslim. It's not so much about which country you're from, I think it's about whether you are Muslim or not.
>
> Focus Group December 2009

> **E**: I think before 9-11 we were all Asian ... now it's just them or us.

> **U**: Like that Sikh guy who's joined the BNP, they're united by the common hatred of Muslims. I think they're trying to now promote him to say 'look we've got our token Sikh guy who's part of the party'.

There is an argument that Islam, more than other religions, is a 'way of life' or complete code of personal conduct, and that more than ever in current times, to be a Muslim has also become a political statement. This identification with wider international issues has been called 'imaginaries from the margin' by Pnina Werbner (2002:101), who, in her work on diasporic Pakistanis in Manchester, draws a parallel between their identifications with homeland struggles and diasporic Jewish support for the Israeli extreme right or Irish-American republicanism. We found in our conversations with young people not only that particular age groups (especially older teenagers and younger adults) were particularly exposed to prejudice against Muslims, but also that this experience seemed to politicise young people and affect the way in which they could explore their faith. Many young Muslims reported how constant confrontation with anti-Islamic prejudice has made them much more political:

> I think Muslims are now compelled to have an awareness of politics as well, because of the questions we always have to answer. Such as 'why did 9/11 happen, why did 7 July happen?'. And I feel that if Muslims don't research these questions, and have answers to these questions prepared, it's almost like people are going to continue with the stereotyping, what they've got in their mind.
>
> You kind of have to become political. I was never political, but people expect me to have an opinion on what happened.

In addition to this, such experiences also hampered young people in the exploration of their faith; they were afraid of coming across as, or being classed as, extremists, and young men in particular tended to self-censor the events they went to, or the people they got involved with:

> I'm not involved in any of the groups [Islamic groups] at Kingston. I sometime go to talks and lectures, and I go to the Islamic week. But I'm not really part of the society. That's like … I think mum would be very worried about extremism, she's always saying don't get too involved with any group. Do what you need to do, you know go and pray or, OK, go to some talks if you want to. But even if I go to a talk I have to tell them what it is. Everyone knows that universities are hotspots for youngsters to get into radical stuff, so you're careful. My mum was more worried about my brother, when he started at university. She was much more worried about him getting involved than me. So he didn't really go to talks or even pray. But he isn't really religious, so it didn't matter. But it was still funny that my mother was so worried that she'd rather have him out of that scene altogether. Even if it was a talk, she'd ask him a 100 questions – what is it about? who is he? do you really know who he is? where is he from, what's his background? So before he answered all these hundreds of questions he'd just rather just not go. He is more religious now. But my mum was fine with that, because it happened after uni, and in a more private way, so that was fine.
>
> *Was uni a reawakening?*
>
> **U**: Very definitely. I was at the University of Manchester and they've got quite an active I-Soc. I knew I wanted to be Islamically involved but I hadn't realised how to do it in Manchester, because I felt really ostracised by them and castigated – if you didn't wear a headscarf you weren't really part of that posse, and you wouldn't really be integrated into that posse until you had a headscarf – after that it's fine, you're in. I mean even girls with headscarves have preconceived ideas about those who don't … and at the time I was very … you know, hair straightened, I was very fashionable. When you looked at me you wouldn't say 'Muslim', you'd say 'ok, second generation Asian' … so I think they do harbour prejudices. It was only when I came back wearing a headscarf that my concept changed. I think I had preconceived ideas as well about them. I created barriers to impede myself, to hinder my chances of becoming involved Islamically so …

I don't know. I've always had conservative ideas, I just didn't know how they would materialise.

E: I started at Strathclyde, so when I came down to Manchester Met for postgraduate study I didn't really know much about my religion until I went to that uni, which is really weird. It was through people I met more than I-Soc, because I wasn't really involved in that that much. Stuff like, I knew basics, like one god and things like that, but I basically had no idea about things like schools of thought …

FAITH AND DIASPORA IN SUBURBIA

There are obvious broad parallels to be made between Jewish residential settlement and that of Asians. Thus Lipman (1966) contested the domination in Jewish social history – particularly that emanating from America – of the study of the 'ghetto', and to redress this imbalance mapped out what he saw as the underestimated history of Jewish suburbia, drawing particularly on demography and occupational history among the Jews in England during and since the Emancipation in the 1800s. And the research of Sharman Kadish (2011) documents a rise and fall of UK suburban jewry.

The trajectory of London's Jewish community began in London's East End, from where there was a movement northwards to leafier suburban locations, which could be seen as moving up the London Transport northern line – although inroads were also made in other parts of the capital. However much of the imagined geography in popular folklore of this community is now out of date. Many of the suburban areas of London known for Jewish settlement have seen declining numbers. Gants Hill, Barkingside and Ilford (London Borough of Redbridge) to the north east, and Golders Green, Hendon and Wembley (Barnet/Brent) in the north west were once seen as classic sites of Jewish suburbanisation from the inner-East End, but since the 1970s and 1980s Jews from these areas have continued their outward trajectory to areas such as Radlett, Elstree and Stanmore in South Hertfordshire. All were built as affluent neighbourhoods. And, as always, education has continued to have an umbilical connection with faith. Kenton (Middlesex by postcode but north west London in spatial positioning) is the present location of the Jewish Free School that was originally founded in Spitalfields in 1817. Other private Jewish secondary schools exist in Hendon and Bushey in Hertfordshire.

Present faith communities have changed the contours of long-presumed suburban geographies on a number of levels. There is evidence of many migrant communities of faith in the suburbs: in many cases people have bypassed the inner city and migrated directly to the suburbs in order to join their co-religionists. For example for many Tamils and Koreans, Kingston is a point of first arrival rather than the final stage in an outward journey from the inner city. Furthermore, contrary to the longstanding presumption that minority ethnic populations are synonymous with 'multiple deprivation districts', Kingston is third least deprived of London boroughs, while neighbouring Richmond-upon-Thames is second (the largely financial district, the City of London, is least deprived). The National Census of 2011 is likely to indicate further shifting patterns, given that the Tamils and Koreans of Kingston are generally comparatively materially comfortably off, thus further contradicting assumptions about ethnicity and deprivation. There is also a particular role for faith groups within wider urban and transnational networks and suburban geographies. Religion has a key position in education: it governs access to sought-after church schools that are known for their discipline and high attainment, as well as offering supplementary schools to other non ecumenical faiths. Many 'faith' schools of non-Christian character are situated in suburban areas.

A number of contributory factors make up identity in the twenty-first century complex globalised world, and for many in suburbia identity is a complex intertwining of Britishness and Diaspora Culture. Among the discussants that we spoke to, nationality of origin, religion, language and political affiliation were all obvious markers, but there is a need for further research on how these interact with Britishness. Many aspects of what we term 'Muslim culture', 'Tamil culture' or 'Korean culture' in Britain have acquired a specific identity in diaspora. Identifications, interactions, belonging and belief across the groups studied here are shaped both by events, places and people far beyond Britain's boundaries and by the way these are experienced within British-based communities. It is a daily process for all our respondents to negotiate, construct and re-construct their relationships between their immediate surroundings and their wider diaspora origins – home and away. Other academic work illustrates this point; for example Kurien (2007) has traced the US Hindu immigrant experience of two-way traffic between India, in its influence both on American immigrant communities and the dynamics of Indians 'back home'.

Whilst the sociology of religion is by no means a new subject, having preoccupied all three of the subject's founding fathers, Marx, Weber and Durkheim, multi-ethnic diversity means that it has become an even more complex question; and there is a growing number of studies of religion and suburbia which recognise this, for example Dwyer et al (2012) and Shah et al (2012). This chapter has shown how religion can become an ethnic category as well as a simply spiritual or faith one – as Solomos and Back (1996:125) remind us, 'ethnic identities are ascribed and they are always articulated in particular situational contexts'. There is currently a view that non Christian religious identification can be an obstacle to integrating into what is vaguely conceived of as 'the British way of life', particularly for followers of the Islamic faith, who some seem to believe to be unintegratable. But the interview data presented here, rooted in the subjective self-positionings of respondents, demonstrates the dangers of seeing a binary opposition between 'ethnic minorities' (by implication black) on one side and the 'white British majority' on the other. Most of those we interviewed have constructed their own versions of identity which accommodate the reality that it is possible to inhabit and draw on multiple identities and belongings simultaneously.

In conclusion, then, the various religious based practices we have described in this chapter undermine the case that within the contemporary suburban landscape the garden centre or shopping mall has replaced the church. Contemporary suburbs cannot be understood in terms of a straightforward relationship between secular materialism and faith/spirituality, where the former has killed the latter. Congregational prayer does take place still, but not always in churches, and the sites of worship that do exist are often recycled buildings – while religious buildings can also be the setting for wider community functions such as birthday parties. Religious significance in suburban life carries on from birth to death to death. And here the Kingston Mosque committee member quoted earlier in this chapter neatly encompasses the role of globalised media as a key channel for his congregation to maintain diaspora identities in the tension and negotiation surrounding burial: 'I do funerals and go into people's houses which would surprise you … in some houses the tv is on 24 hours a day'.

There are a number of material and spiritual practices at work in the contemporary suburb. A multi-layered and complex relationship between belonging, citizenship and suburban space is being played out, and this chapter has begun to probe some of the intricacies of these interactions.

REFERENCES

Alderman, N. (2006) *Disobedience*, Viking.

BBC (2010) 'Boris Johnson criticised for "Kosovo" benefits remark', 28.10.10: www.bbc.co.uk/news/uk-politics-11640219.

Bhatt, C. (2010) 'The "British jihad" and the curves of religious violence', in *Ethnic and Racial Studies* Special Issue: Migrants and Minorities Mobilization, Volume 33, Issue 1, January 2010, pp39-59.

Bourdieu, P. (1986) 'The forms of capital', in Richardson, J. (ed.), *Handbook of Theory and Research for the Sociology of Education*, pp241-258, Greenwood.

Bright, M. (2005) 'Leak shows Blair told of Iraq war terror link', *Observer*, 28.8.05: www.guardian.co.uk/politics/2005/aug/28/uk.iraq.

Bruce, S. (2000) *Choice and Religion: A Critique of Rational Choice Theory*, Oxford University Press.

Bruce, S. (2002) *God is Dead: Secularization in the West*, Blackwell. Also see http://politics.guardian.co.uk/foi/images/0,9069,1558170,00.html.

Cantle, E. (2007) 'A Window on Extremism: Young People in Hounslow – A study of identity, social pressures, extremism and social inclusion., commissioned by London Borough of Hounslow.

Dobriner, W. (1963) Class in suburbia, Prentice-Hall.

Dwyer, C., Gilbert, D., and Shah, B. (2012) 'Faith and suburbia: secularisation, modernity and the changing geographies of religion in London's suburbs, in Transactions of the Institute of British Geographers.

Edmunds, J. and Turner, B. (2002) *Generations, culture and society*, Open University Press.

Fishman, R. (1989) *Bourgeois Utopias: The Rise and Fall of Suburbia*, Basic Books.

Hall, P. (2007) *London Voices, London Lives*, Policy Press.

Hall, S. and Du Gay, P. (1996) *Questions of Cultural Identity*, Open University Press.

Howse, E.M. (1953) *Saints in politics: the* 'Clapham Sect' *and the growth of freedom*, George Allen and Unwin.

Hussain, E. (2007) *The Islamist: Why I Joined Radical Islam in Britain, What I Saw Inside and Why I Left*, Penguin.

Institute of Race Relations (2010) 'Evidence to the UK parliamentary select committee inquiry on preventing violent extremism', *Race and Class* Vol. 51, No. 3, pp73-80.

Jackson, A. (2007) 'The Bucks Herald 1963 – Present day', 15.3.07: www.bucksherald.co.uk/newspaperhistory/The-Bucks-Herald-1963-.2051918.jp.

Kadish, S. (2011) *The Synagogues of Britain and Ireland: An Architectural and Social History*, Yale University Press.

Khan, K. (2009) *Preventing Violent Extremism (PVE) & PREVENT: A response from the Muslim* Community: www.an-nisa.org/downloads/PVE_&_Prevent_-__A_Muslim_response.pdf.

Khan, S. (2008) 'Fairness not Favours', Fabian Society.

Kundnani, A. (2008) 'Islamism and the roots of liberal rage', *Race and Class* 50 (2), pp30-68.

Kundnani, A. (2009) *Spooked: How not to Prevent Violent Extremism*, Institute of Race Relations: www.irr.org.uk/spooked.

Kurien, P. (2007) *A Place at the Multicultural Table*: *The Development of an American Hinduism*, Rutgers University Press.

Lipman, V. (1966) 'The Rise of Jewish Suburbia': www.jhse.org/book/export/article/17248.

Lott, T. (1996) *The Scent of Dried Roses*, Penguin.

Open Society Institute (2005) *Muslims in the UK*, Policies for Engaged Citizens, Open Society Institute.

Putnam, R. (2000) *Bowling Alone: The Collapse and Revival of American Community*, Simon & Schuster.

Taxpayers Alliance (2009) *Council Spending Uncovered II – No. 5: Preventing Violent Extremism Grants*: www.taxpayersalliance.com/Prevent.pdf.

Solomos, J. and Back, L. (1996) *Racism and Society*, Macmillan.

Shah, B., Dwyer, C. and Gilbert, D. (2012), 'Landscapes of diasporic religious belonging in the edge-city: the Jain temple at Potters Bar, outer London', in *South Asian Diaspora*, Volume 4, Issue 1, pp77- 94.

Tomkins, S. (2010) *The Clapham Sect: How Wilberforce's circle changed Britain*, Lion.

Waller, R. and Criddle, B. (1991) *The Almanac of British Politics* (4th edition) Routledge.

Werbner, P. (2004) 'The Predicament of Diaspora and Millennial Islam: Reflections on September 11th 2001', *Ethnicities* (4), pp451-476.

5

Consuming suburbia

Steadily the suburbanite fills every inch of available space with the 'latest' in furnishings and equipment, and the overall impression is one of cramped clutter.

Scott Donaldson (1969:73)

Shops are now becoming woefully alike so that when you have gone round one town's shops you have gone round all.

1950s grammar school teacher quoted by Kynastan (2009:399)

Consuming suburbia makes an interesting narrative: the suburbs were often sold as consumer paradises. But the reputation of the suburbs as places of mindless consumption has already been called into question in a number of ways in this book; and in recent years shopping centres in the suburbs have also been through substantial changes. Already deeply affected by changing patterns of shopping, local high streets have been under pressure from the economic downturn and our recessionary climes. Indeed many local authorities have put murals or pictures of functioning shops into the windows of vacant premises on suburban high streets in order to disguise the blight.

The central importance of shopping in modern lives was demonstrated in an extreme form in the 'riots' of August 2011, when the term 'shopping with violence' made its appearance. In many ways this was more of a shopping spree than a riot, and a large number of suburban shopping centres were involved. The buildings attacked were not symbols of authority: they appeared to have been selected for what they sold. The actions of those arrested amounted mostly to the illegal acquisition of material goods. Looters targeted high-value goods where they could, and where supermarkets were looted it was cigarettes and alcohol that were taken. The old suburban areas and their shopping parades were already looking shabby, but the 'riots' helped draw attention to this decline.

Many of the old suburban areas were already showing signs of wear and tear: the 'riots' simply helped to draw attention to one of the most visible signs of suburban economic downturn – the built-environment indicator of empty shops. The cumulative effect of all the shop closures is a degradation of public space. Allied to Cameron's 'broken Britain' is the notion of a 'boarded up Britain', signalled by empty shop fronts in suburban town centres, in the wake of closures of branches and entire chains of once well-known high street traders such as C&A, HMV and Woolworth. The suburbs are shaped by their shops, which are often a focal point for those who live there, and help give areas distinct identities for those passing through. But in many cases suburbia has not been weathering recession well, even though it was designed to connote stability, with all the reassuring echoes of continuity that are so prevalent in its architecture. Threats to suburban town centres have come from multiple directions, including the out-of-town mall, Tesco-isation and internet shopping: and the cumulative effect of all this threatens to undermine the sustainable and social capacity of local suburban communities.

This chapter draws on a series of examples to consider the importance of retailing to the function and character of the contemporary suburb – including the Trafford Centre in Manchester (a strategically placed ring-road-bisecting mecca for Asian filmgoers across the North West, amongst other things). Are retail giant chains taking over? How justified are fears that many suburbs are becoming identikit multiple-branch 'Tesco towns', from out-of-town megastores to the suburban 'Metro' model? The way in which ethnic commerce has transformed several suburban parades, for example Ealing Road in Wembley and Wilmslow Road in Rusholme, Manchester, will also be considered, including recent instances of local authority assistance in an effort to make them into hubs for the consumption of exotic produce. The chapter will include a case-study of Chorlton in South Manchester and draw on interview data compiled from a focus group conducted with four residents in September 2008.

THE ROLE OF SHOPPING IN THE SUBURBS

Suburbs were seen as embodying consumption by many who have written about them in the past. The very process of suburbanisation had marketing at its core, with individual house builders selling the dream of a location bound up with social status – as seen for example in the posters displayed at the London Transport Museum exhibition of 2009 on Suburbia. Also on view at the exhibition were creations by London Transport itself, inviting Londoners to leave behind the urban drudgery of the city (unnamed locations of smoking chimneys and satanic mills) and trade the monotony of the slice of terrace for a spacious house in an idyllic location such as Hounslow or Edgware. Such marketing techniques have been used ever since. In the mid-1990s, on my regular journeys on the District Line across London to Barking, at around the Canning Town mark, where construction of the new Jubilee Line was underway, I would spy out of the carriage window new house building going on, complete with a tempting banner displayed above 'If you lived here, you would be home by now'.

Suburban homes past and present, according to accepted norms, are populated by social climbers constantly craving status symbols in the form of worldly goods. In his novel *Kingdom Come*, J.G. Ballard described a fictional shopping mall that was taking over its surroundings in South East England (2006:64): 'Over four decades ago every citizen of Brooklands, every resident within sight of the M25, was constantly trading the contents of house and home, replacing the same cars and cameras, the same ceramic hobs and fitted bedrooms. Nothing was being swapped for nothing. Behind this frantic turnover, a gigantic boredom prevailed'. The idea here is of mindless accumulation of goods for the sake of accumulating. The passage is almost identical to that of US professor Scott Donaldson four decades earlier (1969:74), who wrote: 'The suburban house is a museum in more than one sense. Not only does it serve to display the latest in technological products, such as electric toothbrushes, Exocycles and self rotating chairs, but it also shows off the most up-to-date cultural products.' Just as mortgages in the inter-war years helped to make home ownership a reality, in the postwar years hire purchase aided the purchase of objects with which to fill them. The products may have changed since, but the sentiment has not. The suburbs have traditionally been seen as a 'step up' from the city, a place of aspiration and improvement.

But though consumerism – at least until recently – has been increasing, the old suburban shopping centres and high streets have not in the main benefitted from this. They have been strongly adversely affected by the growth of out-of-town shopping and the advent of the retail park – linked closely to the coming of the car economy – and by the rise of online shopping.

Lury's study of consumption (1996:29) cites the claim of Nicholson-Lord (1992) that shopping is the second most popular leisure activity after watching television, but at the same time he lists new flexible forms of shopping, including mail order, shopping malls, car boot sales and second-hand shops. Since this was written, two decades ago, we have also seen the rise of the online market, which arguably has been the biggest threat to the suburban high street, in a far more advanced version of the old mail order catalogues. All this has meant that in the UK high street there are now multiple store closures. Thus, for example, according to the 2010 BBC documentary *Turn Back Time*, the UK had 5,500 record shops in the 1970s, a number that by the time of the programme's making had reduced to 270.

Meanwhile the closure of another victim of the financial crisis and changing shopping habits, the Woolworths chain, offers an interesting insight into the varying fortunes of different shopping areas – in terms of what replaced it and where. In Chiswick, London W4, a suburb popular with media and celebrities, it became the upmarket Waitrose supermarket. A few miles to the west in West Ealing, London W13, what was once Woolworths is now Poundworld. In other areas stores have remained unlet. While some areas go downmarket others make the reverse journey. Miranda Sawyer starts her book as she revisits her hometown of Wilmslow in Cheshire, where the shops have changed beyond recognition to more upmarket outlets. In other places the new suburban shopping destination of choice is the mall, which seems to have eroded the suburban high street's popularity – for example Bluewater in Kent, Meadowhall in Sheffield and Westfield in East and West London.

There has long been a sociology of consumption, going back at least as far as Marx's analysis of the fetishisation of the commodity, in which he argues that the commodity has an exchange value that is different from its use value: consumerism and the social value of objects begin to overtake value deriving straightforwardly from usefulness. Marx stated: 'Since the aim of capital is not to minister to certain wants, but to produce profit, and since it accomplishes this purpose by methods which adapt the mass of production to the scale of production, and not vice versa, a rift must continually ensue between the limited dimensions of consumption under capitalism and a production which forever tends to exceed this immanent barrier' (1972:256). This means that capitalism will always seek to increase the desires of consumers by whatever means it can. Indeed many commentators have seen a switch of emphasis within capitalism, away from production and towards consumption. According to Bauman (1982:96): 'Consumption replaced production as the arena of power-conflict critical for social order and its dynamics'; and he pointed to 'a constant growth of consumer power' (p97). Marx's fellow founding father Durkheim saw the objects of the sacred as symbols of representation with the power to shape society: and this could be applied to the spoils of capitalism and fruits of consumerism. Twentieth-century sociological theorists looking at consumption included Veblen, whose *The Theory of the Leisure Class* (1899) coined the term 'conspicuous consumption', for example when people used silver cutlery when stainless steel would perform the same function. Indeed there are links here to Bourdieu's (1984) concept of 'distinction', which argued that different class identities are reflected in taste preferences. Social, economic and cultural capital can be bound up in the purchase of goods.

Most people's main everyday interface with the process of consumption takes place through the act of shopping, however – seen by most commentators as a gendered experience. In popular cultural representations of suburbia, when the action moves away from the home we tend to see women pictured at the supermarket: this is the closing scene for example in *Stepford Wives*, both the original 1972 version and its 2003 remake. In *Desperate Housewives* the supermarket is the place where the largely house-bound mother-of four Lynette is seen at the end of the first series grudgingly telling a former work colleague she has bumped into that raising kids was the 'best job I've ever done' – uttered through gritted teeth. And in series three it was scene of a hostage siege at gunpoint. The housewife performing the weekly shop also features strongly in Friedan's work. And shopping has now also become a leisure activity: it can extend into an experience that one can make day of – sometimes in one shop alone. Miller et al (1998) describe how the pleasurable aspect of shopping with the advent of midweek extended hours also arouses guilt amongst mothers, who felt they were selfishly spending time on themselves rather than the needs and wishes of their family.

Cut-price Swedish furniture Ikea is a pioneer of the day-long shopping experience. The Ikea business model demands that the shopper does not just 'pop in' for the one item that they need, but is given an obligatory route to navigate through the vast showroom (with arrows helpfully supplied to direct shoppers); it becomes almost a tour of exhibits. A child-minding service helps relieve parents of unruly offspring, so that they can make that 'big' purchase (sofa, kitchen, bathroom, etc) unencumbered by unruly offspring. Buyers also need to walk through the 'market-place', which houses inexpensive small-sized impulse buys, on their way to the tills. By then they are most likely to have acquired additional bathroom mats, lamps and potted plants that it may not have been their original intention to acquire. There is also a restaurant.

In 2005, when Ikea's branch in the north London suburb of Edmonton was unveiled, several people were injured in the opening day rush. The scramble to seek bargains, spurred on by widespread promotion of offers for one-day-only cut-price sofas, was soon labelled by the press as a 'riot', and it can in some ways be seen as a prefiguration of the 'shopping with violence' that took place in the riots of August 2011. Casey (2010) draws on this event to argue that it challenges perceptions of who it is that potentially constitutes the mob, and whether the mob should necessarily be seen as romantic rebels or victims of an oppressive capitalist state: new thinking is required to take into account subjective understandings of the mob – and for our purposes that includes their location within suburbia.

The term 'exurban' or 'edge city' (Garreau 1991) has been employed by sociologists to describe the post-suburban landscapes of retail and leisure parks that are located away from both city centres and their suburbs, usually near to freeways or motorway junctions. These brownfield developments have much in common with the siting of Ikea stores, which are also often built in wastelands off suburban areas, as they require a large land mass: the stores are housed in aircraft hangar-like structures. Ikea in Croydon, opened in 1992, is housed in a 1950s-built power station on the Purley Way, in a neat summation of the way industry and old forms of energy are now being replaced by a consumer economy. Indeed in 2005 Gordon Brown and Tony Blair paid a visit to the store as part of a charm offensive in marginal seats in the run-up to the election: modernity and being 'in touch' with the shopping public were the underlining principles of the visit. Geraint Davies, then Labour candidate for Croydon Central, was quoted as saying: 'The reason they came to Ikea was it is a forward-looking modern store for modern families. Not like Surrey Street Market, where Michael Howard visited, which is full of rotten bananas' (*Croydon Guardian* 2005). Expansions to the store, making it 23,000 square feet in size, have now made it the fifth biggest employer in the Croydon Borough (*Croydon Guardian* 2006). Nearby is a retail park, including Next and other chain stores, accessible to those who have their own motorised vehicle transport.

The New Economic Foundation has coined the term 'clone town Britain' to describe another feature of the modern high street – their gradual takeover, at least in the still viable town centres, by the same chains in every town:

> In place of real local shops has come a package of 'identikit' chain stores replicating on the nation's high streets. The individual character of many towns is evaporating. Retail spaces once filled with independent butchers, newsagents, tobacconists, pubs, book shops, greengrocers and family owned general stores are filled with supermarket stores, fast food chains and global fashion outlets.

More recently we have also seen the emergence of a different model of high street – largely featuring pound shops, charity shops, betting shops and pawnshops, as well as all the other businesses that ply their wares to the poor, often including the new cut-price fashion chains such as Primark. Both clone town Britain and these newly impoverished high streets are suffering from the new patterns of shopping which focus large numbers of shoppers away from the old high street stores.

The department store Allders in Bromley had for many years been a local landmark, with a plaque to H.G. Wells adorning it, as it was the site of his first home, and an H.G. Wells cafe in honour of the south east London suburb's most famous son. It closed down in 2005. A Facebook campaign started to persuade Primark to take over the site, and they also took over the old Beales store in Ealing Broadway. The leaflet promoting the grand opening of the Peacocks Centre in Woking in 1992 proclaimed it a major redevelopment of Woking town centre, based on five flagship stores: of these The Reject Shop is now TK Maxx; the C&A branch closed, along with all other C&A UK stores in 2000/2001 and Primark now occupies the space; Allders went into administration in 2005; and the Peacocks branch became Debenhams. The Woolworths unit is now occupied by Next. Marks and Spencer also left the centre in 2009, since replaced by H&M. Woking was probably once seen a commuter town, but the fast rail connection to London seems to have recast it as a London suburb. (The town's most famous sons are probably the Jam, who met at Sheerwater comprehensive. Paul Weller, in his long career since, has always positioned himself as a suburban artist and has released a book of lyrics entitled *Suburban 100*. He has lamented (Gilbert 2010): 'Woking's spirit was destroyed when the town planners carved it up in the 70s'.)

On the other hand, 'ethnic' commerce has reinvigorated many suburban high-streets, including Rusholme – scene of Manchester's 'curry mile' – and Green Street in East Ham, London. Carey and Ahmed (2006:8) vividly describe the composition of the latter:

> The number, concentration and sheer variety of south Asian shops (and stalls in the Queen's Market), including beauty and hair-dressing salons, 'high' and 'low' fashion outlets, jewellery, household and electrical, furniture, telecoms, Internet cafes, money exchanges, music and DVD outlets, opticians, pharmacies, photographers, printers, travel agents, Indian and Pakistani sweet shops, grocers and food stores (including several halal butchers and fishmongers), wedding and birthday party specialists and Islamic book and clothing shops offering consumers a wide range of goods and services at highly competitive prices exceeds anything available in comparable shopping areas of Tower Hamlets or, indeed any other area of east London.

The traditional components of 'butcher, baker and candle-stick maker' are here complemented and/or replaced by restaurants, specialist hairdressers and grocery retailers. These shops are providing goods and services that are not available elsewhere, and this is a strong point in maintaining their viability. The injection of variety has also been encouraged by local government. Local small businesses asserting their identity in an area by their visible presence can be a powerful counterweight to the proliferation of chain stores that many worry are resulting in depressingly standardised suburban high streets.

There has also been a movement against the retail giant Tesco in recent years, part of which has been based on the way that many suburbs are becoming identikit 'Tesco towns'. The gentrified suburb of Chorlton in South Manchester, and Mill Road in Cambridge, were both recently sites of vigorous defence campaigns to a planned Tesco opening. The company has responded with several attempts at corporate social responsibility, including the funding of academic posts at the University of Manchester to encourage scholarship in 'sustainable consumption'. The Tesco business model exerts a double pincer movement on the high street. Its 'Tesco Metro' shops compete with corner shops and the 'Mr Patel' type open-all-hours independent Indian family-owned newsagents that have been a familiar part of the postwar suburban landscape; while the large 'Tesco Extra' stores take people right away from the high street – and often have petrol station forecourts. The much quoted figure that Tesco now takes one out of every £8 spent in the British retail sector (Hollingshead 2007) is in part explained by this diversification, which also includes financial services and insurance – a move also made by Asda and Sainsburys.

THE CHANGING SHOPPING EXPERIENCE: CASE STUDY OF CHORLTON

Factors that contribute a strong identity for an area, a sense of its uniqueness, include its architecture, and, in terms of shopping centres, the availability of products and services that cannot be obtained elsewhere. Chorlton in South Manchester is an area that has long prided itself as a distinctive part of the city with its own identity (as seen for example in the Chorltonweb forum). Its residential housing is typically comprised of chunky late Victorian and Edwardian redbrick terraces, with some areas of semi-detached houses in 1930s streets. Aside from this – which is fairly typical of the architecture of the time – another facet of Chorlton's distinctiveness stems from environmental features, such as the natural beauty of Chorlton Water Park. Another thing highly rated by residents is the fact that the area's shopping parades retain a variety of differentiated locally owned, independent and specialist outlets, which have helped to stamp their identity on the neighbourhood. The area has a reputation of being cosmopolitan and socially diverse, and as having a strong sense of community, as opposed to the stereotypical idea of the suburb as monocultural, amorphous and alienating. Its residents frequently have undertaken higher education, and many are linked to the universities of Manchester, either as past graduates or present employees. Savage et al (2005) in their empirical work on Chorlton found that locals had consciously chosen to live there, rather than having just ended up in the location by chance. In interviews residents often compared it to London, going as far as naming distinct comparable neighbourhoods and sites of the capital, including Camden, Carnaby Street, Islington and Hampstead – though, as Savage et al (96) note: 'Chorlton cannot legitimately claim London's degree of cultural distinction, precisely because insofar as Chorlton is attractive as a copy of an urban original, it cannot claim ultimate authenticity.' In a *Guardian* property feature Dyckhoff (2006) named the area's advantages as 'Guardian-reading heaven … it's genuinely all cooperative grocers, Bush-baiters and lesbian single mums galore.' One local commented that it is: 'probably the most varied and interesting suburb of Manchester, being an eclectic mix of 'grew up heres', nouveau intellectuals from the Beeb, students and a large lesbian/gay community. It's also famous for being kid-friendly'.

On the negative side, however, Dyckhoff identified the area as being 'a tad self-righteous'. Furthermore: 'Crime's gone down but it's still a problem in neighbouring areas … Suburban ennui in parts.' In 2010 the *Guardian* named the M21 postcode as the country's most burgled, citing figures from a survey by moneysupermarket.com, based on reported home insurance claims. The paper quoted many residents reacting in disbelief, maintaining that their area was a safe one. It commented: 'The area has gained a reputation as a bohemian part of Manchester, with independent shops and restaurants and more affordable house prices, attracting BBC workers, students and a large lesbian and gay community. Many proudly boast that a local newsagent is the biggest seller of *Guardians* outside of London' (Collinson 2010). The crime figures perhaps show the mixed profile of the area, which borders on some 'undesirable' socio-economically deprived neighbourhoods, such as Moss Side, and social housing estates such as the Nell Lane and Merseybank.

Once the area where the Bee Gees grew up, Chorlton has been intensely gentrified since the 1980s. The current stereotypical

Chorlton resident is a middle-class professional who celebrates cosmopolitanism and needs to be near the city centre. There are residential areas closer to the city centre than Chorlton, including Moss Side, which borders the university area, or Hulme, Whalley Range or Old Trafford, all of which are on the route into 'town'. However the distance from Chorlton to central Manchester is still small – much shorter than, say, from Hampstead to the city of London. There are also several south Manchester suburbs much further out on the route to Manchester airport and beyond in Cheshire. Yet to my mind Chorlton is the start of the Manchester suburbs. It feels somewhat self-contained, if not quite as physically isolated as, for example, Wythenshawe. There is now a Chorlton stereotype that fits the characterisation of the 'new' middle class – rich in cultural capital if not possessing great amounts of material wealth – as written about by Butler (1997) and Butler and Robson (2003). However just as the area's self-image in campaigns such as 'Keep Chorlton interesting' emphasises its disdain for standardised shops, there is also increasing heterogeneity amongst residents. Focus group participants acknowledged a growth in the number of Asian residents, and that there was a side of Chorlton based on publicly owned and former council property that did not fit with the current stereotype.

A common complaint about suburbia is the amorphousness of its planned streets of identical housing, which is thought to inculcate conformism and boredom – though this book has argued throughout that contemporary suburban environments are increasingly socially diverse. Sometimes, indeed, residents consciously celebrate this 'ordinariness', and are happy to 'buy into' a neighbourhood where they can unproblematically blend in (Allen et al 2007). But Chorlton appears to be a suburb where residents see themselves as non-conformist. Of my focus group, one member came to the area having originally squatted as a student in the infamous, now demolished crescents of Hulme a couple of miles further into Manchester on the same arterial road as Chorlton, while another had joined a housing co-operative in the area. Here it should be also noted that the city of Manchester itself has also long had a reputation for progressive local government and tolerance of minorities.

Among the specific elements that symbolise Chorlton as a shopping neighbourhood are the Barbakan bakery and Unicorn delicatessen, and I was fortunate enough when I convened a focus group of local Chorlton characters in September 2008 to have been able to include representatives from both these shops, each of whom had been vocal in the campaign opposing Tesco. Victor has lived in Chorlton since the late 1970s and works at Barbakan as second in command. Andy has been in Chorlton since the late 1980s and founded Unicorn. The other two members of the group were Chris, a graduate of Manchester University who has stayed in the city since then, opting first for a postgraduate career before arts management/consultancy and now work in market research; and Bernard, a professor of sociology at the Metropolitan University. The median age was fifty. The dynamic of the group, all of whose members knew each other prior to the interview, and which was in no way intended to be representative, flowed more as a conversation than as a group responding under laboratory conditions. (Since the discussion took place, Labour made a clean sweep of Manchester council in the local elections of May 2011, unseating all the authority's Liberal Democrats, and Chris became a councillor.)

Andy began by reminiscing about the 1980s, when the Labour-run city council set itself against the prevailing political climate of Thatcherism from the centre:

> **A**: When I first came here it was when the council had that slogan 'defending jobs, defending services'.
>
> **C**: Richard Leese [then council-leader, now knighted] calls it our Chinese period.
>
> **B**: For disability access the town hall was pioneering ...
>
> **C**: And the BME workforce ...
>
> **A**: It was a place with a reputation.

The conversation seemed to construct Chorlton as a destination its own right rather than – as is sometimes unkindly suggested by local media – as somewhere favoured by those who cannot afford nearby Didsbury, a longer established and desirable suburban area of South Manchester. It was described in terms of other parts of London and in relation to other parts of Manchester.

> **A**: When I try to describe it to outsiders, if we trade with a new

company, I say 'it's a bit like a nice bit of north London'. People certainly choose to be here.

C: Didsbury's naff. It's maybe like Finchley.

Independent shops are seen as crucial to the feel of the area:

A: There's small shops, nodes where you can go and where stuff is. The image of slightly trendy well-informed people.

V: ... there are various businesses [that give Chorlton its reputation]. It used to be Chorlton Wholefoods. When Unicorn first opened up ...

Did you see them as competition?

B: It was the right time.

V: Only hindsight can tell that ... Anyone can be a competitor ... Estate agent windows say 'Chorlton is full of independents'. I thought we all depend on each other. I call it inter-dependence.

B: Co-impetition.

V: He does a great service, all the organic stuff – no honey because of the exploitation of bees. My boss [Barbakan] goes down the quality road as the way forward. Twenty years ago there was a man selling local honey in a local shop and I asked him 'where do you get your honey?' He wouldn't tell me that. You wouldn't get that now.

BL: There is a greater enemy.

RH: Tesco?

BL: It's not just Tesco, it's about large chains bringing people to a locality.

Victor explained the profile of the shops which had flourished against the odds. Beech Road is the main hub of the alternative commerce of the area, but this has radiated off into other parts and into the adjoining area, the more inner-district of Whalley Range, which is also undergoing gentrification as a result.

V: The good thing is that individuals can see a way forward to renting a unit and setting up a stall. Here you have independent flowers, independent gift shops.

B: Also independent surgical instruments in that one there [points to shop with shutters up]. My son is training to be a doctor and he needed a stethoscope. He did a search of places in greater Manchester and it was here! People come into Chorlton – shop-owners, shopkeepers. They still see it as a place to come and make a buck or two.

V: There's 'Limited Resources', an organic vegetable place, 'Wild at Heart', an organic meat shop …

B: The Chorlton effect has gone down towards Manchester Road, and there's the Hillary Step, and Palermo in Seymour Grove that do Tapas.

Chorlton's reputation as a haven for alternative independent retail was less esteemed by Andy, who thought this notion was somewhat overplayed. Whilst he praised the area's viability and by extension vitality, he tempered this with the observation that Chorlton was still prone to other problems that the rest of Manchester suffered from, such as lack of retail choices, and parts of the area were still blighted by a poor physical environment.

A: I think it's symbolic having a viable district in Manchester. That's quite something.

B: It's a local honey pot now, for want of a better term.

A: It's become a cliché, Chorlton as bohemian, but there's plenty of grime here. Just walk up the street, there's lots of trashy pound-shops. It's as grim as anywhere else. It has some decent food options, though not loads, but most don't have any. Mike Gayle has written novels set in Chorlton spoofing local bean-shops. He's coming next week to do a reading.

B: I assumed all that was happening everywhere.

A: There are plenty of grim pubs, as grim as anywhere in the city, which I always tend to think is a measure of what real life is like.

There was also a recognition that the blanket term 'Chorlton' masks discrepancies: the Chorlton Park estate, bordering the Water Park, was formerly council-owned and now has largely been purchased by residents under the right to buy. However other parts of Chorlton with low density council-built houses are still in public ownership. These areas were to some extent noted for their incongruity – comparison was made to the large post-war estate of Wythenshawe – but in contrast to comments I had previously come across from private residents, who saw social housing as a blight on their areas, there was a sense of frustration that the 'other side' was not being sufficiently involved in Chorlton community activities, even though there had been efforts made.

> **C**: There's a whole swathe of housing here that is similar to lots of other estates. The Nell Lane estate is in the bottom 1% of most deprived and Merseybank the bottom 5%.
>
> **A**: It's a bit of Wythenshawe in Manchester. I wouldn't wander round there at night; horrible mugging scally kids.
>
> **C**: In Hough End fields there was an attempt to do a reggae sunsplash thing. The local vicar stopped it going ahead as it would attract drug addicts. It's next to Nell Lane, where there's the most drugs and stuff. There is not much right to buy. Not like Merseybank.
>
> **A**: If the aim of social housing is breaking people off into blocks of greyness, it's got a lot going for it.
>
> **C**: I was in Wythenshawe for Ipsos Mori the other day, and there is no right to buy. They were going 'would you buy round here?' 5% makes such a difference. They all have LCD tv screens, mind you.
>
> **B**: There's a huge distinction between the right to buy of Chorlton Park and Chorlton. There is a community café in the Merseybank estate, but the Lib Dem councillors have been terribly unhelpful. They didn't resist Tesco. The population that side is the same. We tried to have a fair trade stall on that side.
>
> **C**: On Merseybank the most right to buy has been exercised across the edge.

> **B:** They are excellent quality houses. We did a study. They should be listed.
>
> **A:** They were built when there were decent planning regs.

Bernard saw the campaign against Tesco as a way of involving people more in associative networks:

> My take on it was different. I just like community activism, people getting organised who weren't organised before. It's my way of getting people to relate to one another.

The Tesco campaign had in the end been lost, and a new cause had been taken up, the Chorlton precinct:

> **B:** It's like once Polio's cured you move on to another disease. The credit crunch has slowed things up, but the redevelopment is in the hands of the city regen people. Then there's the 2011 metro that the Lib Dems are opposing on the grounds of street parking.
>
> **A:** It's not a great design, and it's not public space but private. The Keep Chorlton Interesting people are pushing for whatever it becomes to be viable. It's amazing how you can feel about something when it might be demolished and something else put in its place.

Cosmopolitan values and embracing diversity were voiced by the focus group, but often in terms of regret at the lack of involvement by other groups (namely Asians and Chorlton Park estate dwellers) in community actions. This was thought to have been for cultural reasons – a lack of identification with and unwillingness to join forces with people who are perceived as white middle-class do-gooders – or because of a general fall in volunteering and erosion of the public realm. There was also a feeling that new geographical areas of non-standardised retailing were growing up to service new populations, such as Clarendon Road in neighbouring Whalley Range, which was now populated by Asian owned fresh fruit and vegetable outlets. It seemed that niche markets could still sustain more individual high streets.

> **V:** There's a tremendous amount of Asian families in Whalley Range, Clarendon Road. It's just another world. When the hairy

bikers [television chefs] came in to film at Barbakan they wanted to go to Rusholme and get some shots of the Curry Mile. I said 'forget that, you can get it 200 yards away'. And there's the Hindu temple down the road. Chorlton has a large number of Buddhist temples.

B: One of the things I was going to do with the civic society was to do a survey to get people involved, there were very few Asians involved.

R: Are there a lot?

C: Oh yes, extended families, extended houses, like in Egerton Road.

B: One of the things I do as part of the civic society is to review all planning applications for Chorlton. There's been a big change from building flats to extensions, often unfriendly extensions for example ones that block light.

C: It's along certain roads, like Egerton South, where it's changing. It's good change.

V: But with the food and drink festival we've not been able to persuade any of the Asian businesses.

(The Hindu temple on Wilbraham Road is a centre of worship for the local Hindu community who have origins in the subcontinent, while the Buddhists referred to are more likely to be white converts.)

Andy defined Chorlton as a place with a wide variety of food options, although his project Unicorn has undoubtedly contributed to the reputation of it as a 'foodie' area. I asked him why he had chosen Chorlton for the siting of Unicorn:

A: Well it could have been anywhere on the Mersey Valley really, say, Prestwich or somewhere like that. I was walking back with my son from school one day and we saw the boards up. It's unfortunate in a way that we are here, because it goes with all that cliché of being the alternative suburb, but then again we would be one of things that changed the area. I would've been quite happy for it to be somewhere else. For me in Manchester the prices were ok, and, second it was not a complete nightmare. I basically bought land at the edge of the city to sell food … It's better to live somewhere where there's a choice of decent food. Do you really want to eat porridge every day or Pot Noodle? People live in food deserts now all over Manchester. Where you live determines how well you eat.

C: If Tescos arrived next door and sold the same food as you would you think 'our work is done'?

A: If the food on offer in the UK gets better it's got to be a good thing. In terms of ownership, it is notable that Peel Holdings [owners of Manchester's Trafford Centre, see below] own a lot of the docks. I find the tie-up with logistics companies worrying.

The attractions of the 24 hour city had also permeated Chorlton. As Chris commented, it was now 'a night-time destination':

B: Places get known for different things. There's one down there that's known for folk music.

A: The local paper had something about Didsbury chains: the Slug and Lettuce etc. What was once the most desirable suburb, you know, people [forever] looking for 'the new Didsbury', has just become the same as everywhere.

C: In Didsbury there's hardly any independents now. In a more rural place, you know, you might all go into the local town for a night out. Didsbury used to be the place for a Wythenshawe night out, a student night out ... whereas if you go out here it'll be a night out with other Chorltonians rather than a mixture of tribes. There's not the huge swathe of people you see in Didsbury.

A: It's cheap, ok-ish housing that got gentrified. It was Hebden Bridge before. Then certain functions arise – Barbakan's been there a long time. There are several critical things ... you get two or three things that are novel and good, and then you've got a certain critical mass and people move there and stay there.

Allen et al (2007) found that cost was a key consideration in their respondents' choice of residential location. Chris thought that rising prices in Chorlton would displace younger buyers from the area to other neighbourhoods, whereas he had bought before the major inflationary movements in the area. Now people in their position would be going to Slade Lane in Longsight.

OUT OF TOWN SHOPPING AND RESISTANCE MOVEMENTS

The advent of 'out of town' areas for shopping, business and leisure in the last two decades is another development that threatens the capacity of the English suburb to provide leisure and retail facilities. Different uses can be made of areas on the peripheries of cities: they can be where the people of the suburbs work – industrial estates, business parks or silicon-valley style science parks; or they can be or where they play, with recreational shopping and leisure facilities such as multi-screen cinemas, restaurants and bowling alleys. These out of town centres are challenging the expected function of the city centre as well as that of the suburbs. They are often modelled on similar layouts – functional and impersonal, with vast acreages of carpark tarmac. Whereas the suburb was always defined in relation to the city centre and fostered by public transport connections, the 'out of town' landscape is often centred on lateral links to other suburbs by motorway network, thereby maximising the number of people arriving by private car. Physical isolation was a complaint made by early suburban settlers and was a constituent part of the 'new town blues'. The new out of town areas have no residents. Their isolation is mediated through their connections to other similar areas.

In the opening page of *Kingdom Come* (Ballard 2006:3) explains: 'Beyond Heathrow lay the empires of consumerism … a dormant people who had everything, who had brought the dreams that money can buy and knew that they had found a bargain.' Further descriptions continue: 'The shoppers grazed contentedly like docile cattle' (p11). The reader of the book today might visualise Brooklands as like the Westfield centres in London (both squarely in the inner city though having a feel of outer-suburbia). When I initially read the book, however, I imagined it as set at Manchester's Trafford Centre, which is sandwiched between a sewerage works and Europe's biggest industrial estate – the long-established Trafford Park.

For many years Manchester's Arndale Centre, in the centre of Manchester, was the main draw for shoppers in the region. On the front page of its website in 2008 the Arndale claimed to be 'the UK's largest inner-city shopping centre', and emphasised its central location and size. It is frequented by people from Manchester's suburbs, facilitated by the fact that it is the termini for many major bus routes from outlying areas. Miranda Sawyer (1997) describes how, as a child growing up in Wilmslow, south of Manchester in the Cheshire hinterlands, coming to the Arndale was an exciting vaguely exotic experience. Savage et al (2005), however, found that their respondents had a different notion of it. They describe it as 'the universally disliked Arndale Centre' ... 'built as a shopping centre in the heart of Manchester in the 1960s as a beacon to modern planning, now taken to represent its failure as well as the loss of the "old" Manchester... Not a single resident had any affection for the Arndale' (Savage et al 2005:112). Today it is rivalled by the Trafford Centre, which is built firmly on the car economy and is comparatively poorly served by public transport. A 2008 television programme claimed that a quarter of Britain's population lived within a 90-minute drive of the centre (BBC 2008). This explains why the centre is a hub for shoppers beyond the immediate Manchester area.

During the 1990s, urban and out of town developments became increasingly bold, and the Trafford centre's architecture is a good example of this departure from the old identikit model. It is distinctive both in its large scale and in its pastiche of previous building styles; there are Roman-style columns, and the food court is overlooked by a Titanic-style ocean liner mock up. The centre still continues to grow, and it has recently added an extra wing that includes Manchester's answer to the Legoland theme park. Its history, on the other hand, is rooted in the collapse of manufacturing industry in the 1970s and the rise of the service economy since. The parent company is Peel Holdings, and it is an unashamedly commercial venture: there are no museums, library or any other public/civic institutions on site. The company also owns Manchester Airport, and has been increasingly vocal in public lobbying in recent years, particularly in opposing the proposed Manchester congestion charge.

The centre is a symbol of New Britain and the coming of the consumer society; it represents a distinct shift from the old north west's manufacturing base. Its emergence has been aided and abetted by the relaxation of planning laws, set in train by Thatcher accelerated under New Labour, and eagerly embraced by Cameron. According to Dykhoff (2003:233): 'New Labour governments of the 1990s essentially gave up on manufacturing and did all they could to encourage the notion of London as a consumerist playground'. The same applies outside the capital. Shopping as a leisure activity is promoted by the Trafford Centre as it is by other out of down developments, including Bluewater in Kent, Meadowhall in Sheffield, Lakeside in Thurrock, Merry Hill in Birmingham or the Metro centre in Gateshead, to name but a few examples. The Trafford Centre in particular, with its domed appearance, immediately visible from the sky when taking a flight back into Manchester from abroad, is a graphic illustration of how Manchester, home of the industrial revolution, has reinvented itself in a post-industrial era.

Chorlton derives its distinctiveness and authenticity from the fact that it has constrained the number of retail multiples there. The Trafford Centre however is in many ways the opposite.

V: The perfume shop in Chorlton can't have certain franchises because they're owned by the Trafford Centre. Some of the local shops do suffer.

A: When it opened it was feared that it would suck up the life out of the surrounding neighbourhoods, which it was feared would suffer significantly.

Were you against it at the time?

A: God yes. There was Tory Trafford Borough council and Peel holdings on one side, versus a plan from the council to do something around Shudehill with the Co-op in the city centre ... It went all the way to the highest level of the UK legal system. Maybe they had deeper pockets, you know if you've got the right barristers and consultants you're away ...To me anything that generates more traffic has to be opposed. Manchester has the highest asthma levels and you're selling retail trash nobody needs. It'd be great to see the figures [since the credit crunch]. Bluewater has seen fairly drastic levels of falls in profits. In the paper the Trafford Centre have been very bullish, but there are still no figures.

C: There's less cars around there [since the downturn].

A: There's no real substance to it, it's high end. What's the point of an out of town shopping centre?

Some areas, such as Chorlton, have managed to continue as successful and distinctive shopping centres in spite of the giant presence of the Trafford Centre. Others are under threat, both from the competition of out of town shipping centres and from the recession.

IS THERE AN ALTERNATIVE?

There are a variety of alternative responses to the consumer age, including moves towards more ethical shopping and support for fair-trade products. Among the alternatives has been the rapidly growing phenomenon of farmers markets. London Farmers Market (LFM), for example, links a series of markets across the capital where, at odds with the onward march of globalisation, the local is stressed in produce terms. At an event at West Ealing Farmers Market off the Uxbridge Road W13 in 2010 their spokesman enthused, 'The council has been really supportive, it's been going nine years now, was one of the first ones.' All of the produce is grown no further than one hundred miles away. At the top of the side street where the market takes places every Saturday is a fruit and vegetable stall that is present all-week round but happily co-exists with the farmers market. The LFM spokesman commented, 'People know where they can get the more regular veg from, and down here people come for farmers type veg. The two are complementary. He knows we're good for him as on Saturdays there's increased footfall.' West Ealing has suffered from the exodus of many well-known names in the past decade: Marks and Spencer and W.H. Smith shut up shop long before Woolworth, and the farmer's market is a welcome sign of new shoots in the area.

During 2010's West Ealing Apple Market, sponsored by the farmers market, I was able to speak to various people involved, including craft stall-holders at the nearby craft market and the West Ealing Traders Association representing local shops. The council regeneration officer introduced us to a butcher on a parallel street where a steel band was playing in the pedestrianised street facing West Ealing Library and Sainsburys.

> I love West Ealing, it's a really vibrant, cosmopolitan community. When I first came here I had four shops, but now this is only one. I went on the council's marketing course and it made me think. I've been here 40 years, started as a butcher's hand and now I've got two

> sons ready to follow me into the business. The trade we've usually relied on is west Indian and Irish, but the course did make me think. There is a dearth of traditional English butchers so when I get my fibreglass sign tomorrow that's what it will say, 'traditional English butcher'.

This attempt to stamp distinctiveness onto the business on a micro-scale has the potential to be scaled up to other retail areas, which may be able to stake out a unique claim to be areas worthy of visiting for purchases, rather than being bypassed with fast suburban transport links to city centres or other retail hubs. But it will be an uphill struggle.

A number of tendencies have markedly shaped the suburban landscape in recent years. These include shifts from traditional to online operations and increased pressure for residential development, as well as changing labour markets and subsequently altered patterns of work/life balance. The recent economic recession has also cast serious doubt over both the growth model of commercial investment and the suburban home as an automatically appreciating asset. The perverse effects of the dual-earner household on housing costs have made it necessary for couples to work round the clock to service rents and mortgages. As a result, for many suburbia has gone from paradise to pressure cooker. The future of suburban shopping will vary from place to place, but there is likely to be a split between different types of retail area: some areas will establish themselves as 'destination' shopping areas, while others will be restricted to shops for necessary local goods.

Many lamentations for the suburban shopping of the past revolve around an idealised version of the old suburban high street, the emergence of which in its 1860s beginnings was itself a consequence of social change. (Then it provided a more permanent way of selling produce than from market stalls, as suburbanisation took root and the average person could no longer grow their own food and/or keep livestock.) It remains to be seen whether current developments will leave behind human-scale places in which people are able to supply their daily needs. Calthorpe (1989:470) noted 'a growing sense of frustration – placelessness – with the fractured quality of our suburban megacenters. The unique qualities of place are continually consumed by chain-store architecture, scaleless office parks and monotonous subdivisions.' Some of these developments we have looked at can be described as post-suburban, but they can also co-exist with the more traditional set-up. There is still a place for good quality shops, and shops that supply particular needs for particular groups, as well as services that people can access on foot. Suburbs must embrace social transformation if they are to survive as viable retail centres. Otherwise they will wither and die.

REFERENCES

BBC 2008, *Britain From Above*, BBC2 24.8.8.

Ballard, J.G. (2006) *Kingdom Come*, Fourth Estate.

Bauman, Z. (1982) *Memories of Class: The Pre-history and After-life of Class*, Routledge & Kegan Paul.

Benjamin, A. (2007) 'Taking on Tesco', *Guardian*, 21.3.07: www.guardian.co.uk/society/2007/mar/21/communities.supermarkets.

Booth, C., Darke, J. and Yeandle, S. (eds) (1996) *Changing places: women's lives in the city*, Paul Chapman.

Butler, T. (1997) *Gentrification and the Middle-Classes*, Ashgate.

Butler, T. and Robson, G. (2003) *London calling: the middle classes and the re-making of inner London*, Berg.

Calthorpe, P. (1989) *The Next American Metropolis: Ecology, Community, and the American Dream*, Princeton Architectural Press.

Casey. E. (2010) 'Struggle and protest or passivity and control? The formation of class identity in two contemporary cultural practices', *European Journal of Cultural Studies*, vol. 13 no. 2, pp225-241.

Carey, S. and Ahmed, N. (2006) 'Bridging the Gap: The London Olympics 2012 and South Asian-Owned Businesses in Brick Lane and Green Street', The Young Foundation.

Collinson, P. (2010) 'Manchester's bohemian suburb tops house theft list', *Guardian*, 6.8.10: www.guardian.co.uk/uk/2010/aug/06/house-thefts-worst-areas.

Corrigan, P. (1997) *The Sociology of Consumption*, Sage.

Crera, P. (2011) 'Boris Johnson recruits troubleshooter for the suburbs', *Evening Standard*, 11.2.11: www.thisislondon.co.uk/standard/article-23922624-boris-johnson-recruits-troubleshooter-for-the-suburbs.do.

Croydon Guardian (2005) 'PM makes pitstop at Ikea', 5.5.05: www.croydonguardian.co.uk/news/593829.pm_makes_pitstop_at_ikea/.

Croydon Guardian (2006) 'Ikea is bigger than ever', 1.5.06: www.croydonguardian.co.uk/news/742402.ikea_is_bigger_than_ever/.

Dyckhoff, T. (2008) 'Let's move to … Chorlton, Manchester', *Guardian*, 9.12.08: www.guardian.co.uk/lifeandstyle/2006/dec/09/homes2.

Fong, Eric, Chen, Wenhong, Luk, Chiu (2007) 'A Comparison of Ethnic Businesses in Suburbs and City', *City & Community*, Volume 6, Number 2, June 2007, pp119-136.

Garreau, J. (1992) *Edge City: Life on the New Frontier*. New York: Anchor Books.

Gilbert, P. (2010) 'Review: Lives. Paul Weller: Woking Arts Centre 6.6.10', Q Magazine.

Hollingshead, I. (2007) 'The day I moved to Tescoland', *Daily Telegraph*, 21.2.07:

www.telegraph.co.uk/news/features/3631576/The-day-I-moved-to-Tescoland.html.

Lury, C. (1996) *Consumer Culture*, Polity Press.

Malik, K. (1994) 'Asians denounce media myth of the corner shop: One in five driven to seek self-employment' *Independent* 12.6.94.

Marx, Karl, Capital Volume III, Lawrence and Wishart 1972.

Miller, D., Jackson, P., Rowlands, M., Thrift, N., Holbrook, B. and Rowlands, M. (1998) *Shopping, Place and Identity*, Routledge.

Mort, F. (1996) *Cultures of consumption: Masculinities and social space in late twentieth-century Britain*, Routledge.

Reeves, D. (1996) 'Women Shopping', in Booth, C., Darke, J. and Yeandle, S. (eds) (1996).

Savage, M., Bagnall, G., Longhurst, B. (2005) *Globalization and Belonging*, Sage.

Simms, A. (2007) *Tescopoly: How One Shop Came Out on Top and Why It Matters*, Constable.

Turner, G. (2008) 'The cosmopolitan city and its Other: the ethnicizing of the Australian suburb', *Inter-Asia Cultural Studies*, Volume 9, Number 4, December 2008, pp568-582.

Veblen T. [1889] (2009) *The Theory of the Leisure Class: An Economic Study of Institutions*, Oxford University Press.

Weller, P. (2007) *Suburban 100*, Century Press.

6

Extremism in the suburbs

Suicide bombers from the suburbs

Daily Mail headline 2005

Part of the problem identified by suburban detractors is the perception of suburbia as ultimately a site of boredom, of unremarkability. A multitude of adjectives have been used to convey this, for example as reflected in the headline on the BBC website in 2005, which stated in a matter-of-fact way '"Dreary" suburb may get protected', in reporting on a campaign to make a part of North West London's Harrow into a conservation area. There has also been a vein of popular cultural material on suburbia that is about the hidden stories of what lies beneath the ostensibly idyllic suburban landscape. When Bertrand Russell came up with the short story title 'Satan of the Suburbs' (1953), it was meant to highlight the incongruity of devilish goings on in the outer reaches more frequently perceived of as being innocuous, inoffensive and generally mild. This chapter turns to manifestations of extremism in the suburbs in recent years, including Islamic fundamentalism and far right politics. The extent to which fear in suburbia now clusters around extremism as well as the more enduring suburban phobia of crime (Taylor 1995) can be seen in the fact that Poynting et al (2004) called their Australian based study *Bin Laden in the Suburbs: Criminalising the Arab Other*.

Perhaps historically shocking happenings inscribe themselves most deeply into our collective psyche when they are named after dates that have memorable cadence: six years after the events of 9/11 occurred in New York in September 2001 came what became known as 7/7 in London: similarly seen as a turning point for many. This series of domestic mainland acts of terrorism occurred on 7 July 2005. As the identities of the bombers who caused death and injury on the London transport network were uncovered as British-born young men of Pakistani origin from Yorkshire, their suburban origins were remarked on. Tales of young men who had betrayed their outward ordinary appearances with their extraordinary deeds unfolded in the news media. The *Daily Mail* 13 of July 2005 talked of:

> Normal people leading normal lives, good people from good families – one loved cricket, another was a young father. A third happily told his parents last week that he was off to London 'with his mates'. All three had a deep Islamic faith, but no one thought of them as radicals.

The article detailed the mundanity of their lives – how one came from a fish and chip shop-owning family, whose business was to serve up the longstanding epitome of British takeaways. Its pen-portraits deftly presented its readers with a new enemy within: young British-born men who hated the country of their birth so much they were prepared to kill fellow citizens and be killed in defining themselves in opposition to it. The implied rhetorical question was how could 'they' (second generation Muslims in Britain) do this to 'us' (the majority)? One image that continually replayed on news bulletins showed an iconic red London bus ripped apart by a bomb – the destruction of one of the most reassuring images of Britishness, and all its associations with safety and security. As we have seen throughout this book, stereotypical notions of 'the suburbs' in the UK have long been seen as component elements of quintessential Englishness. The former premier John Major famously engaged in crystal ball gazing in outlining all that was good about Britishness: 'Fifty years on from now, Britain will still be the country of long shadows on cricket grounds, warm beer, invincible green suburbs, dog lovers and pools fillers' (Major 1993 – evoking Orwell 1943). Yet recent years have seen our received notions of the concepts of 'suburbia' and 'Englishness' become somewhat unsettled. In July 2008 the *Sun* newspaper (6.7.08) depicted a map of knife crime incidents in London which showed such activity clustering around the periphery.

Whilst the post-devolution climate has encouraged the assertion of Scottish and Welsh identities, and Britain's multiculture has seen the rise of 'hyphenated' identities such as black British, Englishness as an entity has been left rather trailing in their wake. And in the mean time this lack of attention to the nature of Englishness has for several decades coincided with a focus on regenerating run-down inner city areas rather than improving the suburbs, which are perceived to be comparatively 'unproblematic'. Taken in combination, this means that relationships of identity and belonging in the suburbs have been particularly under-examined. This chapter considers suburban extremism as manifested both in the far right political activity of the BNP and in Islamic fundamentalism. It also takes a look at attitudes to recent immigration by Poles to the suburbs. For although the debate on this recent wave of white migration in some ways differs from the old discourses on commonwealth immigration, and the old solutions of 'repatriation' are more difficult to apply given EU rules, it was Eastern Europe that provided the flashpoint to the 'Mrs Duffy' incident of the 2010 general election, when Gordon Brown became embroiled in a conversation on the merits and de-merits of post-2004 accession and settlement rights.

THE BNP

Other academics and think tanks have explored in detail the BNP's electoral fortunes and appeal in the UK (Goodwin 2008; 2010, James 2009, Renton 2005). This chapter will not attempt to revisit this theme, but instead presents interview data from four suburban locations on the party's tactics in those areas: the east London localities of Dagenham and Redbridge, the outer south east London areas of Bexley and Bromley, and the northern borough of Bury.

Dagenham is an area that has been considered classic enough to have inspired two well-known sociological studies. Following the much celebrated *Family and Kinship in East London*, Peter Wilmott also published studies of first Woodford and then Dagenham, as 'old'/private and 'new'/council housing suburbs. His (1963:1) study of Dagenham largely focused on the Becontree housing estate, a vast acreage of inter-war housing built by the London County Council to rehouse east-end slum overspill. He described the area as one of 'endless thoroughfares lined with straight rows of little houses … the general effect of monotony': '… the general atmosphere of a vast flatness, openness and uniformity is overpowering' (Wilmott 1963:4). He quotes interviewee Mrs Adams, reduced to tears on returning from a walk while the estate was still being built: 'The workmen said, "what's the matter ducks?" I said, "I can't find my house" (1963:8).

Dagenham is today a very different area. Fords – around whose factory the Becontree estate was built – now employs only 4000 employees, down from its peak of 40,000. Large numbers of council homes have been sold off under right to buy schemes, many to buy-to-let owners. The relatively homogenous nature of its original white working-class residents has been supplemented with recent generations of settlers of many different ethnic origins. It is now a classic of suburban change. One response to these changes has been increased support for the BNP, which at one point had 12 BNP local councillors – though the party lost all its seats at the 2010 local elections, as a result of a major popular initiative to combat their influence. Jon Cruddas is Labour MP for the area, and I discussed with him what this support meant, at a time when the BNP held their council seats (and when he was a candidate for the Labour Party deputy leadership). Cruddas believes that the BNP appeal to people who feel ignored by the mainstream, whose sense of belonging is undermined by a sense of powerlessness:

> I know a lot of people who voted BNP. I know loads of people that vote BNP. My departure point on this is that we haven't got thousands of people that are seriously Nazis ... there's an awful lot of vulnerable people, they feel like they've disappeared off the edge of the political bubble in Westminster, they are disenfranchised ... they feel that the Labour Party has removed itself from them. The BNP come in with messages tailored for that ... They come in and say we're more Labour than new Labour. We're the Labour Party your parents voted for ... there's a lot of material insecurity so a lot of it is a cry for help I feel. Or deep protest, quite profound protest.

> *These people have come straight from Labour?*

> Well a lot of them have. But there's two groups that you can identify here. First is those with absolutely no record of ever having voted before, so they'd be your classic person who's never participated in it, that does respond to the dog whistles of the BNP. And then the other group is those who've sort of been New Labour in the past. Typically in the local elections the Tories and the Liberals don't

really stand. The BNP becomes a repository of all the anti Labour protest.

The whole Olympics thing was built on 'we're such a happy multi-culti city', and in the next-door borough they're the official opposition.

Well, it is a lot more complex than that. You know this city is changing radically. There is something quite palpable happening in the body politic that's got to do with quite a deep sense of dissolution and alienation, but it's not just in Dagenham. I spent a lot of time in the last year going round the country and it is everywhere. The BNP stood in nearly 800 seats and they averaged out everywhere they stood at something like 15%. I think the BNP in Dagenham or Respect four to five miles down the road from here are part of the same reaction to the ever more precise political positioning of the mainstream parties in the interests of attracting marginal voters. They reflect the disenfranchisement of the people, who are disenfranchised because they don't have power in that system. The policy framework is built around the focus groups rather than competing ideologies. That is why such issues as council housing haven't been important for years, because they have no core importance with that very selective part of the electoral landscape. The consequence has been a failure to deal with the material forces that go with appealing to extremism. Because your policy and your political positioning are focused ruthlessly on a different community.

How has it changed your patch since you took over?

Completely. It's changing at such speed it's extraordinary.

What about your road?

Asylum seeker at the end, a few African families. The thing is the right to buy is having an extraordinary effect because people are selling up. A lot of what we could describe as the 'white resident community' are selling up their council houses and they're moving further out towards the coast. Coming in behind them are inner east London who are on a similar journey to them, but they just happen to be black.

Is that what you say on the doorstep to the people who voted BNP?

They say 'you can't get a council house because of all the people moving in'. But it's got nothing to do with that, it's the long-term structural failure to provide low-cost social housing. And I share their frustration and that's why I jumped into this deputy leadership election, to raise some of these issues around housing, working poverty, class.

In fellow outer East London borough Redbridge, the only area that had previously had BNP electoral representation was Hainault, a ward which shared some characteristics in common with Barking and Dagenham, as my conversation with three Labour councillors in 2010 highlighted. The ward had swung between political parties in recent years, as voters struggled to find someone who they felt could represent them:

BW: It's what you would think of as Labour heartland to a certain extent. The thing is, this year I think we were all convinced we'd finish up with three BNP councillors ... well the Tories took it in the end. But one of our people was only 63 votes away. With a little bit of work we could have possibly won it.

BJ: In 2002 it was all three Labour and then it went to mixed Tory/Labour, then 2006 it went two Tories, one BNP – Labour was far, far behind. But then this time the BNP was almost nothing, and Labour and the Tories were quite close. I think the ethnicity of housing itself is probably changing. I think it's got probably the cheapest houses along the central line.

My interviews with the Adab women's group in Bury in 2009 showed the attempts made by the BNP to increase their North West representation:

M: I think there has been a resurgence of the BNP over the last couple of years. When it comes to towns like Rochdale, Bury, Bolton ... up to two to three years ago you'd never find a BNP candidate on the ballot paper, but they started off testing the waters about two years ago, and at the last election I think they virtually fielded a whole range of candidates, a full slate in most of the towns, which is worrying, because I think they're attracting four to five hundred votes in the wards that they're standing in. So it is worrying, but it's difficult times for the country as a whole, with the recession, with people losing their jobs, with us having a devastated economy with the downturn – so people need something to blame.

… in addition to that, with the MPs' expenses people are really out off voting for the mainstream parties, because they feel they've been let down, and quite rightly so, they're right … some changes need to be made in the parliamentary process, in parliamentary activities, to bring those voters back to the mainstream. In the European elections the BNP gained a Parliamentary seat in the north west, which I believe is a protest vote. The other thing is, I think the mainstream parties have been very scared of having a debate on immigration. I think there is a need for a sensible debate to take place, and once that does take place I think people will stop protesting and move away from the BNP.

U: I don't really like the way that Gordon Brown for example is pandering towards that, using that tagline 'British jobs for British people' …

M: No, no, I'm not talking about that. I disagree with that myself.

Protest vote? So it's not for the BNP? What's it against?

E: More the Labour government, just its failures, and it hasn't lived up to its promises. Iraq would come into it I'd say.

M: On foreign soil, the dying of soldiers who are not equipped with the right equipment.

In James Cleverly's constituency the BNP had stood candidates, as he described:

They've always had a fairly strong showing in Welling … As I say that north bit of Bexley doesn't feel hugely different from Barking and Dagenham – it is literally on the other side of the water. It doesn't feel very different. That's what you have to understand. There are wards in that north bit of Bexley that look and feel very similar to Barking and Dagenham, and people's concerns are not dissimilar. But Bexley is a much better run council than B and D. That is a national audit office fact. I would say that anyway, but they really are a better run council, so some of the issues which have caused friction in Barking and Dagenham are not quite so acute here. But there are white working-class people here that once relied on heavy, manual industry, who are struggling financially, and that's where the BNP have traditionally done well. And again – it's expected for me to say Conservatives are always best in every circumstance – but it's traditionally disillusioned former Labour voters that are looking for a natural home, don't feel a natural affinity with the Conservatives, perhaps are looking for solutions, and someone comes up with childishly simple and very distorted solutions – 'I can solve all your problems, all you've got to do is get rid of the darkies you know and everything will come good'. There will always be people that are desperate, and want to buy into very simplistic solutions. And actually the slightly more nuanced, more accurate reflection of what's going on, and the solutions to what's what going on, are just not that sexy. It's a question of 'I will make everything better and will do it tomorrow if you vote for me', or 'You have to deal with it and you have to accept that it'll take you a little while'. Which one would you go for? And the other point that I'd make is that, if you traditionally vote Labour and then you start voting Lib Dem who takes notice? Who cares? Or if you switch from Labour to Conservative, like big chunks of Essex did in the 1980s, excellent, fantastic. But if you're angry, you want to make a statement, you want to be noticed, you want people sweating with blood to find out why you're so disengaged – nothing else works like voting BNP.

Same cry for help as people who join extremist Muslim groups?

It's a different manifestation of the same drivers ... You're a young Muslim lad and you feel you're being discriminated against, not having the same opportunities in life, and then someone presents you with these really simplistic options. It's very compelling. And then suddenly everyone's like 'how did we allow this to happen?

What are we going to about these young Muslim lads'. Same thing with the white working class in these areas. They feel no-one's listening. You vote BNP, everyone beats a path to your door saying how has it come to this? What are we going to do? How do we win them back? That'll get loads of attention. That works …

What do you think of Richard Barnbrook [a BNP Barking and Dagenham councillor and GLA member at time of interview]?

I can't be bothered to vilify him. It's a whole load of effort I could very much do without, to be perfectly honest with you. I treat him with the same courtesy that I treat anyone else, and just let him get on with being incompetent, because he is. Digs his own grave. I don't need to queue up to give him a kicking on the way down. There was a big hoo-ha about who was going to sit next to him, and the Labour lot all left and said we're not having him on our side, he can go over to you other right-wingers. We were saying, no he's left-wing, so we had this big row. And then the Conservative group were all 'I'm not gonna sit next to him' so I said 'Oh bollocks I'll sit next to him, I don't care'. So I sit next to him on the assembly and when I walk in I say 'morning Richard', he says 'morning James', and I cannot believe we spend so much time obsessing with the BNP. I think there are bigger fish to fry. There are more important issues. We should concern ourselves why people are disengaged, but let go of this obsession, this absolute fanaticism, with the BNP. I find it amazing that people get so angry at the BNP, so full of hatred for the BNP. The 'I hate people that hate people' attitude. 'The BNP hate people, that's why I hate the BNP'. Does that not make you the same as them? – passionate hatred but for hatred. Does that not undermine your arguments actually? Let them go on television. Let them spout their nonsense. The best antidote for voting BNP? Watch the videos of Richard Barnbrook performing in the chamber of the London Assembly. I would like to broadcast it on a big screen in Barking and Dagenham and say, 'look, look, that's what you voted for. You wanna vote for them again? Knock yourselves out, 'cos the guy is not championing your views. He is not shaking up British politics, he is not exposing the dark underbelly of incestuous party collaboration. He's just crap.' I don't lose any sleep about the BNP as I've seen them up close and they are not scary, they're just shit/crap/rubbish.

The general view amongst the people I interviewed was that it was in those parts of suburbia where people were suffering from feelings of exclusion and abandonment that BNP extremism was most likely to attract support. Ray et al (2003:119) conducted a study of racist violence in social housing in outer neighbourhoods of Manchester from 1998 to 2000, where residents expressed negative feelings about racism but felt marginalised by public policy concerns:

> While generally disavowing actively racist beliefs and expressing disapproval of violence, racist or otherwise, the adult residents expressed a sense of being overlooked: their estates were seen as ignored by those in charge of regeneration projects and the resources allocated by them; recognition of problems and ameliorative action was seen as concentrated nearer the centre of the conurbation in areas (like Moss side) that had acquired national notoriety. The poverty, decline and increasing criminality (according to older residents) of small, outlying estates went unregarded ... the areas that gained were those with substantial ethnic minority populations, those that lost were white.

Here suburban disaffection was heightened by a sense of being passed over in favour of the inner city. Certainly the relationships between inner city and suburb make for complex patterns of grievance. It is a very wide range of changes that has contributed to the rise of incidences of suburban extremism.

And, as James Cleverly acknowledges, feelings of exclusion – though of a different nature – have also contributed to the rise of Islamic fundamentalism. It is to this phenomenon that we now turn – a phenomenon that, to the surprise of some, is also present in the suburbs as well as the inner city.

ATTITUDES TO PREVENT

As we have seen, a number of the underlying reasons for turning to extreme and simplistic solutions are shared by supporters of both the BNP and Islamic fundamentalism, but it is the Muslim population on which the Labour government's 'Preventing Violent Extremism Strategy' (known more commonly in shorthand as 'Prevent') was focused. (Prevent has subsequently been adapted and continued by the Coalition government.) Among its objectives were community development work among the general Muslim population of the UK, and efforts to identify individuals considered to be 'vulnerable to radicalisation'. In pursuing these aims suburban Muslims were once more engaged, as part of the effort to identify ways of fostering harmonious communities. As noted earlier, I myself was involved in research funded by the programme in the leafy borough of Kingston.

Sadiq Khan MP (2008) argued that, rather than being conceived of in narrow national security terms, the programme needed to make an effort to forge wider links across all communities and to combat inequality, as well as to foster public engagement in foreign policy, an inclusive Britishness, and a rethinking the role of faith in public life. His argument indicates an understanding that the reasons for the turn to extremism need to be understood if it is to be tackled:

> We cannot let how we win votes, or how we tackle terrorism or extremism, become the primary factors when we consider how best to reconnect to constituencies that are often disillusioned, disengaged and disadvantaged ... Instead our priority must be to address major obstacles that prevent many Muslims becoming fully active participants in mainstream civic society, while helping individuals to climb the social ladder and take up new opportunities.

The scheme was controversial from the beginning, however, especially within the Muslim community, which was expected to deliver the programme among its own members – to develop 'good Muslims' and take away influence from 'bad Muslims' (Mamdani 2004). For example a report from Muslim women's group Al Nisa (Khan 2009:6) made these comments:

> Funding grassroots Muslim groups to deliver Prevent is unhelpful as it causes them to lose credibility and trust with the very groups the government wants them to engage. Hardened extremists are not likely to attend projects funded by the government ... There is so much hostility to the strategy amongst Muslims once they become aware of it, that local councils and funded groups are finding implementation difficult, and are resorting to disguising the source and objectives of the funding by being 'economical' with information and using misleading labels.

In the borough of Reading, for example, although a number of local mosques supported the PVE agenda, a Muslim PVE Crisis was launched by twenty Muslim organisations in the area. According to the group's website, it was formed 'in relation to the implementation of the government's Preventing Violent Extremism (PVE) agenda and the dangers that this misguided agenda poses to the community'.

Amongst non-religious groupings, criticisms of PVE have come from across the political spectrum. From the right there was the worry that the good Muslims might not be correctly identified. The Taxpayers Alliance (2009) claimed:

> Giving councils millions of pounds to dole out to hundreds of community groups clearly creates a massive risk that money will be wasted or finance groups hostile to Britain's liberal, democratic values. The Government has failed to avoid endorsing or funding radicals in the past and as such it's totally unrealistic to expect local councils to be able to assess which groups warrant funding. Grants to community groups aren't just risky though, they can also be divisive and wasteful. Politicians of all parties need to acknowledge that the approach has failed, cancel this programme and start focussing directly on stopping terrorists.

Meanwhile the Institute of Race Relations also published a highly critical report, and a submission to the UK Parliament Select Committee inquiry on the subject concluded that Prevent constructed the Muslim population as a 'suspect community', fostered social divisions both among Muslims and between Muslims and others, encouraged tokenism, facilitated violations of privacy and professional norms of confidentiality, discouraged local democracy and was counter-productive in reducing the risk of political violence. The IRR's Kundnani (2008, 2009) has written extensively on what he sees as the likely counter-productive effects of the programme.

Most of our Muslim interviewees did not have much first-hand knowledge of Prevent, but those in officialdom whose roles had been expanded to incorporate the brief – for example from cultural services or arts – were well versed in its aims and objectives and frequently critical of them. One Kingston grants officer voiced the fear that Prevent appeared to be singling out specific communities:

> I was trying to write the guidelines for the grants. I was thinking 'is anyone going to want to do any of this?', because … certainly in the stuff the government set down, it was really difficult not to feel that they were getting at communities really. I didn't like the language that was being used for that, so we tried to put it into a more user-friendly terms, to say we're aware that there may be people who might be drawn into this more extremist behaviour, but putting it into a wider context, for example, wouldn't it be good to do some wider mentoring, getting across more liberal views? Or more interpretation and the religious angle, which was more generally acceptable stuff about being a good citizen, community cohesion or those things, having workshops, having conferences around those kinds of themes. And also some inter-community understanding – that kind of approach, rather than thinking it's got to be about getting young people and saving them from themselves, you know. It does sound a little bit patronising. I do think it has that tone.

The bearded Asian respondent quoted below was being interviewed with regards to a completely different sub-topic of the project, but voiced the ways in which terrorist incidents had changed perceptions of him by others:

> Basically a lot of times I get very good examples of how I am perceived because of my beard. 9/11 took place, 7/7 took place, the amount of times I was abused as Osama Bin Laden or experienced abusive language, you know, 'get out of this country' or whatever it is.

The mosque committee member we interviewed also claimed that attitudes had changed towards him in the five years since his retirement, when he had grown a beard. But he also sometimes seemed exasperated at the tendency of his largely Pakistani congregation to disassociate themselves from terrorist events, thus absolving themselves of any responsibility in the process: 'The newest thing going on in the mosque is … [the view that] "all these troubles internationally, they're caused by Indian Muslims"'. He was also conscious of the need to interact with authorities and even to make sure the environs of the mosque were presentable: 'If you walk to the mosque and there is litter all around it creates, well, a ghetto mentality. I ask the worshippers … why don't you pick it up.' Any impression of dereliction and decay would give out a negative impression of the mosque and religion.

The perception of Islam by the wider community has become more hostile since the 9/11 and 7/7 attacks. And the suburbs have not escaped these effects. Nor have they been without their own Islamic extremists.

INTERVIEW WITH A SUBURBAN 'EXTREMIST': AMIN HOSSAIN AND HIZB UT-TAHRIR

Of all of the Islamist groups in the UK Hizb ut-Tahir is among the best known. There is now a small publishing industry fuelled by ex Hizb ut-Tahrir members who have revealed all after life on the other side (see for example Hussain 2007). The group's strategy in the 1990s, when Kingston's Amin Hossain joined, was entryism into higher and further education courses, and once having infiltrated to identify, persuade and then groom potential members, as Amin described:

> I was 16 when I first came across them at Kingston College and at the time … I was always intensely spiritual, I still am … my experience at the mosque completely fucked me up … It didn't turn me off religion, it turned me off that side of religion, so I thought 'this is bullshit'. And when HT came to me – they have a pseudo intellectual style – it was very stimulating. When you're 16, 17 years old, they come to you and say that all the ideas that you had when you were growing up are a fabrication. Islam is actually this. Islam is actually this. Islam is actually a political ideology. If you look at the history of Islam this is actually what happened. If you look at the life of the prophet, he was a statesman or a politician, he united the tribes … all that sort of stuff. Islam had an empire stretching over a thousand years. Islam gave rise to Algebra. Islam gave rise to astronomy. Islam gave rise to libraries, universities, conquests. So all of these things struck me as really romantic notions of my own identity, that I didn't know, that I was never really exposed to.

The usual procedure with Hizb ut-Tahrir was to serve a two year apprenticeship before acceptance. But Amin was fast-tracked in the procedure for joining and became a full member on beginning his degree course at SOAS:

> I was one of the head recruiters for University of London. I had a team of people and I got to go off and do stuff. I became a member when I came to university, but when I was at college I was what's known as a student member. To be a member you have to swear an oath, you're bound by your word in front of god … I'd organise meetings, I gave talks, I spoke to people, I took them out. They're into cafe culture in HT, they'd sit down, discuss. That's its stuff really. Mostly educated boys, students. Also there were different teams of people at work – a team of people that spoke to people in the city, a team of students that spoke to students, a team of Arabs that spoke to other Arabs … and you had an executive team, an elite team. There was central London, north London, south London, west London, east London, and within central London there's the universities … which is what I was part of. And there's communities … there's north of England, Scotland, different regions.

There is a spectrum of extremist groups, with different organisations adopting different methods. I asked Amin whether HT engaged in activities like paintballing, as seen on some videos:

> HT don't do that. As I say, HT is more intellectual, it attracts people who are less … they're all angry, but they're more … I don't know how to explain. It's not even educated, because they're all educated, but it's … if you're a pseudo intellectual then you'll like HT, because they go into history, they go into philosophy, they go into all that sort of stuff, but these paintballing things are more angry folk that want to go out for a fight. HT is a non-violent organisation. It's not violent at all. It will be violent once you get a state. Its whole point is to get a state where you're ruled by Islam. Once you get a state ruled by Islam then you can be violent, then you can sort of wage Jihad.

This contradicts the notion of the members as testosterone-filled thugs. During the time of this project's compilation, the group Islam4UK, and its parent operation Al Majharoon were proscribed by the government – a move condemned by Amin, who explained the philosophical differences between the groups:

> I don't think anything should be banned. I'm against censorship. With HT, first of all they're not enough of a threat, so if you ban them you're only giving them more legitimacy, because they don't share any love for the government, they don't really give two shits about the government. So if the government turns around and bans them it'd be like a huge victory for them. They'll get more popular as a result of being banned. I don't want them to be banned, they should definitely be debated, they should be given a platform to be exposed. They do go on *Newsnight* every now and again.
>
> Islam4UK is a pseudonym for Al-Muhajiroon, which was set up by the head of HT in this country after he was booted out by HT. He left HT and set up Al Majharoon … The point of difference is that is Al-Muhajiroon is calling for a caliphate here. He became more Salifi, or more Wahabi in his thinking, so he became more literal – it's our obligation as Muslims to set up an Islamic state wherever you are. So that was the initial difference. And then Al-Muhajiroon span put of control. They still maintain a belief in the establishment of an Islamic state now. They're very very Saudi, very very Wahabi, very very Salifi, very Jihadist as well, Jihadist-Salifi. All Jihadists are Salifi. They're an extreme, just like the Tabliq and the Taliban of the Deoband …

There is an argument that Islamic politics in Britain are domestic echoes at home of events abroad, as is frequently the case with other diasporic groups. Thus, although the PVE agenda is firmly entrenched within a UK context, extremist activity often occurs as a consequence of far-off happenings:

> I've got sisters [in their late 30s] and I used to hang round with them a lot and with their friends, we'd go to places like Asian events, loads of events, but it shifted. It shifted with the Rushdie affair. It shifted with the Gulf War. It shifted with Bosnia. These are all in the 1990s. Bosnian Muslims, they're white but they're Muslims getting annihilated, do you see what I mean? Bang bang bang bang bang. The 1990s was the period where radicalisation in Britain prevailed. Now it's been curtailed because there's Prevent,

> think tanks, there's this, there's that. But the 1990s was mental and that's when I got sucked in, I got sucked into the wave. So did a lot of these guys.

Amin attributed the impetus for joining such groups to the existence of what he saw as a pan-Muslim under class – rather than being linked to the social standing of individual members:

> … there is no class distinction between suburban Muslims and urban Muslims or rural Muslims … I don't think it's that. It's less to do with where one is situated in Britain but more to do with Britain. So if you live in the suburbs you'll be radicalised in a different way from what you would be if you were urban, but you'll still be radicalised … but let's not be all Fox news about it and say everyone's radicalised. A lot of us just get on with shit, you know? … but the people that do turn to Islamism do it for a multitude of reasons, and those, as I said, are the result of social, economic and political mismanagement by the powers that be, you know … unintentional mismanagement. Historical process results in their alienation, disenfranchisement. If we take the most extreme example of the Tavistock Square suicide bomb. These guys before they died left a message saying we're doing this for our brothers around the world, we're doing this to fight oppression. This is a profound political message. Their entire endeavour was political, and the constituency that they ascribed themselves to was not in England, necessarily. It's this sort of global umma, global community of Muslims. So they identified themselves as Muslims before anything else, and, more than that, they saw Muslims as suffering the consequences of foreign policies of the sort of post-colonial world. They saw these corrupt rulers that the ex-colonies put in place after they left. It's actually quite a sophisticated political critique of the global world as it stands today. They felt that pain to such an extent that they were willing to give up their lives for it, and that's where the religion comes and kicks in … ideas of afterlife and reward.
>
> Because class … I think all people who are Muslims in the country are immediately underclass. It doesn't matter how rich they are. If you're non-white Muslim in this country you're immediately underclass. You're not even working class, you're less than that. For

> me class doesn't work on the level of affluence per se, and I think Muslims, along with asylum seekers and migrant workers, have the lowest social capital.

Other people involved in terror plots have hailed from similarly suburban locations. As was reported in the *Bucks Herald* newspaper: 'when news filtered through that suicide bomber Germaine Lindsay – the deadliest of the four London bombers – was an Aylesbury resident, the town was stunned … The biggest police operation in Aylesbury's history took place days later when Lindsay's family home was raided by officers led by anti-terror branch officers' (Jackson 2007).

Sadiq Khan (2008) has warned: 'It is beyond doubt that poverty, discrimination and inequality disproportionately affect British Muslims. This is not only unjust, it also threatens to undermine the basic tenets of an integrated society of universal and equal citizenship.' But Khan also says that British Muslims must, in turn, reject the 'single narrative' on Western foreign policy that sees the west as implacably opposed to Islam, and should participate in mainstream British political issues: 'I challenge British Muslims to accept that as strongly as they feel about Iraq or counter-terror measures, poverty and inequality have the biggest impact on the lives of the majority of British Muslims'.

Amin Hossain was critical of think tanks such as the Quilliam Foundation that had been set up to tackle extremism since PVE's institution:

> I read it on … Islamism, fighting Islamism, Islamists, the trouble with Islamists … the problem is ideas from Saudi. No! All of this has a place in the history, but that is not the problem. Do you know what I mean? That's not why people are becoming radicalised. People are becoming radicalised because of the way they feel inadequate in this fucking country because of the way that they're … their exposure to the world, their interaction with British society isn't enough for them for them to feel part of this society and so they look for alternatives.
>
> … But if you look at it, how would one feel so politically and socially disenfranchised to go to that measure? It's not because people are going round and radicalising and saying 'Islam is like

> this', and 'this is what Islam tells you that'. It's not because of that … if they thought their next door neighbour was a good guy, the white guy who lives next door to them and the Nigerian guy that lives next door on the other side and the Jewish person opposite … if they felt they had a part to play in this society, if they felt this society represented their needs, if they felt that they'd learnt from this society, if they felt they'd benefitted from this society, it doesn't matter how much hocus pocus someone comes to you with. If someone sits down and says to you 'kill your Jewish neighbour', you're just gonna say 'why? I'm not gonna kill my Jewish neighbour. I've grown up with him (or her) all my life you know, they come to my house. I'm not gonna blow up the working class Chelsea supporting working class man who lives next door to me. He's looked after me all my life. This can't be religion. If this is religion I don't want anything to do with it.' Do you see what I mean? But the way these people have been socialised is that they have no affinity for anything that is British. They have no affinity for this country, this country has made no efforts to give them affinity. These people are angry. Something's happened.

Acknowledgement of the grievances that result at home from events occurring abroad has taken place at the highest level of the civil service. A leaked letter from Michael Jay, the Foreign Office permanent under-secretary, to the cabinet secretary, Sir Andrew Turnbull from 2004, well before the UK's own 7/7 incidents, warned that British foreign policy could be a driver for discontent in the Muslim community, 'especially in the context of the Middle East peace process and Iraq' (Bright 2005). The letter speaks of 'potential underlying causes of extremism that can affect the Muslim community, such as discrimination, disadvantage and exclusion' and 'the issue of British foreign policy, especially in the context of the Middle East peace process and Iraq'. The letter mentions both Hizb ut-Tahrir and Al-Muhajiroon as potentially benefiting from this in membership terms. Such comments concur with what Amin told us about his reasons for joining Hizb ut-Tahrir. It is probably most accurate to characterise this process as grievance-led, with an added divine dimension – i.e. accountability before your creator. Amin stressed that he had been attracted to Hizb ut-Tahrir for chiefly intellectual reasons. (He had also had negative dealings with Kingston mosque as a child, and claimed that he had been beaten by the man that ran their madrassa-school, which had stopped him attending the masjid altogether.)

Whilst at first sight 'Islamic extremism' appears as one political bloc, we can see that there are differences of strategy, tactics and theological opinion. The exit strategy of Amin Hossain was described as a process rather than a critical incident:

> *Was there a decisive moment when you saw the light? Or were you never convinced?*
>
> I was convinced for a while I must admit, for a year or two I was convinced. It was only after I came to SOAS really. The thing that impressed me about HT was they gave me an idea of my own identity that was based on something that I was completely ignorant of. When I found out more details of that history it appeared to me how erroneous their narratives were, and I started questioning those narratives to them, and nobody really gave me a satisfactory answer, but by then I was bound to the organisation because I thought it was a religious duty. Going back to the earlier point, I wanted to nourish this desire for spirituality and I thought I was doing it with them, so even though I was intellectually unimpressed with them after a couple of years I felt it was my religious duty to be with them – for lack of an alternative, because I thought 'yeah alright they're a bit fucked up but I still gotta'. 'Cos they give you all these things to convince you that you have to be with them, like the prophet wasn't buried for three days after he died because they were appointing the next successor. The prophet of Islam, the greatest guy that ever lived, was not buried for three days because of a political decision – and that's how they frame it.

There is a need for a sensitive exploration of the barriers and discriminatory practices described above that can feed discontent and be a driver to joining extremist groups, and decision-makers need to make a concerted attempt to root out such occurrences with appropriate public policy. But there should also be a move away from exaggerating divisions in British society and accentuating difference. Commonalties need to be stressed in a plural society of self-confident citizens of multiple ethnicities and religious backgrounds, who have no need to resort to extremism as an imagined solution to their problems.

FUTURE FAULT-LINES: CONTINUITY AND CHANGE IN SUBURBIA

The future is likely to see a number of changes in attitudes towards race and migration within suburbia. From the 1992 general election onwards, a generational shift in attitudes to race has appeared to be discernible, with younger people less likely to be attracted towards racist parties. Changing attitudes on the part of the Conservative Party, making it less likely to exploit race as an issue, have sometimes been attributed to Prime Minister John Major having spent his early childhood in Brixton, a south London inner-city neighbourhood with a significant number of black residents. However the Major government was also guilty of failures in the battle against racism. The obstinate refusal of the Home Office to properly investigate the murder of black teenager Stephen Lawrence became one of the final symptoms of his lame duck government, which had lost its parliamentary majority and authority in the country. Soon after New Labour came into power in 1997 they set up an enquiry into the murder, which led to the publication in 1999 of the McPherson report, which for the first time acknowledged the existence of 'institutional racism' (Macpherson 1999). However the reception of the later Parekh report of 2000 in many ways showed the limits of what New Labour would deliver. Changing attitudes among young people are caused by greater familiarity with diversity and wider trends within youth culture, as well as governmental action. Meanwhile a further boost to changing attitudes has taken place at Parliamentary level, where both Conservative and Labour parties contain vastly swelled numbers of Muslims on their benches, which may lead to more recognition of Muslims in both government and opposition policies.

Stephen's murder drew attention to the existence of serious racist problems within the London suburb of Eltham. Writing fourteen years later, in a chapter entitled 'Eltham: Garden Suburb Challenged', Hall (2007:161) begins with a descriptive account of the area's infrastructure before shifting gear by observing that the area has been 'widely represented in the media as a crucible of white working-class racism … of course a caricature, deeply resented by many residents'. Hall's interviewees frequently mention Lawrence in both condemning the case and the effect that it has had on their area's reputation. This shows once more the complexity of the interaction between place and attitudes to race, which is unlikely to get any simpler.

The accession of a number of Eastern European countries to the EU in 2004 brought with it higher levels of white immigration, and this in turn has delivered a new set of stereotypes capable of eliciting extreme reactions. A major response to the large numbers of migrant workers coming into the UK immediately after 2004 was the rise of new discourses of fear and hatred towards the newcomers. The colour of the skin may have changed, but the lack of generosity remained constant. The new focus on 'mass immigration' has both similarities and differences with previous attitudes to difference, but has contributed to a wider resurgence of intolerance. In an article for the *Daily Mail*, written in response to an apology that had been elicited from the paper by the Federation of Poles in Great Britain, for their hostile coverage of Polish migration, spokesman Wiktor Moszczynski (2008a) declared that: 'There have been hundreds of cases of hate crime against Poles in this country recorded in the last 2 years, some leading to death or permanent injury'. Moszczynski makes a link between the attacks and all the negative stories: 'the worst examples linked Poles with words and phrases like 'feckless', 'chancers', 'race riots', 'swamp the NHS', 'fears for schools', 'cut-price treatment', 'push British graduates to back of the jobs queue', 'killers, drug smugglers and rapists' … [all of which] … has made Poles living in the UK feel vulnerable and persecuted.' Certainly negative headlines regarding Poles and immigration generally have been plentiful in recent years, including the *Daily Mail*'s 'Mass immigration "has made the UK's poor even poorer"' (Doughty, 2011); or its headline '10,000 council houses given to immigrants in a year' (Slack and Hickley, 2007); fears about the UK's limited physical capacity have also been raised, for example the *Daily Express*'s characterisation of the UK as 'squashed' and 'crammed', and its question, 'so where will everyone live?' (Ware, 2010); while there has also been scaremongering about British culture being under threat in the face of 'uncontrolled immigration' from McDougall (2010) and McKinstry (2011).

In contrast, Le Grain (2011) has argued that the British workforce needs overseas workers, and Moszczynski (2008b) also powerfully makes this case in the Polish context, including pointing to their positive impact on suburbia in service sector occupations amongst other things: 'Their presence has been hugely popular among the middle classes, who needed plumbers and nannies, and welcomed by the catering and construction industries, local public transport and by Scottish agriculture, which they have saved from extinction'. Their £1.9 billion a year contribution to the Treasury in income tax and national insurance (disregarding council tax at local government level) is also cited by Moszczynski as a positive contribution to the economy. There has been much media discussion during this period of how to evaluate the contribution of migrants to the economy: unfortunately most commentators seem to select the figures which best support their existing opinion.

According to Trevena (2009) most Polish migrants are under the age of 34, with those aged 18-24 the largest category. WRS data show that Polish male immigrants outnumbered females, and LFS data shoes that the high watermark of migration was between 2004-06, when males comprised 61.4% of Polish immigrants. Moszczynski (2011) has also stated that this first post-2004 wave of Polish migrants represented the 'cream' of their generation, who were generally well educated, with a higher level of secondary education than Britons. The 'Polish plumber' stereotype persists only because Poles typically take up jobs that are well below their educational and skill levels, and are considered to be hard-working and to possess a good work ethic. Ruhs (2011) has similarly discussed the position of care-workers in the UK. With an ageing UK population – most of whom are concentrated in the suburbs – this category of worker is likely to be evermore important in future years, and in the big cities such individuals are frequently overseas workers. These are the people whose brown faces now appear at suburban bus stops (see p29).

Though extremism has been the focus of this chapter, and it undoubtedly exists in suburbia in the same way as it does in other areas, it would be mistaken to give an impression of suburbia as a hotbed of radicalism and extreme views. In the long term there is a good chance that new generations will be absorbed into Britain's multicultural suburbs along with the earlier arrivals. The following exchange with councillors in Ilford demonstrates the adaptability of an area which was once rural Essex, but has now become firmly embedded within London suburbia:

KT: We now have a very vibrant multicultural community. The main thing about is that it's always been ... despite severe pressures at times a very ...

BJ: Harmonious ...

KT: ... peaceful community. There've been odd examples, particularly until this election we did have a BNP candidate elected as a councillor for Hainault, which is one of the hard-hat areas I would say ... but even during the problems of the Iraq war and so on we've never really had any major problems, apart from the Preventing Violent Extremism initiative, which quite a bit of money came into the borough to try and develop. I think that's now been buried hasn't it? I think although we made a valiant effort I don't think it was particularly successful here, and certainly a lot of us were quite concerned about the implications as far as the anti-Muslim ethos of the thing went.

But though suburbia is not a hotbed of extremism, spatial patterns of ghettoisation and white flight are in serious need of reconsideration. At the same time there is a tendency among supporters of suburbia to see its contemporary form as multi-ethnic mosaic or tapestry in an unproblematic way, as symbolising a post-racial utopia. The activities of the BNP in Barking and Dagenham, however, together with south London suburban recruiting amongst fundamentalist Islamic groups, suggest that racial hierarchies and boundaries do persist and are simply redrawn. Disenfranchised BNP supporters see the boundaries of white privilege shifting out of their grasp. Islamic radical groups operating out of the suburbs have become more and more visible in national news outlets, as in Luton with the burning of poppies on Remembrance Sunday. Here we see a downside of communities once thought to 'keep themselves to themselves' engaging in the public sphere. The English Defence League have also been able to command column inches and the airwaves. Their reaction to what they see as an encroachment of British values by Islamic ones recalls the sociological literature on skinheads from the 1970s: at that time Clarke (1976:102) described the 'magical attempt to recover community' by skinheads in the face of fragmenting traditional working-class communities, slum clearance, industrial decline, unemployment and corrupt central and local government: all reasons for their attacks on 'scapegoated outsiders' – i.e. immigrant youth. One should, however, be careful about drawing the inference that such aggression is inevitable, which can serve to render it excused.

In some senses the examples described in this chapter, as well as the community protests of chapter three, seem to illustrate suburbia not in its traditional guise as insular but rather as an extroverted place, connected to other localities, be these real, or as Pnina Werbner (2002) put it 'imagined'. Despite being long established as a nation-state, Britain's tradition of citizenship is very young (Huq 2009). If the late twentieth century was about Britain coming to terms with its post-imperial state, the twenty-first century presents new challenges to internal centralised decision-making, as a result of external international obligations as well as moves towards regional government within its own shores. Extremism is both cause and effect in the balancing of competing demands from different groups on a twenty-first century scale. Over the last decade young people have been increasingly vocal in their demands for global justice – but it remains to be seen whether or not the changes to come will further such a cause.

REFERENCES

Bright, M. (2005) 'Leak shows Blair told of Iraq war terror link', *Observer* 28.8.05: www.guardian.co.uk/politics/2005/aug/28/uk.iraq.

Clarke, J. (1976) 'The Skinheads and the Magical Recovery of Community', in Hall, S. and Jefferson, T. (1976) (eds) *Resistance through Rituals: Youth subcultures in post-war Britain*, Hutchinson, pp 99-102.

Hall, P. (2007) *London Voices, London Lives*, Policy Press.

Hari, J. (2005) 'The best way to undermine the jihadists is to trigger a rebellion of Muslim women', *Independent*, 15.7.05.

Huq, R. (2009) 'A Young Concept in a Old Country?: the institutionalisation of the citizenship question in the UK and its generational impact', in *Young: the Nordic Journal of Youth Research* (2009) vol 17 (4), pp443-455.

Goodwin, M. (2008) 'Backlash in the 'hood: determinants of support for the British National Party (BNP) at the local level', in *Journal of Contemporary European Studies* Vol. 16, No. 3, 2008, pp349-363.

Goodwin, M. (2010) 'Who votes extreme right in twenty-first century Britain? The social bases of support for the National Front and British

National Party', in Eatwell, R. (ed) *The new extremism in 21st century Britain*, Routledge.

Hussain, E. (2007) *The Islamist: Why I Joined Radical Islam in Britain, What I Saw Inside and Why I Left*, Penguin.

Jackson, A. (2007) 'The Bucks Herald 1963 - Present day', 15.3.2007: www.bucksherald.co.uk/newspaperhistory/The-Bucks-Herald-1963-.2051918.jp.

James, L. (2009) *In Defence of British Muslims: A response to BNP racist* propaganda, Quilliam Foundation.

Khan, K. (2009) 'Preventing Violent Extremism (PVE) & PREVENT: A response from the Muslim Community':
www.an-nisa.org/downloads/PVE_&_Prevent_-__A_Muslim_response.pdf.

Khan, S. (2008) *Fairness not Favours*, Fabian Society.

Kundnani, A. (2008) 'Islamism and the roots of liberal rage', *Race and Class* 50 (2), pp30-68.

Kundnani, A. (2009) *Spooked: How not to Prevent Violent Extremism*, Institute of Race Relations: www.irr.org.uk/spooked.

Mamdani, Mahmoud, *Good Muslim, Bad Muslim*, Doubleday, New York 2004.

Major, J. (1993) Speech to the Conservative Group for Europe, 22.4.93.

Moszczynski, W. (2008) 'The Polish community and the United Kingdom', *Daily Mail*, 5.8.08: www.dailymail.co.uk/news/article-1039255/The-Polish-community-United-Kingdom.html#ixzz1TnAaummV.

Moszczynski, W. (2008b) 'Why Britain needs Polish migrants', *Daily Telegraph* 3.4.08: www.telegraph.co.uk/comment/3556852/Why-Britain-needs-Polish-migrants.html.

Olechnowicz, A. (1997) *Working-class Housing in England between the Wars: the Becontree Estate*, Oxford University Press.

Orwell (1943) 'My Country Right or Left', in Orwell, S. and Angus, I. (1968) (eds), *The Collected Essays, Journalism and Letters of George Orwell*, Harcourt, Brace & World.

Poynting, S., Noble, G., Tabar, P. and Collins, J. (2004) *Bin Laden in the Suburbs: Criminalising the Arab Other*, Institute of Criminology, Sydney.

Ray, L., Smith, D. and Wastell, L. (2003) 'Understanding Racist violence', in Stanko, E. (ed), *The Meanings of Violence*, Routledge, pp112-29.

Renton, D. (2005) '"A day to make history"? The 2004 elections and the British National Party', *Patterns of Prejudice*, Vol. 39, No. 1, pp25-45.

Ruhs, M. (2011) 'Responding to immigration's perceived economic impacts: What can be done?', paper given at 'Immigration and political trust' seminar, Policy Network, 1.2.11.

Russell, B (1953) *Satan in the Suburbs and Other Stories*, Bodley Head.

Taylor, I. (1996) 'Private Homes and Public Others: An Analysis of Talk about Crime in Suburban South Manchester in the Mid-1990s', *British Journal of Criminology* (1995) 35 (2), pp263-285.

Taxpayers Alliance (2009) *Council Spending Uncovered II – No. 5: Preventing Violent Extremism Grants*: www.taxpayersalliance.com/Prevent.pdf.

Trevena, P. (2009) 'Why do highly educated migrants go for low-skilled jobs? A case study of Polish graduates working in London', in Glorius, Birgit, Grabowska-Lusińska, Izabela and Rindoks, Amie (eds) (forthcoming), *Lost in Mobility Transition?*, Amsterdam, University Press.

Werbner, P. (2002) *Imagined Diasporas among Manchester Muslims*, James Currey & School of American Research.

Wilks-Heeg, S. (2009) 'The canary in a coalmine? Explaining the emergence of the British National Party in English local politics', *Parliamentary Affairs*, Vol 62 issue 2.

7

Rethinking suburbia in an age of insecurity: hard times on the edge?

> Being middle class and coming from cosy suburbia is such a grey area. It's coolest to come from the mean streets.
>
> Phil Cornwell, writer of *Stella Street*

This chapter collects together some of the strands already touched on throughout this book, such as identity, community and culture, to see how these concepts relate to contemporary suburban living as a whole. The suburb – close to the city but distinct from it, and boasting the benefits of general salubriousness, cleanliness, greenery and proximity to the country – is where most people in the UK live. Whereas suburbs have long been reviled by critics for their mass produced architectural uniformity and monotony, they were conceived of as promised land by their creators, and are now attracting interest as sites of political transformation, targeted by all the political parties as key territories to unlock if they are to win power. Suburbs were once stereotypically seen as middle-class and 'safe', yet as old models of hidebound class fragment in the face of ethnic diversity and the economic insecurity characteristic of modern times, it is time for a rethinking of suburbia. Many of the observations made in this chapter apply to society at large, but suburbia makes an interesting case study, precisely because it is seen as desirable, and because it is seen as 'ordinary'. Suburbia, then, has the potential to contribute to a blueprint for community living.

CHANGING VALUES

The suburb as understood in this book is a peculiarly Anglophone concept. As stated at the outset, in other countries the outlying areas of cities are those where marginalised populations are relegated – in Paris for example the poor live in the outer banlieues. But in the UK and US, as well as Australia and Canada, suburbs are about aspiration and progress, security and social respectability. Both suburbia and suburban housing are built on the principle of defensible space. Suburban values are often seen as unashamedly materialist, typified by the phrase 'keeping up with the Joneses'. Indeed many characteristic features of the typical suburban semi are about ostentation and wealth, most notoriously in the form of mock Tudor. The move outwards and upwards was marketed by private house builders as a positive consumer choice, a means of escape from the decaying and insalubrious city.

This suburban celebration of the private, and private wealth, can be seen as being in direct contradiction to centre left values – such as the championing of the public realm, the redistribution of wealth, and solidarity in collective action. Long-term prospects for such values have been on the wane for some time. The decline of Britain's manufacturing base has resulted in a shrunken trade union membership, and the shift from production to consumption has also undermined traditional labour constituencies. Since the Thatcher years there has been an increasing focus on consumerism and individualism. This means that the Labour Party has had to work harder for its votes: its natural reservoirs of support have declined as the suburbs have grown.

A major part of the contemporary political battle is about constructing a set of values that will resonate with the electorate, and these often overlap with quality of life issues. Time and again parties have dreamed up election sloganeering that they hope will convince the 'average' – i.e. suburban – voter to entrust their votes to them. Just like the suburbs, should the population be seen as conservative or as ready for change? In 2005 Labour plumped for 'Forward Not Back', emphasising both forward movement and their ability to keep on delivering. In 1987 the Conservatives similarly chose 'Britain is great again, don't let Labour ruin it'. During the post-war period, some of the old suburban values of a work ethic grounded in thrift, hard work and delayed gratification were undermined, as Thatcherism and the onset of popular capitalism urged people to regard their houses as investments, and consumerism took an increasingly strong hold. This made the political balancing act between nostalgia and forward progress ever more difficult to calibrate. The Labour and Conservative

Parties both contain modernising and conservative wings, and the policies of each party reflect a mix of these. If the values of traditional suburbia have included moralism (including religion), capitalism, conservatism and property ownership, some of these – albeit frequently articulated in new ways – have thrived as public policy, while others have receded in importance. Stability for households has been undermined, particularly since Thatcherism defeated the one-nation Conservatives and ushered in a radical and market fundamentalist version of Toryism. Thus, for example, the postwar political consensus mainstay of full employment became expendable under Thatcher – and Cameron appears well attuned to this particular Tory tradition.

Monetary mores also became more lax after Thatcher, as the expectation of house-price growth – running counter to puritan values of hard work – assumed more significance in the economy. Indeed rampant house price inflation has made getting on the ever-escalating property ladder increasingly difficult for newcomers, in the suburbs and elsewhere, while at the same time it has allowed existing home-owners to speculate and trade up, or to monetise the equity in their houses. At the same time, the allowing of council tenants to purchase their homes at a discount opened up suburban home-owning to swathes of new people who had previously rented all their lives, a deft piece of politics. Home-owning in the suburbs became more complex, along with political allegiances. All these changes, though full of contradictions in their effects, have tended to benefit the right. Labour has never quite found the means to counter the totemic policy of popular capitalism, or to match it with a new kind of 'popular socialism', of the kind which fed into the creation of the NHS.

Economic uncertainty has affected life in the suburbs in recent years on a number of levels. Shop closures have changed the physical appearance of high streets. The iconic pictures beamed all over the world by the BBC of a queue of Northern Rock depositors waiting to withdraw their funds during the run on the bank were taken in Kingston upon Thames, at the intersection of suburban London and Surrey Home Counties. Such images were a further death blow to the quaint old suburban values of investing and saving for a rainy day. Credit (in earlier times known as debt) has largely replaced savings as the preferred from of finance both in the suburbs and elsewhere (though the easy availability of credit is now itself also being discredited). Consumer demand and upwardly spiralling house prices have increased the personal debt of the average Briton to unprecedented levels over the last two decades, while the country's national debt has rocketed to £1.5 trillion, double its GNP. All over the UK yellowing newspapers in suburban gutters, copies of free-sheets like the *Metro* discarded by commuters on train carriages heading suburb-wards, and billboards on the streets of suburbia, are all screaming apocalyptic warnings of job losses and savage cuts. Other effects have included more pressure on state primary school admissions in suburban boroughs fuelled by population increase (including from new accession EU countries) and less people choosing to educate their children privately in the downturn because finances are tight.

Ideas of politicians as upholders of civic responsibility have also taken a battering. In January 2011 the exemplary custodial sentence meted out to former Bury MP David Chaytor was a reminder of the expenses-gate that had rocked the UK three years earlier. Greed was manifesting itself all the way across British society. *Telegraph* columnist Peter Oborne (2011) noted at the time of the August 2011 riots that there was 'something very phony and hypocritical about all the shock and outrage expressed in parliament':

> the criminality in our streets cannot be dissociated from the moral disintegration in the highest ranks of modern British society. The last two decades have seen a terrifying decline in standards among the British governing elite. It has become acceptable for our politicians to lie and to cheat. An almost universal culture of selfishness and greed has grown up.

We also now live in a media saturated world, so that all this greed is constantly being exposed in what is frequently also a persecuting press, at whatever level of society.

Such chaos and immorality enhances the appeal of an innate suburban small-c conservatism – something that the big-C Conservative Party have certainly spotted in recent years. After some early image rehabilitation, including photo opportunities with husky dogs to prove his 'green' credentials, Cameron soon moved on in his speeches to stressing suburban values. He told the 2009 Conservative Party conference: 'This is my DNA: family, community, country. These are the things I care about. They are what made me. They are what I'm in public service to protect, promote and defend' (Cameron

2009). New Labour had also returned to tapping into such values, for example by repeatedly emphasising 'hard-working families'. At the same time the parties also have to appeal nakedly to people's baser acquisitive instincts, something Labour failed to do with their 2010 slogan 'A Future Fair For All', which was trounced in the suburbs and elsewhere by the Conservatives' policy of changes to inheritance tax and the promise of tax breaks for married couples.

Values reflect times and circumstances, and in contemporary politics there is a need to address risk. Traditionally times of insecurity favour a conservative and inward-looking moral framework, but when cuts in living standards are extremely widespread there is also an opportunity for the left to point to inequality and growing poverty, including within the 'squeezed middle'. The UK joint research councils have in recent years launched a programme to address Global Uncertainties. Its founding questions include an exploration of the 'risks and threats communicated, constructed, represented and received by key actors and communities, using different media and cultural forms for different audiences, including the use of language, images and symbolism'. In France – another country that, like the UK, has been dealing with the stresses of exchanging a colonial past for a European present – the term 'l'insecurité' has been part of political dialogue since the 1990s, and refers to a clutch of issues that include immigration, unemployment and law and order matters. The 'Risk Society' theorised by Beck (1992) refers to transformations in social structure that have made the world feel riskier for most people since the collapse of the postwar consensus. Recent years have seen a list of new concerns added to the insecurity agenda, including national 'defence-of-the-realm' type issues (see McGhee 2010). Labour in government responded to the national security agenda with a series of illiberal measures, which the Conservatives opposed. Politicians one might not instinctively have thought to have been liberal, such as David Davis MP, were passionately making the case for an acceptable balance between national security needs and the protection of civil liberties and human rights. These issues have not easily fitted into to traditional left/right categorisations; whether a party is in government or not appears to be part of what decides a given political stance, but there are also the old issues within all the mainstream parties of competing conservative and liberal attitudes on social and civil liberties issues. The strengthening and comeback of all things religious has added to this picture – a conservative stance on Islam could equally take the form of support for its strengthening of family, faith and moral values or of hostility to its perceived nurturing of extremism. On the other hand a radical stance could include opposition to Islam's conservative values at the same time as protest at racism towards Muslims.

At times the arithmetic of local needs measured against global responsibilities seems to have become rather complex, as evidenced in the Preventing Violent Extremism programme, under whose auspices organisations had to bid for funding at local borough level. There has been heavy resort to the invocation of community on all sides as part of the ideological repertoire for combating a wide range of insecurities, and Prevent is no exception – though describing a group as a community is not always welcome if a whole community appears to be being identified as politically extreme/and or physically violent. And there are further contradictions here: other community groups complain that they cannot unlock money for projects given its parameters. What we can be certain of is contradiction and uncertainty itself.

WHAT'S CLASS GOT TO DO WITH IT?

Danny Dorling (2008) has delineated 'families, which we still call middle-class, [who] usually have two jobs (the British norm), two or more cars (the norm), a small semi-detached or large terraced house, and a combined income that pays for the mortgage, food, fuel and a couple of holidays a year (one of them somewhere warm)'. This description of conforming family norms could be seen as a cataloguing of middle-class suburban lifestyle traits – you are more likely to live in semi-detached housing in the suburbs, and though the first wave of suburbs had to be within walking distance to the railway station, cars now define the modern suburb, and garages and driveways became part of the building pattern of post-1930 developments. But local authorities also built suburbs for the working classes, such as the cottage estates at Becontree and Wythenshawe. Doreen Massey (2002:462), in her essay on the latter in Manchester, where she grew up, notes how it was originally conceived of as sunlit uplands by 1930s planners, 'fuelled by idealism, by an idea of what the public sector might be at its best' (467), in direct opposition to the city slums that had so horrified Marx and Engels. Needless to say the modern older suburb is no longer uniformly middle-class territory, and nor is the working-class variant solely working-class, partly because of issues of location and the right to buy (see p25; 63–4). Class itself is becoming more and more indistinct. At the same time the housing market is becoming increasingly inaccessible to single-earner or low income households. In Haringey or Northfields in north and west London respectively, the capability of financing a mortgage on a modest suburban terraced London home (with much smaller square footage than an American suburban villa), once built to house commuting clerks, would now require the sustenance of two substantial incomes.

Is class now an anachronistic relic of the past? Dorling (2008) commented: 'We used to have many popular guides to the British class system that told you how to appear just a slight cut above. But in 2008 those at the top have to try to appear like the rest: chummy and normal.' Perhaps the most obvious manifestation of this superficial symptom of a post-class society could be seen in the coverage of the romance and wedding of Prince William and his bride-to-be Kate Middleton. Although the headline news at the time of their engagement was 'royal to marry commoner', in their televised engagement interview, Middleton – the descendant of miners who had attended exclusive private schools – sounded distinctly more plummy in her accent than the more relaxed prince, who dropped his consonants more liberally and employed more vernacular. The arcane nature of British class culture has been widely pondered on, and has been the occasion for many a classic British comedy. In cultural terms it can seem to have less of a hold on life-chances than before. Indeed television programmes such as *Who Do You Think You Are?* and online searchable archives on ancestry show both a voyeuristic interest in the class background of the individuals concerned and a range of stories of social mobility – though such stories tend to emphasise individual rather than collective generalities. At the same time real inequality is on the increase.

Perhaps the best approach to class is to understand both that it has become much more complexly articulated in recent years, and that our understandings of it have also become more nuanced. Thus, for example, American feminist bell hooks (2000) has pointed out that gender and racial inequalities are more visible than class stratification; but the Australian theorist David Bedggood (2007:132) maintains that 'social classes are alive and swinging' and that the persistent inequalities of global capitalist society flow from class relations of production. However even though occupational status has long been held to be a significant factor influencing life chances (Erickson and Goldthorpe, 1996), occupational groupings are now more fluid than before – for example, are those in service sector jobs and call centres white or blue collar? Class is undergoing fluidity and flux. The title of Kalra's 2000 study of Asians in the labour market of Oldham in Greater Manchester, *From Textile Mills to Taxi Ranks*, neatly captures this change. But the old homogenous idea of the working class which at one time the Labour Party was conceived of as representing no longer exists (and probably never did). Many Labour strategists today believe that it needs to learn how to engage with aspiration: the offer of equal access to life-chances can all too often look like a process of 'levelling down' to the status conscious of suburbia.

If class is fragmenting, what can be said of community? Many of the traditional bases of suburban identification have eroded. In particular, the family – the cornerstone of the communities studied in the sociology pioneered by Wilmott and Young – has fragmented dramatically, as Ulrich Beck noted over a decade ago (1999, see p26). The new constellations of relationships Beck refers to have only become more complex since then, with the increasing proliferation of non-traditional family forms.

Other institutions that once sustained community are also under threat. The IPPR have recently lamented the decline of the pub because of its community remit (Muir 2009), noting that there are now some 39 pubs a week closing their doors. The Church too has seen attendance decline in an age of existential arguments based on rationalism, science and progress. Trade unions and political parties, too, command fewer and fewer numbers. It seems the British are less and less a nation of 'joiners'. It is possible that looser forms, such as community politics, could be the beneficiary of the malaise surrounding traditional politics, with local issues becoming rallying points, as in defensive campaigns to oppose planning applications. Obama's presidential campaign was substantially based on the principles of community organisation and harnessing support from existing campaigns of solidarity at local level, and to some extent David Miliband's Labour leadership bid and resultant offshoot organisation

'Movement For Change' had something of the same character; while Ed Miliband has also acknowledged the need for change in Labour Party culture. When David Miliband came to the meeting of Labour Party members in my Ealing house he asked: 'How many times have you been to a meeting where the first item on the agenda is the minutes of the last meeting?'. The implication was that more time should be spent in working towards achieving defined goals, with less effort expended in procedural wrangling/time-wasting. However, though forms of organisation could undoubtedly be improved, there are also structural reasons for the contemporary decline in participation.

THE DIVERSIFICATION OF SUBURBIA

Patrick Keiller's film *London* (1994) bleakly documents the latter years of pre-New Labour rule in the capital with an acceptance that 'the centre of the city continued to decline and activities previously thought of as occurring in the centre now began to take place in the suburbs'. Although some of these predictions of one-way atrophy have not been realised, partly due to revitalisation through the restoration of a London-wide tier of strategic government, London has definitely also seen a growth of vitality and an expanded social diversity within its suburban populations. Suburbia has always been highly differentiated, but this is even more the case today. Population displacement frequently continues along the familiar arterial roads and transport links: African-Caribbeans have moved from inner city Brixton to suburban Croydon, Asians have moved from the East End to South Essex. Other communities have settled in suburbia as their first point of arrival, such as the South Koreans in New Malden, Kingston. Once seen as a gendered space, with its privatised homes providing the habitat of the housewife, these long-ascribed roles are also breaking down. The distance between home and work is dissolved in our networked society; in the twenty-first century technology allows working from home for all genders. Globalisation and cosmopolitanism also underscore the modern suburb; shopping parades include restaurants from a wide variety of international cuisines, not the least of which is chicken tikka masala, declared the national dish by the late Robin Cook. Today Pizza Hut and Pizza Express are part of the familiar background on every high street, and yet as recently as the 1950s, in *Panorama*'s celebrated April Fools Day joke, the British public could be persuaded that spaghetti grew on trees.

In *Dunroamin*, a 1991 BBC documentary, Ann Leslie stated that Asians were 'ideally suited to suburban life' because of their cherishing of the values of hard work and respectability, and their ambition for their children. Certainly Asian suburbanisation has been marked in recent years. But it would be a mistake to see Asians in Britain as embodying the declaration by croquet-playing John Prescott that 'We are all middle-class now'. Within this bloc term there are many variations: the London Borough of Tower Hamlets, for example, is one of the poorest municipalities in the country, where Bangladeshis suffer multiple deprivation, including poor health, poor education and over-crowding. And the 2001 riots in Bradford, Burnley and Oldham, in which Asian youth were prominent, showed how structural decline had affected Pakistani and Bangladeshi communities in the former mill-towns of the north. (Ironically, the cotton industry jobs that those young people's parents or grandparents came to take up, from Sylhet or the Punjab, have now been outsourced back to the subcontinent.)

As we have seen, religious observance has also survived and indeed been revived in the suburbs through diversification. Catholic churches have been revitalised by successive waves of migrants, recently including large numbers of Polish immigrants. But it is the rise of Islam in the UK – followed by Pakistanis and Bangladeshis who started to arrive in large numbers in the 1960s, through to the more recently settled Somalis – that has caused the most alarm. Indeed the crucial post-millennial fault-line appears to be around religion rather than race/ethnicity.

One response to this increasing diversity has been anxiety about multiculturalism, particularly against the backdrop of heightened security concerns in the era of the 'war on terror', and this has been visible in a number of suburban locations. In late 2010 Luton was named as the base of the perpetrator of the failed Stockholm terror plot, and it had also been Luton station from which had set out the 2005 London bombers. As well as being the home of a substantial Asian population in its suburb of Bury Park, Luton has also been the site of two recent English Defence League demonstrations. Post-industrial economic woes form part of the background to this narrative: Vauxhall had once been the town's biggest single employer, with a thriving car plant where workers of different ethnic and religious backgrounds used to mix on the production line, but it has shed many workers over the past decade. In discussing the issue of fundamentalist-Islam terrorists, Luton Labour MP Gavin Shuker told the *Economist* (18.12.10): 'It's not that multiculturalism is failing ... people are simply feeling economic pain. The challenge is to prevent a few hotheads exploiting a bigger disenchantment with politics itself.' Some of the same motivations drive BNP and EDL recruitment.

In the public policy context 'community cohesion' became a government buzzword following the 2001 disturbances and the multitude of reports that followed in its wake, best known of which was the Cantle commission. But since then terrorism has become a factor in considerations – though the Preventing Violent Extremism strategy can appear to be in conflict with cohesive communities, particularly when it is seen as being a cover for 'spying' on Muslims. A number of strands have fed into an evolving public discourse which increasingly points to the failures of multi-culturalism: the events of 9/11 in the USA and 7/7 in London; the problems of urban and suburban decline; and the increased numbers of migrant workers following the accession of EU countries to the EU. All these have been drawn on in a way that funnels a wider anxiety and insecurity towards a concern with issues of race and immigration. The widely reported select committee report 'Community Cohesion and Migration' (2008) included a case-study of Peterborough, which claimed that a third of residents surveyed agreed with the statement that different ethnic groups were opposed to one another. The negative effects of migration named included car crime, prostitution, benefit fraud, street drinking, overcrowding, litter and fly-tipping. Police listed an increase in cannabis-growing, trafficking of eastern European women, drink-driving and knife crime as by-products of immigration. The report concluded that central government needed to adjust its local support grant to help councils manage migration and to compensate for communities that were bearing the pressure of suddenly increased migration. There clearly does need to be a reconsideration of what constitutes cohesive communities (or whatever the new government language for these may be), but it should be seen as a goal for all rather than something that affects other people living elsewhere.

PROSPECTS FOR LABOUR IN THE SUBURBS

Twenty-first century suburbia is not simply a promised land. It is a place of contradictions with its fair share of problems. Many suburban-dwellers lie awake at night fretting about how to cover the mortgage payments and afford the middle-class lifestyles that should go with owner-occupation. An *Economist* (18.12.10) feature on the allure of Christmas baking rightly claimed that 'Britons yearn for tradition, but these days live busy, rather atomised lives'. The piece also referred to 'their tiny, expensive homes' in which further belt-tightening must necessarily take place as a result of straitened financial circumstances. Labour ought to be in a position to exploit the Coalition government's economic mismanagement and counter the argument that severe pain must be felt by all. The suburbs have featured heavily in Labour's post-election analyses, including in Ed Miliband's acknowledgment of the 'squeezed middle' and Liam Byrne's essay (2002) on the way to win back 'Motorway Man and Woman', written for the Blairite think tank Progress. For Progress this includes prioritising a politics of aspiration; while in a blogpost for the Labourlist site John Healey (2010) pointed to 'the "just coping class" in Britain today' and urged the leadership to 'make income insecurity as great a Labour concern as income inequality'. Another contribution to the same site (Ferguson 2010) reported Experian findings that 57 per cent of Middle Britain struggle to find enough hours in the day to manage life. If Labour can bring back together the coalition of middle and working class voters that New Labour managed to hold together for some time, it will need to address insecurities among mortgaged home-owners as well as rent payers.

Suburban electoral behaviour is conditioned by various factors; voters tend to unite as a power bloc when their living standards are under threat. Labour needs to make sure that Conservative accusations that it was asleep at the wheel when global financial crisis hit do not stick. The sizeable housing bubble created a correspondingly loud popping sound when it burst, and this particularly affects the suburbs. The housing market, suburban or otherwise, should not be seen primarily as guarantor of economic growth. Labour will need to find new solutions to address the housing shortage, and here it must not forget to address the long-term neglect of social housing, whose decline has fed into the disillusionment that for some has led to the BNP.

The BNP itself seems to have been contained for the moment after its lacklustre 2010 General Election performance. Many of their successes – including in Epping, home of Wilmott's 'Greenleigh' estate of former Bethnal-Greeners – were in the 'Thames Corridor', a band of constituencies to which East Enders have moved throughout the post-war period (Gable, 2004), particularly after the closure of the Port of London, after which many dockers moved out to Tilbury and Thurrock. The disillusionment with mainstream parties felt by many within this East End diaspora was not helped by what Eatwell (2000: 187) sees as a failure by both parties to engage with racism: 'What the Conservatives and to a lesser extent the Labour Party have done is to *manage* racism. In doing so they have legitimized certain forms of racism'. Labour needs to resist the strategy pursued by Mitterrand in France in the 1980s and 1990s, when he deliberately allowed the extreme right grow in order to deflate the mainstream centre-right. The threat of the BNP has indeed redirected the attention of Labour strategists, including Jon Cruddas, to the grievances felt by large sections of working-class people who feel abandoned by the metropolitan elite. And Labour should be proud of the way in which a rainbow alliance of campaigners from inside and outside the party defeated the cries of right-wing populism in 2010.

Events in Arizona in early 2011 and the rise of aggressive groups like the English Defence League show the dark and violent extremes that widespread disaffection can lead to. Equally, those seeking to express themselves in pressure group politics need to be convinced that without voting in elections things will not change. Harnessing the opposition in the country to coalition cuts could be fertile territory for pushing the Labour message. After all, popular opposition to the poll tax paved the way for the demise of Thatcher and gave a new meaning to the words 'community charge'. Restoring confidence in Westminster politics can be achieved. Voters, however, need to be treated with dignity – as people not as occupants of a spreadsheet column. Labour needs to demonstrate that it is 'on their side' and working with communities – doing things *with* people and *for* people rather than *to* them. The idea of citizenship is a relatively new one in the UK, but could be one area that Labour could make its own.

Ed Miliband has rightly identified the civil liberties agenda as one that needs to be reclaimed by the party, which at many times in the past decade seemed to neglect these fundamental freedoms in the name of the 'war on terror'. Labour also needs to send out a clear message that its 50% tax band for the super-rich will be reinstated, and to make the accompanying argument that such taxes are justified by the gross income inequalities produced by unchecked capitalism. The Labour Party is still seen in the public imagination as identifying with benefit claimants – a category that of course also inhabits modern suburbia and is not simply confined to the inner city – but Labour's policy review must come up with a welfare programme in which the benefits system makes work pay, while also recognising that those unable to work need to be able to live. There is a wide range of policy that the current Labour leadership needs to address.

In plotting a winning course for the next general election Labour is faced with two possibilities: either to concentrate on mainstream voters in marginal, often suburban, seats (which the Conservatives tried to with Lord Ashcroft's campaign) or to shore up the core vote (who, advocates of this strategy claim, have been deserting Labour in droves since 1997, preferring to stay at home and sit on their hands). But of course any new strategy needs to come up with policies that appeal to both groups, and this could be achieved with a policy programme that defines and encapsulates a newly invigorated popular socialism. It would also be a mistake to make presumptions on electoral attitudes on issues such as race: the settled UK Asian community often have the most anti-immigration stances. Indeed Conservative pandering to social conservatism might be a misjudgement, given that opinion polling has shown that attitudes once thought to be 'socially liberal' are now more widespread, and have increasingly become 'the norm' (Reeves 2007), for example in changing attitudes towards homosexuality.

At a time when old institutions (church, state, parliament, party, union, etc) are holding less and less sway with the British voter, Muir (2004) has pondered what there is left we can all coherently unite around. Multiculturalism is often approached as a problem, to be therefore treated in problem-solving terms, but among other possible answers Muir has identified multiculturalism as a potential answer, along with cosmopolitanism, heritage, arts/culture hybrids and sport. Multiculturalism is certainly a brave suggestion given that it has fallen from favour if not all but been discredited in the post 7/7 climate. Class consciousness also seems to be on shaking ground as a left totem now that workers have largely become consumers. Suburbs are today inhabited by diverse people, for whom the bases of their identity are complex, and who have to negotiate increasingly atomised and time-poor lives. Shoe-horning them into constructed categories around which to cohere seems somewhat forced: genuine community cohesion is more likely to be forged over time and through dialogue with difference rather than the construction of borders. Perhaps the mistake is to seek one banner around which Britain's diverse multi-faceted mosaic can all unproblematically unite.

There is also a high degree of internal diversity within groups such as 'the Asian community', 'people of Turkish origins', 'Maghrebians' and the like, which makes the idea of homogeneous communities more redundant than ever. Indeed 'mixed race' is the census category most likely to grow as a demographic in forthcoming years. Such groupings identify more with the Labour Party than others, but Labour needs to build on and earn their support and not take them for granted – and without being held back through fear of alienating the 'white working class', elements of which have increasingly presented themselves as victims.

The other story of the May 2010 elections was the impressive Labour performance across the country in the council elections: Ealing, Harrow and Liverpool were among the authorities where Labour made sweeping gains. Indeed Labour now has a strong local government base which needs to be built on rather than ignored. The party is not running on empty. Far from the embarrassing 'loony left' Labour Town Halls of the 1980s – themselves a caricature – local Labour group leaders need to use their positions to propagate responsible stewardship of borough finances in delivering high quality public services, using their leadership as an opportunity to popularise the Labour brand in the country in the run up to the next round of elections. Encouraging active citizenship and greater political participation have the potential to be just as important to the new politics of Labour as solidarity and collective action were to its original remit.

Now more than ever before it is the suburbs not the industrial heartlands that will be the most volatile battleground in deciding the election outcomes. Suburbia needs to be reconstructed as a vibrant place of possibilities, rather than a place that is neither here nor there, or as the last relic of Englishness. At the same time it would be mistaken to view the social upheaval of recent years as being wholly beneficial for the suburbs. Modernity has taken its toll there. The promised utopia of cool Britannia and its attendant urban regeneration, with shiny new arts centres and pedestrianised squares broken up by greenery, has not manifested itself in many of the outer reaches of the cities – in fact it has sometimes adversely affected them, leaving empty retail units that engender suburban decay. (Boris Johnson has commissioned reports into the state of outer London, and given the impression of being concerned about the problems of suburban blight: Labour needs to match and better this.) Thinking local is a cause to be championed even if we also need to be aware of international agreements.

We are often told we are in an era of so many things (globalisation, diversity, technology … take your pick) but they are all ways of trying to understand the increasing complexity of our lives and all point to issues that need addressing head-on in order to address the concerns of the average voter – which today above all means those who inhabit the contested territory of 'suburbia'.

REFERENCES

Beck, U. (1999) 'Goodbye to all that wage slavery', *New Statesman* 5.3.99: www.newstatesman.com/199903050020.

Bedggood, D. (2007) 'Stratifying Class', in Matthewman, S. et al (eds), *Being Sociological*, Palgrave-Macmillan, pp131-148.

Benedictus, L. (2005) '"This restaurant is a little bit of Korea brought into a very English town": Koreans in New Malden', *Guardian*, 21.1.05: www.guardian.co.uk/uk/2005/jan/21/britishidentity9?INTCMP=SRCH.

Blond, P (2010) *Red Tory: How Left and Right Have Broken Britain and How We Can Fix It*, Faber.

Bourdieu, P. (1984) *Distinction: a Social Critique of the Judgement of Taste*, Routledge.

Callinicos, A. (1993) *Race and Class*, Bookmarks.

Cameron, D. (2009) 'Putting Britain back on her feet', speech by David

Cameron, 8.10.09: www.conservatives.com/News/Speeches/2009/10/David_Cameron_Putting_Britain_back_on_her_feet.aspx.

Cooper, J. (1979) *Class, A view from Middle England*, Eyre Methuen

Coote, A. (2010) 'Ten Big Questions about the Big Society', New Economics Foundation: www.neweconomics.org/publications/ten-big-questions-about-the-big-society.

Dorling, D. (2008) 'Cash and the class system', 24.7.08, *New Statesman*: www.newstatesman.com/society/2008/07/middle-class-british-income.

Doward, J. (2011) 'Britain's changing ethnic map: how suburbia has been transformed', *Observer*, 10.4.11: www.guardian.co.uk/search?q=new+malden+%2B+korea&target=guardian.

Eatwell, R. (2000) 'The Extreme Right and British Exceptionalism: the primacy of politics', in Hainsworth, P. (ed), *The Politics of the Extreme Right from the margins to the mainstream*, Pinter.

Economist (2010) 'Season's eatings: Old and new traditions blend in a modern Christmas ritual', 16.12.10: www.economist.com/node/17733514.

Fox, K. (2004) *Watching the English: the hidden rules of English behaviour*, Hodder & Stoughton.

Gable, G. (2004) 'Disaster in Dagenham', *Searchlight*, October 2004: www.searchlightmagazine.com/index.php?link=template&story=113.

Hall, P. (2008) *London Voices, London Lives: Tales from a Working Capital*, Policy Press.

Hattenstone, S. (2010) 'Yvette Cooper: 'There's nothing better than politics', 4.12.11: www.guardian.co.uk/politics/2010/dec/04/yvette-cooper-guardian-interview?INTCMP=SRCH.

hooks, b. (2000) *Where We Stand: Class Matters*, Routledge.

Hutton, W. (2010) 'Of Course Class Still Matters – it Influences Everything that We Do,' *Observer*, 10.1.10: www.guardian.co.uk/commentisfree/2010/jan/10/will-hutton-class-unfair-society.

Kalra, V. (2000) *From Textile Mills to Taxi Ranks: Experiences of Migration, Labour and Social Change*, Research in Migration and Ethnic Relations Series, Ashgate.

Lamont, M. and Lareau, A. (1998) 'Cultural Capital: Allusions, Gaps and Glissandos in Recent Theoretical Developments', *Sociological Theory*, 6 (2), pp153-168.

Leo, J. (2007) 'Bowling With Our Own', *City Journal*, 25.6.07: www.city-journal.org/html/eon2007-06-25jl.html.

Lanchester, J. (2011) 'Restaurant: Su La, New Malden, Greater London', *Guardian*, 7.5.11:

www.guardian.co.uk/lifeandstyle/2011/may/07/su-la-london-restaurant-review?INTCMP=SRCH.

Massey, D. (2002) 'Living in Wythenshawe', in Borden, I., Kerr, J. and Rendell, J. and Pivaro, A. (eds) (2002) *The Unknown City*, MIT Press.

McGhee, D. (2010) *Security, Citizenship & Human Rights: Shared Values in Uncertain Times*, Palgrave.

Mikes, G. (1966) *How to be an Alien: A Handbook for Beginners and More Advanced Pupils*, Penguin Books.

Mikes, G. (1986) *How to be a Brit*, Penguin

Miles, R. and Phizacklea, A. (1984) *White Men's Country*, Pluto.

Modood, T. (1994) 'Political Blackness and British Asians', *Sociology*, November 1994, vol. 28 no. 4, pp859-876.

Muir, R. (2009) *Pubs and Places: The social value of community pubs*, IPPR.

Oborne, P. (2011) 'The moral decay of our society is as bad at the top as the bottom', *Daily Telegraph*, 11.8.11: http://blogs.telegraph.co.uk/news/peteroborne/100100708/the-moral-decay-of-our-society-is-as-bad-at-the-top-as-the-bottom/.

Perri 6, Fletcher-Morgan, C. and Leyland, K. (2010) 'Making People More Responsible: The Blair Governments' Programme for Changing Citizens' Behaviour', *Political Studies*, Volume 58 Issue 3, pp427-449.

Prince, R. (2008) 'School pupils to get a daily "culture hour"', *Daily Telegraph*: www.telegraph.co.uk/news/newstopics/politics/1578531/School-pupils-to-get-a-daily-culture-hour.html.

Reeves, R. (2007) 'Middle England: they're nicer than you think', *New Statesman*, 25.10.07: www.newstatesman.com/politics/2007/10/middle-england-class-social.

Strangio, S. (2011) 'Occupy Wall Street meets Dhaka', *The Diplomat*, 5.11.11: http://the-diplomat.com/2011/11/05/occupy-wall-street-meets-dhaka/.

Taylor, M. (2010) 'English Defence League: new wave of extremists plotting summer of unrest', 28.5.10: www.guardian.co.uk/uk/2010/may/28/english-defence-league-protest-bnp.

Wallace, W. (2005) 'The collapse of British foreign policy', *International Affairs*, Volume 81(1), pp53-68.

Walford, G. (2005) 'Introduction: education and the Labour Government', *Oxford Review of Education*, 31: 1, pp3-9.

Wark, P. (2008) 'Are we all middle-class now?', *Times*, 19.3.08: http://women.timesonline.co.uk/tol/life_and_style/women/the_way_we_live/article3576387.ece.

Wind-Cowie, M. (2010) *Civic Streets: The Big Society In Action*, Demos: www.demos.co.uk/publications/civicstreets.

Young, H. (2008) 'Inside Track', 15.11.08: www.guardian.co.uk/books/2008/nov/15/politics-the-hugo-young-papers.

Postscript

The grass on the other side

He put her in a ranch house on a hill
She could see the valley barbecues
From her window sill
See the blue pools in the squinting sun
Hear the hissing of summer lawns

Joni Mitchell, *The Hissing of Summer Lawns*, 1975

Having been brought up in the interwar west London suburbs, in a 1930s semi on an infill development to the north of Ealing Broadway, I had always thought that the density of the city – in terms of socio-cultural practice as well as houses per hectare – was an exciting prospect when set against my daily surroundings of tree-lined rows of houses with their sacred front gardens. Indeed the lawn was in some ways emblematic of suburban existence, offering an individual section of greenery a short hop away from the city via arterial roads and/or public transport – in our case via the twin lifelines of the A40 and the Central Line at Hanger Lane. The standard of maintenance of the patch of grass at the front of the house served as a barometer of the inmates' ability to adhere to suburban ideals.

Yet in the same streets today many front gardens have been concreted over and transformed into car-ports; people-carriers are squeezed into spaces where grass once grew. Since the 1970s and 1980s the placid suburbia of my recollection has given way to a more pressurised environment, where, most typically, dual-earner families work round the clock to service the mortgage and provide for their offspring. Some households have multiple cars, as grown-up children, unable to afford the exorbitant cost of relocating and living independently, remain in the parental home, trying to save up for a deposit.

Behind other doors are single-parent families – it has been said that divorce has helped keep the property market from complete stagnation during the recession. It is not only the spacious Victorian villas in the centre of Ealing that have become subdivided into money-spinning flat conversions for their freeholders. The trend has spread even to modest turn-of-the-century redbrick terraces in once less well-to-do South Ealing.

In short, just as the global postcolonial city is constantly subject to defining and redefining, so too are the suburbs today shaped by diversity at every level. Shifting demographics, altered and technologically-driven work and leisure practices, new migratory trends and changing patterns of consumption, make them far more complex than their old pattern as clusters of housing for strictly nuclear individual families, marketed as an antidote to the evils of the city.

The lawn has been a recurring suburban motif in postwar western culture (Taylor 2008). In episode one of *Desperate Housewives* from 2004, Gabrielle Solis is seen mowing the lawn in evening dress and stilettos in the middle of the night, in order to cover up her affair with her toyboy gardener. Joni Mitchell's 1975 album *The Hissing of Summer Lawns* contains ten songs chronicling affluent suburbia, where the hissing of sprinklers soundtracks the summer months. On the foreground of the cover a giant snake is carried by a group of African tribesmen across a large green space; behind them is a row of respectable suburban residences and behind that the city. Tracks such as 'The Jungle Line', in which Burundi drums pound away throughout, continue the theme of wilder processes working away behind the surface tranquillity of the suburb. The title track tells of a woman trapped in suburban life. Another track also neatly juxtaposes the effervescence of city excitement and suburban *ennui*:

> *Under neon signs*
> *A girl was in bloom*
> *And a woman was fading*
> *In a suburban room.*

The lines from the title track quoted at the beginning of this postscript could be straight from the pages of Betty Friedan's *The Feminine Mystique*. On another track, 'Harry's House/Centerpiece', a husband flies off on a business trip while his wife is left managing the unruly kids:

> *She is lost in House and Gardens*
> *He's caught up in Chief of Staff.*

The 2011 Disney/CGI animation film *Gnomeo and Juliet* translated Shakespeare's tale of star-crossed lovers in Verona into a story about gnomes in the neighbouring gardens of two semi-detached houses in suburban England, whose rivalry reflects the pettiness of their home-owners. Front gardens also feature in the Yorkshire-set film *Rita, Sue and Bob Too* (1986). Bob and his status-conscious wife Michelle live on a smart new-build suburban cul-de-sac where an elderly neighbour perpetually hosing his lawn looks on at the to-ing and fro-ing between the bickering couple. The lawnmower becomes a weapon of war in this neighbours-from-hell tale.

In June 2012 @ellesonshine tweeted: 'I had a dream last night I had a beautiful husband, a few kids, and a white picket fence. Nightmare, really'.

SUBURBAN REVANCHISM

In recent decades the idea of suburban dysfunction in popular culture has become a popular one – to the point that this now exists as a category in the Netflix film catalogue. Included within the list are *American Beauty* (1995); *Stepford Wives* (1975, remade 2004); *Far From Heaven* (1950s-set but created in 2002); *Revolutionary Road* (1961 novel, 2009 film); *A Single Man* (1964 novel, 2010 film); and *The Ice Storm* and *Virgin Suicides* (both 1997 films from early 90s novels). The idea of suburbia as sedate yet soul-destroying has not always prevailed however. The benefits of suburban life were stressed in the popular culture of 1950s and 1960s films and sitcoms, which portrayed the suburbs as virtuous: they were the de facto backdrop for most of them for years. The promise of suburbia as conceived of by its creators is easily forgotten today, but the view of suburbs as promised land was widespread in the immediate postwar period. What many of the new cultural critics of the 'suburbs as hell' seem to overlook, however, is that suburbs today are nothing like those of the 1950s and 1960s.

In *Suburgatory*, a comedy series launched by ABC in the US which made it to E4 by 2012, a number of suburban clichés are present. The title echoes Bertrand Russell's short story of 1953, *Satan in the Suburbs*. The story line involves a single father who moves his only daughter from the big bad city of New York to a 'white picket fence nightmare' suburb. Before long he is becoming like the neighbours, who sprinkle their lawns with hoses in unison. The spotless set feels like the type of place we have witnessed before, in David Lynch's *Blue Velvet* or in *Desperate Housewives*. The considerable degree of criticism the show received is evidence that attempts to be cutting edge in mocking suburbia are becoming as clichéd as the suburban clichéd way of life they set out to attack. Other US situation comedies of recent years, *Weeds* and *Breaking Bad*, have attempted to introduce an element of drug-related variability into the standard suburban set-up.

Siegel (2008) has noted that 'suburb-phobia' has become an increasingly culturally acceptable attitude: 'In *Revolutionary Road*, the two principal characters are brought down by lawn sprinklers and station wagons'; and he pours scorn on this 'Killing Me Softly' strain of anti-suburbanism. But he also quotes from Sylvia Plath's (1963:109) autobiographical novel *The Bell Jar*, in which Esther Greenwood states:

> I stepped from the air-conditioned compartment onto the station platform and the motherly breath of the suburbs enfolded me. It smelt of lawn sprinklers and station wagons and dogs and babies. A summer calm laid its soothing hand over everything, like death.

As befits twenty-first century news media, the readers' comments posted 'below the line' of Siegel's online article are often more interesting than the piece itself. One tea-party-type writes:

> What is wrong living in a neighbourhood where families stay together, church is important and work is imperative? I like my SUV, boat, jet ski and trips on jets to other countries. But somehow Hollywood sees this as bad.

Another more leftish poster points out that the suburbs should no longer be associated with the cloying atmosphere of respectability: whereas once their inhabitants were prosperous, they may now be barely scraping enough to make a living, because of failed neo-conservative economic policy. (This state of affairs has led to the coining of the term 'slumburbia'.)

CONCLUSION: KEEP OFF THE GRASS?

In the 1920s Stanley Baldwin spoke of his desire that every working man from the city should have a bit of garden to call his own (Hunt 2004:333). And the BBC's 1970s sitcom *The Good Life* was about a couple who took the suburban dream to its logical conclusion by growing their own produce and keeping livestock in their suburban back garden. But the history and representation of suburban greenery often stray from such visions.

The title of the US sitcom *Weeds* refers not only to the 'weed' that the main character sells but to the moral decay that is infecting the contemporary suburb as it becomes overgrown. Its title sequence is accompanied by the song 'Little Boxes', originally written by Malvina Reynolds for Pete Seeger, about the little boxes that all look the same, the suburban dwellings on the hillside. J.B. Priestly also despises the place 'where the smooth wide road passes between miles of semi-detached bungalows, all with their little garages, their wireless sets, their periodicals about film stars, their swimming costumes and tennis rackets and dancing shoes' (1943:401).

An entire 1979 episode of the BBC sitcom *Terry and June* was entitled 'The Lawnmower' – again about a neighbourly dispute over this appliance – and there is also the 1992 *The Lawnmower Man*, a science-fiction horror film. In one episode of *Mad Men* series 2 (2009), a scene of blood-splattered carnage results when a drunken secretary loses control of a lawnmower at an office party. Although this show is chiefly set in Madison Avenue, the high-pressured city environment of advertising is constantly counterposed with the suburban domesticity of the home, where the slick Don Draper steps off the commuter train after a hard day's work/philandering. Here his unfulfilled wife Betty remains, with the children and housemaid.

Contemporary suburbia, as even a cursory google image search shows, often takes the form of houses in line, and 'sprawl' is a term much beloved of science fiction writer William Gibson, whose dystopian vision of the suburbia of the future inspired his 'sprawl trilogy' (1984, 1986, 1988) – referenced by US grunge/art rockers

Sonic Youth on their track 'Sprawl' on their 1988 album *Daydream Nation*, and then by Canadian band Arcade Fire twice on their 2010 album *The Suburbs*, which was accompanied by a 30-minute film *Scenes from the Suburbs* directed by Spike Jonze. Yet this premise of suburban uniformity and unoriginal claims of blandness are in desperate need of revision.

Fear and suspicion in 1960s suburban America can be sensed in the 2009 film *A Single Man*. We see suburbia through the eyes of a gay college professor (played by Colin Firth), and a major focus of the story is the playing out of difference in the suburbs. Portrayals of UK suburban difference are also manifold, including *Bend It Like Beckham* (set in Hounslow), *The Kumars at Number 42* (Wembley), and the fiction of Gautam Malkani's (2006) *Londonstani* and Shukla's (2010) *Coconut Unlimited*.

In Nick Hornby's (1995) novel *High Fidelity*, the thirty-something main character has escaped the Hertfordshire suburbia of his childhood, trading it in for trendy Camden Town, particularly fashionable in the 1990s era of Britpop. But he feels that his sedate existence still constructs him as a suburbanite, despite living near the city centre. He muses:

> … nobody ever writes about how it is possible to escape and rot – how escapes can go off at half-cock, how you can leave the suburbs for the city but end up living a limp suburban life anyway. That's what happened to me; that's what happens to most people.

Camden once was a suburb, built with individual houses and gardens, although London's growth has seen it transformed into an inner-London area. Even though the inner-city/suburban divide is fading fast, it seems that, wherever you stand, the grass is greener on the other side.

REFERENCES

Cunningham, G. (2007) 'London commuting: suburb and city, the Quotidian Frontier', in Cunningham, G. and Barber, S. (eds.) *London eyes: reflections in text and image*, Berghahn Books, pp7-25.

Priestley, J.B. (1933) *English Journey*, Heinemann.

Genzlinger, N. (2011) 'A Worried City Father Seeks Wholesomeness',

27.9.11, *New York Times*: http://tv.nytimes.com/2011/09/28/arts/television/suburgatory-on-abc-review.html.

Gibson, W. (1984) *Neuromancer.*

Gibson, W. (1986) *Count Zero.*

Gibson, W. (1988) *Mona Lisa Overdrive.*

Hornby, N. (1995) *High Fidelity*, Penguin.

Hunt, T. (2004) *Building Jerusalem: The Rise and Fall of the Victorian City*, Weidenfield.

Orwell. G. (1937) *The Road to Wigan Pier*, Penguin.

Malkani, G. (2008) *Londonstani*, Penguin.

Plath, S. (1963) *The Bell Jar*, Faber and Faber.

Poniewozik, J. (2011) 'TV Tonight: Suburgatory', *Time* Magazine, 28.9.11: http://entertainment.time.com/2011/09/28/tv-tonight-suburgatory/#ixzz2267Nd92d.

Priestley, J.B. (1934) *English Journey*, Heinemann in association with Gollancz.

Ramsey, T. (2012) 'Suburgatory: E4, review', 17.7.12: www.telegraph.co.uk/culture/tvandradio/9406937/Suburgatory-E4-review.html.

Shukla, N. (2010) *Coconut Unlimited*, Quartet Books.

Siegel, L. (2008) 'America's long artistic tradition of claiming spiritual death by station wagon', *Wall Street Journal*, 27.12.08: http://online.wsj.com/article/SB123033369595836301.html.

Smith, Z. (2000) *White Teeth*, Penguin.

Stasi, L. (2011) 'Burb's the word', *New York Post*, 28.9.11: www.nypost.com/p/entertainment/tv/burb_the_word_qhWAogkSxiulS3HQ80HMpI#ixzz22607Yukt.

Taylor, L. (2008) *A Taste for Gardening: Classed and Gendered Practices*, Ashgate.

Index